Seven Myths of
Native American History

Seven Myths of Native American History

by Paul Jentz

Series Editors
Alfred J. Andrea and Andrew Holt

Hackett Publishing Company, Inc.
Indianapolis/Cambridge

21 20 19 18   1 2 3 4 5 6 7

For further information, please address
  Hackett Publishing Company, Inc.
  P.O. Box 44937
  Indianapolis, Indiana 46244-0937

  www.hackettpublishing.com

Cover design by Rick Todhunter and Brian Rak
Interior design by Elizabeth L. Wilson
Composition by Aptara, Inc.

Library of Congress Cataloging-in-Publication Data

Names: Jentz, Paul, author.
Title: Myths of history : seven myths of Native American history / by Paul Jentz.
Description: Indianapolis, Indiana : Hackett Publishing Company, 2018. | Series: Myths
    of history series ; v. 4 | Includes bibliographical references and index.
Identifiers: LCCN 2017040028| ISBN 9781624666780 (pbk.) | ISBN 9781624666797
    (cloth)
Subjects: LCSH: Indians in popular culture—United States. | Indians of North
    America—Public opinion. | Indians of North America—Historiography. |
    Stereotypes (Social psychology) | Public opinion—United States.
Classification: LCC E98.P99 J46 2018 | DDC 970.004/97—dc23
LC record available at https://lccn.loc.gov/2017040028

∞

CONTENTS

Series Editors' Foreword

It is with great pleasure that we introduce the fourth volume in Hackett Publishing Company's Myths of History Series, *Seven Myths of Native American History* by Paul Jentz.

The history of the Indians of North America is long and complex, especially when one puts aside stereotypical images of who they were and are and what constitutes "Indian culture." Moreover, the story of their relations with the colonists and settlers of the lands that became the United States and Canada often makes for uncomfortable reading. Beyond that, it is a subject that continues to be bitterly fought over by partisans and scholars on all sides of its many issues. It speaks well of Jentz's devotion to this, his chosen field of historical inquiry, that he has undertaken the challenge of subjecting to analysis seven of the most common misperceptions of the Native Americans who have occupied the lands north of the Rio Grande for thousands of years and continue to reside in numerous sovereign nations and singular communities across this vast expanse.

On a Sunday walk not too long ago, one of the series editors happened across this memorial along the Beacon Street boundary of the Boston Common. It is a memorial he had often noticed but, until that moment, had never viewed in any meaningful way. Sculpted in bronze relief by John Francis Paramino, it was set in place in 1930 to commemorate the founding of Boston three hundred years earlier. Depicted on it is William Blackstone, the area's first White resident, greeting colonial governor John Winthrop and his company of English settlers. Behind Winthrop stand John Wilson, Boston's first Puritan minister, holding a bible, and Ann Pollard, Boston's first White woman (who is incorrectly portrayed as an adolescent). Behind Blackstone, at the far edge of the relief, are two almost totally naked Native Americans, who look on rather impassively. They have emerged from the nearby forest but seem simultaneously to recede back into that environment.

Employing the myths that Jentz deconstructs, what can we say about the First Americans who are portrayed here? Well, they are certainly marginalized, both physically and symbolically. Three large White men dominate the foreground. The two Indians are dwarfed, one by stature (the Indian closer to us), the other by posture (the kneeling Indian). This disproportion seems to be more than accidental. The Indians seem to be little more than a scale against which the newly arrived colonists are measured. Moreover, as they gaze upon the almost larger-than-life Englishmen, who carry to these shores Legitimate Government and True Religion, the two Indians are passive agents in an otherwise active scene. Are they even capable of benefiting from these dual blessings of civilization? It seems unlikely. As we learn in Chapter 4, they

Founders Memorial, celebrating the 300th anniversary of the founding of Boston, Massachusetts. Photo courtesy of A. J. Andrea, © 2017.

are symbolically and collectively "the Vanishing Indian." To be sure, the sculptor has demonstrated his technical skill by investing them with muscular bodies and noble features, thereby making them "Noble Savages," the subject of Chapter 1. But the salt marsh and forest that Paramino shows us, and into which the Indians blend, is largely an empty wilderness ready to be populated by a Christian Chosen People (Chapter 3).

About two miles from Boston Common is the Museum of Fine Arts. At its main entrance stands an imposing equestrian statue known as *Appeal to the Great Spirit.* Created in 1909 by Cyrus E. Dallin, it was the last of his four-part *Epic of the Indian* series of bronze sculptures and was immediately recognized as the best of the four. Indeed, of his more than 260 sculptures, *Appeal to the Great Spirit* is his most highly regarded and even beloved work. Smaller-sized replicas of it can be found across the United States and beyond, including a twenty-one-inch statuette in the White House that once graced the Oval Office of President Clinton. Dallin, a native of Utah, admired the culture of the Plains Indians and surely intended this, and the other three sculptures in the series, as a tribute to the horse-riding Native Americans of North America. Yet, once again employing Jentz's insights, one can perceive certain disturbing features in this work of art.

In harmony with Chapter 5, one asks, "Who is the 'Authentic Indian?'" The model for the man on horseback was Antonio Corsi, an Italian—another example of the

Appeal to the Great Spirit, Museum of Fine Arts, Boston. Photo courtesy of A. J. Andrea, © 2017.

propensity of impresarios and artists of that era to present White men in redface. Beyond that, we might well ask, was Dallin's homage to a people he respected an inadvertent exercise in perpetuating the myth of the Noble Savage—a myth that, regardless of the honorable intentions behind it, robs Native Americans of their full humanity? Even more so, was Dallin a devotee of another mythic view of Native American culture that was already popular in the early twentieth century, "the Mystical Indian," the topic of Chapter 7? These are vexing questions and just two of many that Jentz's penetrating study forces us to confront. And there are no easy answers to them.

Certainly, we are not indicting the city of Boston or its Museum of Fine Arts with the charge of gross ethnic insensitivity. Attitudes and perspectives have changed substantially in that city since 1930, and the MFA's collection of pre- and post-Columbian Native American artifacts is sensitively curated, interpreted, and displayed. Furthermore, there is nothing uniquely Bostonian about these sculptures. Similar, often well-intentioned representations of Native Americans can be found today in almost any city in the United States. It is no exaggeration to say that such subtle (and not-so-subtle) images and the notions that underscore them remain part of our cultural baggage.

Another element of that baggage, and a fairly recent one, is what Jentz terms the "Ecological Indian" (Chapter 6). When we initially composed these words, tribal members of the Standing Rock Sioux Reservation in North Dakota were leading a protest against plans to construct an oil pipeline that they claim will violate the sanctity of burial sites and threaten the drinking water that they draw from the Missouri River. Native Americans from a significant number of other tribes joined with them. Their cause appears to these editors to be righteous, but often the champions of morally and ethically just movements unknowingly shroud their crusades in historical myth and stereotype. An otherwise well-argued op-ed article in the *New York Times* condemning the pipeline project noted, "The Native Americans are the only people who have inhabited this continent in harmony with nature for centuries."[1]

Such a claim lacks a solid historical basis. As Jentz points out, "[Indians'] survival depended on adaptation. This included the need to establish new cultural practices and to invent new technologies, sometimes in response to climate change, but often due to crises caused by Native Americans themselves, including resource depletion and environmental degradation" (page 142). Very much like the Myth of the Noble Savage, to which it is closely allied, the perception of the Indian as an always prudent steward of the environment perversely flies in the face of the incontrovertible fact that historical Native Americans were capable of exercising a full range of human actions, both good and bad.

Another stereotype, which happens to be closely allied with the Myth of the Ecological Indian and is a subset of the Mystical Indian mentioned above, is the currently fashionable vision of "the New Age Indian" (also dealt with in Chapter 7). The epicenter of this movement might well be Sedona, Arizona, which supposedly possesses vortexes that are sites of psychic power into which ancient Indians had tapped. The result is that annually several million "seekers" travel to Sedona in search of mystical insights. Many of them, as Jentz points out, pay obscenely expensive fees to participate in ceremonies that are fraudulently presented as authentically Indian.

How does one counter such misconceptions? The answer is not to destroy or even hide away the *Founders Memorial*, the *Appeal to the Great Spirit*, or similar representations

---

1. Bill McKibben, "A Pipeline to Climate Disaster," *New York Times*, October 29, 2016, A19.

Horatio Greenough, *The Rescue*. Photo courtesy of the Architect of the Capitol.

of Native Americans. They are artistic works of aesthetic and historical value. White-washing the past and relegating its artifacts to the trash bin is bad history and never a good idea. Likewise, the answer is not to censor anyone who articulates any of these mythic and often absurd notions.

Not everyone who reads this book would agree with what we just stated. Many will argue that speech and visual representations that offend should be exorcized from polite society. And there is precedent for such action. Between 1853 and 1958, a statuary grouping titled *The Rescue* by Horatio Greenough stood at one side of the stairs leading up to the eastern entrance of the U.S. Capitol Building. On the other side of the stairway stood *The Discovery of America* by Luigi Persico, which was in place from 1844 to 1958. Protests from various groups led to their joint removal while the Capitol was undergoing renovation, and they were hidden away in storage, never to be put on public view again. Reportedly *The Discovery of America* is in poor shape, and *The Rescue* suffered a crueler fate. In 1976 it was accidently dropped by a crane and broken into several pieces while being moved

Luigi Persico, *The Discovery of America* (1844). Photo courtesy of the Architect of the Capitol.

to new storage facilities farther from the city. Today, only the family dog is intact and can be seen at the Middlebury College Art Museum, where it is on indefinite loan from the Office of the Architect of the Capitol. The surviving dog is totally inoffensive, but the same cannot be said of the rest of the now-broken rescue scene or its companion, *The Discovery of America*.

The Rescue depicts a larger-than-life outdoorsman subduing a tomahawk-wielding Native American while a pioneer woman holding a small child recoils in fear. The rescuer is the total master of the scene and the subdued Indian is at his benign mercy. Commentators have generally agreed that this scene of restrained violence is an allegory. The message is simple: Euro-Americans' enlightened intervention saved primitive Indians from exercising their basest instincts.[2] What we have here is the taming of the "Ignoble Indian" (Chapter 2). In a similar vein, *The Discovery of America* depicts a triumphant Christopher Columbus dressed as a conquistador and holding aloft a globe while a cowering, nearly naked Indian woman cringes to his right. Her posture, softness, and vulnerability contrast

---

2. Paul C. Rosier, *Serving Their Country: American Indian Politics and Patriotism in the Twentieth Century* (Cambridge, MA: Harvard University Press, 2010), 168.

sharply with his superhuman size, bearing, toughness, and air of invulnerability. The message is clear.

Native American visitors to the Capitol were surely offended and humiliated when viewing these scenes. They did not belong at the entrance to a building that belongs to all and represents the highest ideals of American civic life, and their removal in 1958 was justified. But should they have been hidden away? We think not. The historian's mandate is to interpret all of our deeds, good and bad and in all of their complexity, thereby achieving a deeper understanding of who we are and how we got here. With this purpose in mind, we submit that racist works of art and propaganda, such as these statues, must be part of the public record. Their proper place is a museum, where curators can interpret and place them into context for the education of all who view them. Consigning them to the limbo of perpetual storage is an act of historical timidity.

So also, we need more books such as this. Composed in a style that will please a general reader but buttressed by exacting scholarship, *Seven Myths of Native American History* lays bare the cultural history behind the most pernicious and persistent myths regarding the First Peoples of America and corrects the record. Anyone who takes care to read these chapters will come to understand how and why such myths have become embedded in our culture and why they are so wrongheaded.

We, the series editors, are proud to present this book to the reading public. It should be mandatory reading in our schools.

Alfred J. Andrea
Andrew Holt

Preface

Originally, North America's First Peoples did not think of themselves collectively as a single group, much less as a race. Rather, group identities depended on kinship networks. But Columbus famously referred to the people he met on his 1492 voyage to the Caribbean as "Indios," misidentifying them as a collective whole and as inhabitants of the Orient. Therefore, the collective term "Indians" arose both as a European concept and as a case of mistaken identity. Columbus also had the good fortune of living at the inception of the Gutenberg revolution. The printing press assured rapid dissemination of his reports throughout Europe.[1] So began the Indian mythologizing process.

As the number of European voyagers increased, so did the stories about the New World. Along with the stories, printed images of Indians circulated widely throughout Europe. These pictures did not rely on direct observation. Instead, artists drew on existing notions of Eden, where Indians dwelled as blessed innocents, and on the already ancient tradition of the Wild Man, a savage hunter inhabiting the dark woods. Fantasies proliferated.[2]

This book attempts to trace the history of such fantasies and to explore their consequences for Native Americans. Misconceptions about Native Americans have continued, at least in part, to shape North America's post-Columbian societies and economies. Indeed, North American colonial, and later national, Indian policies instituted at government levels often stood predicated on erroneous conceptions about Indians themselves. Policies for Indian removal, the reservation and reserve systems, and the boarding and residential school systems—however well intentioned by some individuals—generally assumed that Indians lacked the intellectual, moral, and cultural capacities required for navigating modernity. Moreover, Indian policy commonly served the interests of settler colonialism at the expense of Native American interests. As White settler populations expanded, they often relied on assistance from their governments. Federally instituted reservations and reserves in the United States and Canada answered the settler's needs. Settlers benefited because land formerly designated Indian Country became available to them. Myths simplify the world, hence their attraction. Premised on convenient myths, Indian policy often entailed lethal consequences for Indians.

---

1. William D. Phillips, Jr. and Carla Rahn Phillips, *The Worlds of Christopher Columbus* (New York: Cambridge University Press, 1992), 35.

2. Olive Patricia Dickason, *The Myth of the Savage: And the Beginning of French Colonialism in the Americas* (Edmonton, Canada: University of Alberta Press, 1984), 79–80.

Therefore, we will examine conjunctions between the history of Indian policy and historical myths about Indians throughout *Seven Myths of Native American History*.

With the mass marketing of newsprint and cheap paperback Westerns that arose in the mid-nineteenth century, myths about Indians saturated popular culture. Indians could be noble, especially if they recognized the superiority of the White world, or they could be ignoble, acting as bloodthirsty savages. Either way, all Indians faced certain extinction, as their primitive pagan ways remained incompatible with the dominant Judeo-Christian values of White North America. These Indian stereotypes, and others like them, long preceded the eighteenth and nineteenth centuries' Industrial Revolution that made mass marketing possible; however, the impact of such stereotypes reproduced on historically unprecedented scales cannot be overstated. Through media saturation, Indian stereotypes became engrained across generations, especially with the twentieth-century advent of cinema, broadcast technology, and the internet. *Seven Myths of Native American History* emphasizes the role of mass media's dissemination of myths about Indians, with particular attention to the cultural impact of the American Western film genre, the Golden Age of which peaked in the late 1960s. Film probably influences culture to a greater degree than any other single media form, and because the American Western became one of film's most popular genres, this book looks in depth at a number of Westerns and their generally stereotyped portrayals of Indians. Cowboy and Indian movies as conveyors of Native American stereotypes have influenced several generations raised on such fare. In many Westerns, even those purportedly sympathetic to Native American concerns, underlying cultural assumptions on the part of the filmmakers perpetuate Indian stereotypes, and these stand in place of portrayals of individual human beings who also happen to be Indians.

As a cultural and social history, this book traces the changes in myths about Indians that have emerged over the years, and it keeps track of certain characteristics that have remained constant in these myths—especially their inherent racism and their foundation in a distorted sense of history. Myths about Indians must be called out and busted, not only because they are historical lies but also because they have historically *caused* severe destruction of Native American lives, and they continue to inflict damage on Indigenous Peoples.

Stereotypes and myths about Native Americans have traveled transregionally and transnationally. Over the centuries, they crisscrossed the Atlantic, and the forty-ninth parallel that delineates much of Canada and the United States has proven to be no barrier to misconstrued notions about Native Americans and their histories. The historical, institutional, and cultural dimensions of the seven myths examined in this book must therefore also be seen in a global perspective.

But a book on historical myths about Native Americans cannot be all things to all readers. One might reasonably argue for the inclusion of far more myths than the seven selected for this slim volume.[3] Moreover, any number of Indian stereotypes not covered in these pages—or covered too slightly for some—may be estimated as missed opportunities. My intention was not to write an exhaustive catalog or a bullet-pointed list but to look in-depth at *some* of the major myths, and therefore to spark discussions—among general readers and in classrooms—that further explore consequences of the multiple misconceptions about Native Americans. Such myths, as distorted images and perverse simplifications of Indian cultures and histories, must be refuted at every turn and replaced by accurately detailed cultural and historical accounts. *Seven Myths of Native American History* attempts to move in this direction. But how these myths arose in the first place deserves study. For by understanding their roots—which often trace back deeply into the European and Euro-American past—we can appreciate the tenacity of historical myths about Native Americans and how such myths have been kept alive across generations.

Paul Edward Jentz
North Hennepin Community College, Minneapolis

---

3. This book focuses on Native American myths that stem from the colonial era and later from the nation-states of Canada and the United States. Regarding myths about Indigenous Peoples in the histories of the Spanish Empire and its successor states, see Matthew Restall, *Seven Myths of the Spanish Conquest* (New York: Oxford University Press, 2004). The Hispanic influence on today's American Southwest makes Restall's work vital to discussions of that region in *Seven Myths of Native American History.*

Acknowledgments

Many thanks to Cary Miller, my Ph.D. advisor at the University of Wisconsin-Milwaukee, for her insight and for her valuable comments on every chapter. Thanks also to my friend and borderlands scholar Andrae Marak, whose suggestions significantly enriched this volume. My gratitude goes out as well to the two anonymous reviewers whose generous observations helped the book along its way. It was my good fortune to have my work shepherded from start to finish by Rick Todhunter, senior editor at Hackett, and to be expertly guided through the intricacies of the book's production by production director Elizabeth Wilson. I am grateful beyond measure to have Alfred J. Andrea and Andrew Holt as my editors. I could not ask for better mentors and role models. I met Andrew only a few years ago, when this book existed merely as a proposal. We quickly struck up a friendship, and his encouragement, acute perception, and gift for drawing out my best scholarship made this book possible. I met Al about ten years ago through our mutual involvement with the World History Association, over which, at the time, he presided. I value his friendship, and I owe much of my training as a historian to him.

For Gayle—

My wife, soul mate, and best friend.

INTRODUCTION

Repeat Something Often Enough and It Becomes True: Historical Myths about Indians

The . . . races who, however variant, were all characterized in the scale of colors above brown, developed a high state of civilization in arts, letters, industry, and Christianity; while these red-skinned forest tribes, coming, as in all probability they did, in small parties, at successive eras, found a stimulus to their barbarism in this very immensity of area. They wandered over the entire continent, from one end to the other, from sea to sea, in the most profound state of moral degradation, and without having reached, by any monuments traceable to them, a state of much civilization in the highest instances noticed, or given proofs of much apparent intellectuality.[1]

Thus wrote Henry Rowe Schoolcraft, an American geographer and ethnologist, in 1853.[2] To the twenty-first-century eye, his language appears both ethnocentric and racially charged, and for good reason. As an embodiment of accepted mid-nineteenth-century discourse concerning the history and cultural conditions of North America's Indians, these words demonstrate some fundamental misconceptions about the First Peoples of this continent. As non-Whites, Indians registered as automatically inferior to Euro-Americans; Indians existed in a state of "moral degradation" and ignorance; and as nomadic forest and plains dwellers, Indians lacked permanent cities, which in turn meant they lacked civilization, civilization being the sole preserve of Europeans and Euro-Americans. Schoolcraft also recommended institutional policies for the benefit of Indians: "Nothing should divert the government or people . . . from offering to these wandering and benighted branches of the human race . . . the gifts

---

1. Henry Rowe Schoolcraft, *Historical and Statistical Information Respecting the History, Condition, and Prospects of the Indian Tribes of the United States* (Philadelphia: Lippincott, Grambo, 1851–57), 3:vi–vii.

2. Having served as U.S. Indian agent and as superintendent of Indian Affairs in the Northern Department, an area covering present-day Michigan, Wisconsin, and Minnesota, Schoolcraft was commissioned by Congress to write a survey of Indians—what would become the six-volume work cited above.

of education, agriculture, and the gospel."[3] Unless taken under the wing of White largesse, the Indians would be doomed. Schoolcraft's ideas expressed here derived from a mythic history, from misconceptions that reach back to the earliest cross-cultural contacts between Europeans and North America's Indigenous populations, and that continue to thrive today.

To demonize Schoolcraft or to exonerate him as merely a product of his time misses the deeper—and more troubling—issues at stake in a mythic Native American history. His words had political consequences because they influenced policy makers. Moreover, they remain emblematic of the civilization versus savagery, Christianity versus paganism, and modernity versus primitivism binaries intrinsic to both past and present assumptions held by many non-Native North Americans and sometimes internalized by Native North Americans as well.[4] The historic wellspring of these dualities flows deeply. Most derive from European sources that in turn often echo ideas found in ancient Greek and Roman thought.[5] And the notion that the forces of civilization would eventually lead to the extinction of Native Peoples remained evident well into the twentieth century, as demonstrated by Diamond Jenness from the National Museum of Canada, who in 1930 prophesized, "Doubtless all the tribes will disappear. Some will endure only a few years longer. Others like the Eskimo may last for several centuries. Some will merge steadily with the White race, others will bequeath to future generations only an infinitesimal fraction of their blood."[6] His prophecy could not have been more false.

Any study of historical myths about North American Indians begins by dismissing a "that was then; this is now" mindset. Some views that originated centuries ago remain just as prevalent today. Moreover, the racism or ignorance that often drives these myths tells us as much about our own time as it does about any point in the past. Myths say much about the culture that invents them, as a culture's fears, anxieties, values, and aspirations often comprise the driving forces behind their creation and popularity.

---

3. Schoolcraft, *Historical and Statistical Information*, 3:8.

4. Much of Schoolcraft's work is problematic, but there is no denying his valuable overall contribution to scholarship, although it owes much to his Ojibwe wife, Jane Johnson Schoolcraft. See Robert Dale Parker, ed., *The Sound the Stars Make Rushing through the Sky: The Writings of Jane Johnson Schoolcraft* (Philadelphia: University of Pennsylvania Press, 2008) and Maureen Konkle, *Writing Indian Nations: Native Intellectuals and the Politics of Historiography: Native Intellectuals and the Politics of Historiography, 1827–1863* (Chapel Hill: University of North Carolina Press, 2004), 160–223.

5. The American studies scholar Roy Harvey Pearce writes, "In spite of the nationalism which forced its growth, the American understanding of the Indian depended on an idea of savagism whose main structure derived from European sources." Roy Harvey Pearce, *Savagism and Civilization: A Study of the Indian and the American Mind* (Berkeley: University of California Press, 1988), 82.

6. Diamond Jenness, *The Indians of Canada* (Ottawa: National Museum of Canada, 1930), 264.

Indeed, Walt Disney's *The Lone Ranger* (2013) illustrates that Hollywood, even as it attempts to avoid Indian myths and stereotypes, ends up only reinforcing them. Since 1933, when *The Lone Ranger* first appeared as a radio drama, Tonto (whose name means "stupid" in Spanish) served as the Lone Ranger's ever-faithful sidekick, a relationship premised on the Indian's constant subordination to the White hero.[7] Through twenty-two years on the radio, and from 1949 to 1957 as a television series (along with multiple films, comics, and books over the decades), Tonto became popular culture's single most identifiable image of the American Indian. A mythical Indian in a mythical American West, Tonto and his unwavering allegiance to Kemo Sabe—his name for the Lone Ranger—provided a comforting romanticized depiction of a Noble Savage who knew his place in America's racial hierarchy. The 2013 film attempts to recognize and to satirize the Tonto stereotype, but it fails more often than it succeeds in the endeavor.

A White actor, John Todd, portrayed Tonto for twenty-one years on the radio; Jay Silverheels, a Canadian Mohawk, played the role on the television series. The film returns Tonto to his radio roots by casting White actor Jonny Depp as Tonto, who also continues the tradition of stoical and article-free Tonto-speak: "Do not touch rock. Rock cursed." The film's humor often depends on Tonto-speak, as displayed in a runaway train episode: Tonto: "We jump." Lone Ranger: "What about the passengers?" Tonto: "They jump." Lone Ranger: "There are children on board!" Tonto: "All jump."[8] Comedy pretends to defuse Indian stereotypes through the very act of employing them.

The film introduces Tonto as a mannequin in a 1933 San Francisco Wild West exhibition hall. His museum case label, "The Noble Savage: In His Natural Habitat,"[9] may be quaint satire but serves more as a feeble attempt to suggest that the notion of noble savagery belongs only to bygone days. Crustily animated when a child in a Lone Ranger costume wanders into the hall, Tonto tells the boy about the "true" Lone Ranger. However, despite attempts to add complexity to Tonto's character, the film cannot break free of its racist source material, which has been reinforced by nearly a century of repetition in multiple media forms. The Lone Ranger as White hero remains center stage; Tonto's role as the Indian remains one of subservience. Indeed, the film stands premised on Tonto's belief in the Lone Ranger's superior status as a

---

7. Tonto did not appear until the tenth episode. Until then, the Lone Ranger spoke to his horse, Silver, or to himself. So in part Tonto replaced Silver as an extension of the Lone Ranger's thoughts. See Kathleen M. German, "Portrayals of American Indians in Early Radio," in *American Indians and Popular Culture: Media, Sports and Politics*, ed. Elizabeth Delaney Hoffman (Denver, Co: Praeger, 2012), 1–15. For an examination of Tonto's subservient nature, see Vine Deloria, Jr., *Custer Died for Your Sins* (Norman: University of Oklahoma Press, 1988), 200–201.

8. *The Lone Ranger*, directed by Gore Verbinski (2013, Walt Disney).

9. Ibid.

"spirit walker. . . . A man who cannot be killed in battle."[10] His death-proof warrior status trumps Tonto's lesser mortal status. Disney's attempt to put a twenty-first-century spin on an antique racist popular myth probably indicates that certain corners of American culture believe the myth still has some mileage left in it.

Tonto's trademark stoicism appears complemented by the taxidermied crow he wears on his head. At film's end he mystically escapes his museum case by transmogrifying into the crow that then wings away over the child's head. The Indian himself vanishes, in accord with the myth discussed in Chapter 4, that of the vanishing Indian who, like the buffalo, faces certain extinction as civilization advances westward. The film attempts to defuse the mythology of a mythical character. At best, it replaces one myth with another. The result: an entertaining conundrum.

The Myth of a Pan-Indian Type

Stereotypes enforce an "Indians did that; Indians do this" mindset, as if Indians everywhere have been more or less the same throughout history, and their interests remain more or less the same wherever they live. In part, the reductive term "Indian" itself gets in the way. But the reductive thinking that stems from it cannot be excused simply because Indigenous Peoples have used and continue to use the term to self-identify. What often gets lost for non-Indians is that there are today 567 federally recognized Indian nations in the United States and 634 First Nations in Canada.[11] All of these nations have unique and often competing interests, and each nation encompasses any number of bands and communities. Each nation has its own distinct identity and history, and each is concerned with its own individual social, cultural, and economic issues. The ethnic, cultural, and linguistic diversity between—and within—these nations further complicates any easy assumptions about a generalized Indian type.

Myths about groups of people ignore individuality and diversity within those groups; moreover, myths often serve political and social agendas designed to denigrate those groups as somehow less than human and as a dangerous "Other." Myths about Indians constitute an erroneous "common knowledge" about them. By deconstructing these errors that have been repeated either innocently or venomously from one generation to the next, this book attempts to introduce the historical reality and diversity disguised beneath the mythic surface. That said, a number of group terms remain common, and most are used throughout the present study—First Peoples, First Nations, Indian, Indigenous Peoples, Native American, Native North American, American Indian, Native, Aboriginal, and Amerindian. All of these terms possess

---

10. Ibid.

11. National Congress of American Indians, http://www.ncai.org/about-tribes (accessed November 17, 2017). First Nations, http://www.thecanadianencyclopedia.ca/en/article/first-nations/ (accessed November 17, 2017).

distinct historical backgrounds and cultural connotations and remain problematic to one degree or another. The term "tribe" refers to members of a group who share a common culture, and reservation governments are also referred to as tribal governments. These governments retain inherent powers repeatedly affirmed to them by the U.S. Supreme Court and by Congress in hundreds of treaties, also by the Canadian Parliament, and before that the Crown. Reservations—and in Canada, reserves—stand as only portions of an original Indigenous homeland that stretched throughout the continent. Although treaties and laws have established contracts between Indian nations and the federal government that recognized the sovereignty—the right of self-government—of these nations, both the United States and Canada have been historically reticent in recognizing that sovereignty. Indeed, both federal governments have engaged in efforts to erode what amounted to provisional sovereignty in the first place. Yet long before the U.S. and Canadian governments existed, tribes existed as fully sovereign political entities.

Moreover, the sovereignty that tribes work to preserve today places them mostly within federal, not state, law. The complex legal history and the wide range of jurisdictional lines drawn between tribal, federal, and state governments has usually confused the general public's understanding of treaty rights. Such misunderstandings—willful or not—often give rise to a racist resentment against Indians, and this stands at the core of what could be called the Myth of the Coddled Indian. This myth sees Indians as actually having too many rights, a situation that allows them to live—and live well—off of government checks and casino profits. But the Myth of the Coddled Indian could not be farther from either historical fact or current reality.

North American society has a long history of denigrating minorities. Indeed, a myth prevails that all minorities have it easy because they live as benefactors of government largesse; so, the myth goes, they are better off than White people who have to struggle to make a living. Blurred notions also prevail that some shared agenda exists between Native Americans and African Americans. Actually, however, Native Americans have not historically embraced desegregation as have African Americans. For example, the hiring practice usually followed in tribal governments is to give preference to tribal members for positions in tribal schools. This practice helps to resist assimilation policies and pressures. Other minorities in the United States have historically attempted to gain greater inclusion in American society—in other words, to assimilate. But tribes seek to maintain national sovereign identities and rights in the face of overwhelming pressure to disappear. Sometimes tribes seek similar goals as other minority groups and work together with them, but many issues also separate them. Primarily, tribes always seek to maintain sovereignty above all other issues. The sovereignty of Native nations fundamentally differentiates them from other minority populations. Sometimes non-Native Americans grumble, "They were defeated. They shouldn't have any rights." Aside from its racist viewpoint, this ignores the fact that most tribes signed land cession treaties peacefully without going to war with the

United States. And even for those tribes that did go to war, the Constitution upholds all treaties as the law of the land.

Westward across the Atlantic: Europeans and the New World's "Barbarians and Cannibals"

By the time Jacques Cartier first sailed into the Gulf of St. Lawrence in 1534, and certainly by 1607 when John Smith helped establish Jamestown in the muck of the Virginia swampland, they, and the increasing number of colonists in their wakes, arrived steeped in preconceptions about Indians. After all, mythologized notions about the Indigenous Peoples of the New World had been floating around the European homelands of the colonials for generations. For example, between 1502 and 1529, Amerigo Vespucci's letters—or letters ascribed to him—saw widespread publication in cities throughout Europe. His often fantastical reports about the New World's exotic peoples sustained and advanced the distorted, popularized, and intellectualized images of Indians.[12]

In 1504, a letter attributed to Vespucci described an encounter with what appear to have been Arawaks or Caribs, the two ethnolinguistic groups of the Caribbean:

> They all go naked [and] the color of their skin inclines to red, like the skin of a lion, and I believe that, if they were properly clothed, they would be white like ourselves. . . . They have neither king nor lord, nor do they obey anyone, but live in freedom. . . . They do not bring men to justice, nor punish a criminal. . . . Their mode of life is very barbarous, for they have no regular time for meals, but they eat at any time that they have the wish, as often at night as in the day—indeed, they eat at all hours. They take their food on the ground without napkin or any other cloth. [In] making water they are dirty and without shame. [They] are lascivious beyond measure. . . . We did not find that these people had any laws. . . . In conclusion, they live, and are content with what nature has given them.[13]

As naked barbarians, Indians lack shame, which marks them as heathens in a Judeo-Christian worldview dependent on the inherited shame of Adam and Eve's original sin in the Garden of Eden. But Vespucci holds out hope, as Indians could be turned from red to white if properly clothed (in Christian beliefs as well as dressed in all other Western values and clothing). But any civilizing transformations will remain difficult tasks because Indians possess no sense of discipline or right order. They constantly engage in sex (being "lascivious beyond measure," thereby guilty of the moral

---

12. Olive Dickason, *The Myth of the Savage and the Beginnings of French Colonialism in the Americas* (Edmonton: University of Alberta Press, 1984), 7.

13. Amerigo Vespucci, *The Letters of Amerigo Vespucci and Other Documents Illustrative of His Career*, trans. Clement R. Markham (London: Chas. J. Clark, 1894), 6–8.

failing of lust); they eat at all hours (the moral failing of gluttony); and they have neither laws nor king (both of which receive their blessing and ordination from God). Clearly, they belong to the lower animal realm of nature, not to the elevated civilized plane of humanity.

Along with nudity, reported cannibalism imprinted itself on the European imagination. In one late sixteenth-century tale, Caribs died after dining on a missionary; thereafter, they swore off eating men of the cloth. Drawing upon a treasury of Greco-Roman myths regarding wild peoples who inhabited lands far beyond the pale of civilization, early modern European authors described people whose faces grew in their chests. Others, so they soberly reported, possessed ears large enough to be used as blankets, some hopped about on only one foot, and some did not even eat food and lived only on odors.[14]

Beginning in the late sixteenth century, Richard Eden, Samuel Purchas, and other influential English writers published books and pamphlets encouraging colonization in the New World. The French travel narratives of Baron de Lahontan and Jean de Lery, along with philosophical literary artists like Montaigne, tended to use native culture as a foil to critique French society. But on the subject of Indians, both English and French writers depended on fictional creations that relied on stereotypes, which in turn relied on misinformation reported by travelers.[15]

Thus the Indian mythologizing process itself can be traced to the earliest years of the North American colonial era, and the myths grew in size and depth as the Age of American Colonialism progressed. Each time a ship's crew returned to European ports from American shores, sailors spread tales of the New World's exotic inhabitants. The stories spread and grew embellished not only by word of mouth. From the very beginning, their credibility seemed confirmed when reported, sustained, and reinforced in various mass media. With the multiplication of mass media forms over the centuries, the myths sank deeper and deeper into the Eurocentric cultures of North America's colonists and, later, of the White citizenry of North American nations.

Colonial and Federal Indian Removals and the Myths That Drove Them

Many North American colonists, particularly those who commanded great wealth, saw limitless possibilities for profiting through land speculation, and this was especially the case for the wealthy—and politically well-connected—colonists east of the Alleghany Mountains. But that land must first be acquired from the Indian nations

---

14. Dickason, *Myth of the Savage*, 20–22.

15. For extensive discussions regarding early European intellectualization of North American Indian histories and cultures, see Karen Ordahl Kupperman, *America in European Consciousness, 1493–1750* (Chapel Hill: University of North Carolina Press, 1995).

who knew it as their homeland for thousands of years before the Europeans arrived. Generally, justification for taking that land relied on the myth that Indians lacked the intelligence and industry to make full use of its resources. This myth did not recognize the fact that the continent's original inhabitants had, in a variety of environments, expertly domesticated the land and knew full well how to make it productive. However, Native People never received market value for their land. The speculators—land companies and colonial and, later, federal governments—who acquired it always intended to resell it at a higher, market-driven value. Regardless of the dominating power exercised by these entities, Native People skillfully negotiated for the best agreement achievable under very difficult and often disadvantageous circumstances while clearly articulating the importance and extent to which they used the resources of the land negotiators desired. When negotiations failed or seemed unnecessary, colonial powers did not hesitate to exercise military force to remove Indians from their land. Later, federal governments commonly employed their militaries to enforce removal policies. Both colonial and federal removal campaigns inevitably caused great hardship and death.

In both Canada and the United States, a popular misperception has it that the former treated its Indigenous Peoples more humanly than the latter. In fact, although Canada and the United States arose along different historical trajectories as nations, their westward expansions followed roughly similar economic and cultural contours. Moreover, Indian removal imposed by both Canadian reserve and U.S. reservation methods shared a similar dual purpose: to isolate the perceived savagery of Indian cultures and to clear the way for White settlers. The violence that accompanied Canadian removal and assimilation policies differed only slightly from the violent tactics often employed south of the border.[16] Otherwise, as has been asked, "Why would Aboriginals have willingly given up 95 percent of the territory they had possessed since time immemorial?"[17]

The Western

Thousands of Westerns have been produced over the past century, and many have followed a simple two-stage formula: (1) Whites and Indians engage in conflict, and (2) Whites win. Several film titles advertise Hollywood's limited selection of

---

16. Andrew R. Graybill, *Policing the Great Plains: Rangers, Mounties, and the North American Frontier, 1875–1910* (Lincoln: University of Nebraska Press, 2007), 47.

17. Mark Cronlund Anderson and Carmen Robertson, *Seeing Red: A History of Natives in Canadian Newspapers* (Winnipeg, Canada: University of Manitoba Press, 2011), 4. Also instructive is Anderson and Robertson's argument regarding the rule of three that operates in Canadian mainstream culture: "Aboriginals, when compared to white Canadians, exemplify three essentialized sets of characteristic—depravity, innate inferiority, and a stubborn resistance to progress. These representations cross-pollinate and contain within them a wide variety of elements" (6).

tribes required to drive plotlines: *Apache* (1954), *Comanche!* (1956), and *The Great Sioux Massacre* (1965), which would be Custer's Last Stand (known to the Lakota victors as the Battle of Greasy Grass). Plains Indians remained as the most recognizable group to generations of White audiences raised on Westerns, and all Plains Indians tended to blur into a single type. Give a headband, feather, face paint, and a buckskin shirt to a White actor and you have an Indian.[18] The Western formula invariably requires that the Indian, as a primitive savage, must be vanquished to save the wagon train, or settlers, or railroad, or telegraph lines, or fort, or all five at once.

By the late 1960s, the popularity of Westerns as movie house features began to wane, although for the generations born after the Golden Age of Cowboy and Indian movies, cable television networks continue to broadcast them. In part, the increasingly controversial Vietnam War led to the Western's demise. As protest against the war mounted, a cultural analogy between North American Indians and the Vietnamese people gained traction. Both groups appeared as victims of aggressive American government policies: national interests led to wars against Indians; similar interests led to the deaths of Vietnamese civilians. Therefore, the Manifest Destiny–inspired formula of the old Hollywood Western grew increasingly untenable at the box office. A new approach to the Western came with *Little Big Man* (1970), which recounts the adventures of a fictional White survivor from the 1876 Battle of Little Big Horn. The film's sympathetic portrayal of the Cheyenne, and the graphic violence perpetrated upon them by the U.S. cavalry, deliberately equates the immorality of White wars against Indians with that of American policy in Vietnam.[19] Thus, the film uses Indians only allegorically to make a protest statement against the Vietnam War. Moreover, the historical Little Big Man, an Oglala Lakota warrior, bears no resemblance to the film's fictional hero.[20]

Adherence to myths about Indians plays well in Hollywood, if equipped with updated stereotypes. *Dances with Wolves* (1990) has been praised for its sympathetic and detailed depiction of Lakota Indians as they lived in 1863. The story concentrates on a lieutenant in the U.S. army who becomes enamored of the Lakota and appropriates a Lakota identity, largely because of his growing disgust with the White world's violence against Indians. But the film merely reverses stereotypes. While the Lakota represent civilization and a well-tuned sense of justice, the Whites embody barbarism

---

18. Jacquelyn Kilpatrick, *Celluloid Indians: Native Americans and Film* (Lincoln: University of Nebraska Press, 1999), 51.

19. "The Hollywood Projects," http://thehollywoodprojects.com/2011/07/22/penn-2-little-big-man-1970/ (accessed August 6, 2015).

20. *Little Big Man*, http://www.american-tribes.com/Lakota/BIO/LittleBigMan.htm (accessed May 28, 2017).

and ignorance.[21] Thus the film concentrates on another myth—Whites as inherently evil Indian haters.

People often glean their understanding of history not from reading scholarly texts but from consuming popular culture, and here film plays an outsize role. Notwithstanding the history courses from their school years, which in some cases may have provided them with a good understanding of North American Indian history, people generally maintain a passive and indiscriminate reliance on the powerful historical illusions presented to them on the screen. So, because of films with problematic portrayals of Indian history, viewers are likely, to one degree or another, to buy into cinematically perpetuated stereotypes about Indians.[22]

Indians and the National Narrative

In part, however, the attraction and tenacity of historical misconceptions about Native Americans stems from the way in which history has traditionally been taught in the United States and Canada. Although, in recent years, grade school and high school curriculum changes in both nations have included Native American histories, resistance to curriculum changes also continues.[23] On a deeper level, classroom misconceptions rest on a problematic master narrative, or national history, centuries in the

---

21. Kilpatrick, *Celluloid Indians: Native Americans and Film*, 124–30.

22. The examination of the cultural role of cinematic stereotypes about Indians has been the focus of extensive scholarship. A few such studies include Angela Aleiss, *Making the White Man's Indian: Native Americans and Hollywood Movies* (Westport, CT: Praeger, 2005); Denise K. Cummings, ed., *Perspectives on Contemporary American Indian Film and Art* (East Lansing: Michigan State University Press, 2011); and Michelle H. Raheja, *Reservation Reelism: Redfacing, Visual Sovereignty, and Representations of Native Americans in Film* (Lincoln: University of Nebraska Press), 2010.

23. For example, as reported by CBC Radio on June 10, 2015, the history of the residential school era was largely absent from the textbooks and curricula used to teach history in Canada's schools. However, a recommendation of the Truth and Reconciliation Commission's final report is to change that and to make lessons about residential schools mandatory from kindergarten through Grade 12. Anna Maria Tremonti, "History of Residential Schools Ignored in Canadian Curriculum," http://www.cbc.ca/radio/thecurrent/the-current-for-june-10-2015-1.3107341/history-of-residential-schools-ignored-in-canadian-curriculum-1.3107389 (accessed June 10, 2015). Truth and Reconciliation Commission of Canada, "Truth and Reconciliation 2015 Report," http://www.trc.ca/websites/trcinstitution/File/2015/Findings/Calls_to_Action_English2.pdf (accessed June 10, 2015). See report by Shannon Speed, director of Native American and Indigenous Studies at the University of Texas at Austin, "'Pro-American' History Textbooks Hurt Native Americans," http://www.huffingtonpost.com/shannon-speed/proamerican-history-textb_b_6199070.html (accessed June 10, 2015) and Georgianna Lincoln, "Lack of True Indian History in Textbooks," *Authentic Alaska: Voices of Its Native Writers*, ed. Susan B. Andrew and John Creed (Lincoln: University of Nebraska Press, 1998), 91–95.

making.[24] Generally, a national history tells the story that a nation wants to believe about itself, a story that softens the past by turning historical figures into either heroes or villains. The heroes turn into statues in public squares, villains provide scapegoats, and the nation's sense of its own righteousness prevails. Thus national histories tend to rest on mythical foundations, so when Indians appear in the story, they often do so within the confines of myth.

English philosopher John Locke (1632–1704) provided one source for certain scholarly misconceptions about Indians. His *Second Treatise of Civil Government* (1690) argues that Indians could not claim ownership of the land because they only hunted on it without improving it. Locke claimed that Indians lived as part of nature and maintained only elementary levels of social and political organization. Taught in both French and English universities, and by the mid-eighteenth century in North American colonial schools as well, the *Second Treatise* formed part of the training for missionaries and officials before they came to North America and before they headed out to Indian Country.[25] Lockean rationalization reinforced negative stereotypes about Indians. Such misconceptions helped to justify aggressive North American westward expansion, which advanced apace with the institution of reservations and reserves.

But centuries before Locke, indeed beginning with their first contact with North America's Native Peoples, Europeans created a misconception echo chamber fed by the writings of political and economic philosophers, the journals of sea captains and their crews, popular printed and painted images, plays, novels, poems, newspaper articles, and political agendas. The volume increased across the centuries and continues to play out through electronic media.[26] The net effect has been to drown out the historical record.

Regarding North America, the imperial narrative trajectory of Spanish, English, French, and Dutch histories focused on colonial settlement. This approach marginalized Indians, discounted their histories, and generally characterized them with a repertoire of some of the same stereotypes that remain current today. North America's national histories picked up where the imperial histories left off. National histories begin their stories more or less with the country's European and Euro-American

---

24. Daniel K. Richter summarizes, "The 'master narrative' of early America remains essentially European-focused. While American Indians might make 'contributions to the dominant culture' . . . Native Peoples remain bit players in the great drama of a nation's being born and spreading, for better or worse, westward across the continent." Daniel K. Ricther, *Facing East from Indian Country: A Native History of Early America* (Cambridge, MA: Harvard University Press, 2001), 8.

25. Cary Miller, *Ogimaag: Anishinaabeg Leadership, 1760–1845* (Lincoln: University of Nebraska Press, 2010), 239.

26. Kathleen M. German explores some of the consequences stemming from electronic dissemination of myths about Indians. Kathleen M. German, "Portrayals of American Indians in Early Radio," and "American Indians in Silent Film, 1894–1929," *American Indians and Popular Culture: Media, Sports, and Politics*, Vol. 1, ed. Elizabeth Delaney Hoffman (Denver, CO: Praeger, 2012), 1–32.

founders in order to explain how the nation came into being. These histories tend to position First Peoples as the tragic victims of inevitable westward expansion and as the casualties of progress, and they discount or ignore the fact that, from the moment of contact with Europeans, Indians assessed the newcomers according to their own social, economic, and diplomatic priorities.[27] Accordingly, Native People calculated the value of alliances with the new European groups. Tribes would question the value of potential trade agreements with colonials, and they would need to know the value of military coalitions as well. In other words, could these new people help us defeat a neighboring enemy, or could they help us with our own expansionist policy? Both Euro-Americans and Native Americans exercised active historical agency.

Nations—They Get in the Way

The three North American nation-states—Canada, the United States, and Mexico—established their borders within the past few centuries, and Indigenous Peoples, who lived in North America for many thousands of years before these nations drew their lines on the map, tend now to be identified with one modern nation-state or another. Legally recognized as these relatively recent national jurisdictions might be, they become problematic as we think back historically to times before their existence, yet we anachronistically retain today's cartographic boundaries as we think of these Native Peoples.[28] One corrective to this anachronistic way of perceiving the past is borderlands scholarship, which delves into issues of modern political boundaries and the communities that existed before national boundaries and whose economic, social, and cultural patterns continue to straddle them. Hence the concept of transnationalism recognizes and looks beyond borders, even as, for some Native Americans, national borders have profound consequences for their communities.

For example, the Mohawk Nation at Akwesasne spans the border between the United States and Canada, namely New York State and Ontario. The Mohawk consider it a single community, regardless of its division by an international boundary. But political and law enforcement decisions made by the United States and Canada have sometimes made the border itself all too apparent to the Mohawk. Particularly, the Seaway International Bridge across the St. Lawrence, over which the Mohawk by law have crossing rights between their Canadian and American land, has often been the site of controversy. In 1968, Akwesasne protestors blockaded the bridge, calling for an end to duties charged to the Mohawk people on goods at the border.

---

27. For an analysis of the manipulation of language that gradually erased Indians from local and national histories, see James Joseph Buss, *Winning the West with Words: Language and Conquest in the Lower Great Lakes* (Norman: University of Oklahoma Press, 2011).

28. Andrae Marak and Gary Van Valen, "Introduction: Transnational Indians of the North American West," in *Transnational Indians in the North American West* (College Station: Texas A&M University Press, 2015), 5.

Disputes over border-crossing rights continue to this day. Akwesasne leaders argue that the 1794 Jay Treaty between England and the United States guarantees duty-free crossing for Indigenous Peoples.[29] An oral tradition among the Akwesasne concerns their concept of the border at the time it was drawn up at the end of the American Revolutionary War. As recalled in 1959 by Philip Kakwiranoron Cook, a chief of the St. Regis Mohawk Tribal Council:

> The Indians understood that the boundary would come to the edge of the reservation lands and then would project 8 feet into the air until it reached the other side of the Indian lands then back down to the ground where it would be in the way of the white man. The Indian had a unique way of thinking. It seems that he realized that an Indian would never grow as high as 8 feet tall, and he would never grow high enough to bump into that boundary.[30]

In other words, how could a border imposed long after a Mohawk community had been established in any way divide that community? So an understanding of North American Indian history must reimage borders, which are culturally porous and impermanent. Borders simultaneously exist and do not exist. But by relying on hard-and-fast borders between nations, national histories—and the national identities that emanate from them—can be ill equipped for understanding the lives of people between those borders. However real national identities might appear, national histories also contain an element of myth that often cannot be readily apparent or easily separated from the facts. In this way too, the historical record of Native Americans becomes blurred into a mythic past, particularly regarding their pre-European contact history.

Moreover, the concepts of empire and the borderlands of empires require refocusing our work. For example, the North American West stands heavily imprinted by the Spanish Empire and by its successor state, Mexico. However much coveted by the French Empire, the West stood mostly outside of its grasp, as the French beachhead generally remained east of the Mississippi and north of the Great Lakes. But between these two powers stood another, an empire that not only rivaled but often forced the Spanish and French empires to do its bidding—the Comanche Empire.[31]

---

29. Steven Henry Martin, "A Border Runs through It: Mohawk Sovereignty and the Canadian State," *Briarpatch*, July 11, 2010, https://briarpatchmagazine.com/articles/view/a-border-runs-through-it (accessed May 10, 2017).

30. Philip Kakwiranoron Cook, qtd. in Darren Bonaparte, "Akwesasne: A Border Runs through It: Documents Shed Light on Historic Divisions at Akwesasne," *Indian Country Today*, February 25, 2017, https://indiancountrymedianetwork.com/news/opinions/akwesasne-border-runs/ (accessed May 11, 2017).

31. Pekka Hämäläinen makes a compelling argument for characterizing the Comanches as an imperial power, one different in certain characteristics than the European empires that colonized North America yet one that followed their same ideas of conquest, expansion, and transregional control. Pekka Hämäläinen, *The Comanche Empire* (New Haven, CT: Yale University Press, 2008).

Two of ten bronze panels on the main entrance door of the Cathedral Basilica of San Francisco, Santa Fe, New Mexico. During the church's restoration in 1986, Donna Quasthoff was commissioned to sculpt panels depicting significant moments in the cathedral's history. The first panel illustrates the rescue of the statue of the Virgin Mary during the Pueblo Revolt of 1680. The second panel portrays the retaking of Santa Fe by Spanish troops in 1692. Because the Virgin Mary is believed to have secured a supposedly bloodless reconquest of the province of Santa Fe de Nuevo México, she and her statue were given the honorific title *La Conquistadora*. The chapel containing the rescued statue of the Conqueress is a major site of veneration today. Conspicuously absent from the panels are the Pueblo people, except as implied agents of destruction, as suggested by the flames from which the Spaniards flee. Photos courtesy of A. J. Andrea © 2018.

Originating as a tribe of hunter-gatherers on the central Great Plains, the Comanches likely fled political turmoil there and migrated to the northern canyonland frontier of Spain's New Mexico colony in the early 1700s. For about two decades, in alliance with the Utes, who had also recently migrated to the region, they coordinated a lucrative trade in horses and slaves by plundering both commodities from other tribes and from Spanish colonies. By the mid-1700s, the Comanche Empire stretched throughout areas of present-day New Mexico, Colorado, Kansas, Oklahoma, and Texas. The empire's rapid expansion and economic durability relied primarily on horses.[32]

Introduced by Spaniards in the sixteenth century, horses transformed the West economically and culturally. The tempo of these changes increased dramatically following the 1680 Pueblo Revolt that was focused in present-day northern New Mexico. Roundly defeated by the Pueblo peoples—who rebelled against Spanish colonial

---

32. Ibid., 24–27. Numic-speakers, both the Utes and Comanches likely originated in the same Sierra Nevada area, migrated separately, but centuries later reunited.

injustices—and sent fleeing southward back into present-day Mexico, the Spaniards left in their wake hundreds of horses. Herds quickly multiplied, and when Spanish colonials finally returned to reestablish their New Mexico colonies, they confronted a new political landscape, one shaped by the growing numbers of horses. Not only chastened by the Pueblo Indians, with whom they now established a relationship built more on accommodation than on the religious persecution and labor exploitation that had sparked the revolt, the Spaniards also confronted the increasingly powerful Comanche Empire.

Ironically, the Spanish colonists bore a certain responsibility for the rise of Comanche power. The Comanches entered the region on foot. Dogs provided their only assistance for transporting their belongings. But within a generation, equestrianism—introduced by the Spaniards—transformed the Comanches into a transregional empire. A horse could drag a 300-pound load on a travois, four times the carrying capacity of a large dog, and per day could cover at least twice the distance as a dog. Thus with horses the Comanche could now move more hides, meat, and household items across greater distances. So their trade network expanded and, as horse-mounted hunters, they could search out a wider range of animals, particularly bison. They also hunted slaves. Navajo, Pawnee, and Apache villages all fell victim to Comanche-Ute slave raiders, who sold them to Spanish traders, who in turn sold them throughout their own empire.[33]

Horses made the Comanches not only mobile but politically powerful as well, with an expanding kinship network uniting a multiregional empire. Meanwhile, Spain's northern colonial outposts cycled through periods of military assaults against the Comanches and political appeasement of them. But Spain's endeavors in New Mexico also included a strategic defense against French imperial designs in the West, so vigilance against their European rivals further burdened Spanish military resources.

In many ways, however, colonial claims made by both the Spanish and the French empires stood as cartographic fictions, especially because their colonial populations remained insignificant compared to the Native population base. In reality, Indians, not European colonials, controlled the land. Only through maintaining alliances with Native American nations could either European power hope to maintain a North American presence. So for nearly 150 years, the Comanche Empire remained the paramount power in the West. Indeed, initially the Comanche controlled the provisions they received as tribute in several treaties made with the Spaniards, although over the decades fortunes shifted for both powers.

Not until the mid-nineteenth century, with the westward advance of American settlers, did the Comanches sign a removal treaty. By 1875, the Comanches had fully relocated to a reservation in southwest Oklahoma.[34] Today, Comanche Nation

---

33. Ibid.

34. Brian Daffron, "Ten Things You Need to Know about the Comanche Nation," *Indian Country Today*, October 16, 2014, https://indiancountrymedianetwork.com/news/native-news/10-things-you-need-to-know-about-the-comanche-nation/ (accessed May 27, 2017).

enrollment totals 15,191. The Comanche Nation College opened in 2002, the first tribal college in the state. In 2008, the Nation founded Comanche Nation Enterprises, with subsidiaries that include Comanche Nation Construction and other enterprises that enrich the nation. The Comanche both control and are continually expanding their own educational and healthcare systems and employment opportunities for tribal members throughout the professions. In short, the end of the Comanche Empire did not mean the end of the Comanches as a people. Yet a common misperception has it that Euro-American expansion westward inevitably caused the extinction or near extinction of Indians, a guiding error perpetuated as the Myth of the Vanishing Indian, as will be examined in Chapter 4.

The potency of misconceptions, of myths about Indians, includes the notion that they have no history and possess only a "memory culture."[35] This idea originated in the first decades of the twentieth century through the work of anthropologist Franz Boas. His study of American Indians led him to conclude that history—defined as acknowledgment and study of change over time—could not be perceived or transmitted in an oral culture. In other words, Indians did not possess a historical consciousness. Their oral culture could not sustain a record of historical changes experienced by that culture.[36]

However, recent scholars have been overturning Boas' theory. By examining a wide range of oral, documentary, and material evidence, they now recognize Indian histories as dynamic as that of any people anywhere else in the world. Also, as with all human beings, Indians possess what is known as "historical agency." That is, they do not merely passively react when confronted by outside forces. As groups and as individuals, they have been shapers of their own world, and they continue to shape their own world today.[37]

The Indian Gaming Industry

One area that drives many misconceptions about Indians today concerns the Indian gaming industry. Contrary to popular belief, the industry has not provided a significant revenue stream for most Native Americans.

The origins of the Native American gaming industry date to the late 1970s, when several tribes experimented with bingo operations. Then came the 1987 Supreme

---

35. Peter Nabokov, *A Forest of Time: American Indian Ways of History* (Cambridge, UK: Cambridge University Press, 2005), 12.

36. Ibid., 13.

37. Germane here is Philip J. Deloria's comment on historical agency: "The world we inhabit is the shared creation of all peoples, though the costs and benefits have been parceled out with astonishing inequality, as well as the notions about who has been active in that creation and who has been acted on." Philip J. Deloria, *Indians in Unexpected Places* (Lawrence: University of Kansas Press, 2004), 6.

Court decision in *California v. Cabazon Band of Mission Indians,* which gave Native American tribes the legal right to establish gaming enterprises on reservation land without interference from the state. The ruling rested on the band's argument that its sovereign status meant that the state could not interfere with its affairs. But, as noted earlier, Native American tribal sovereignty has historically been an ambiguous and provisional affair. Federal and state governments have often only grudgingly recognized it. Thus, one year after *California v. Cabazon,* Congress passed the Indian Gaming Regulatory Act (IGRA). This act requires tribes to negotiate a compact with their respective states regarding the distribution of most gaming profits within the tribe. In part because it interferes with tribal sovereignty, IGRA remains controversial.[38]

Intended to strike a balance between state and tribal interests, IGRA has not been particularly successful in allaying the fears that some states have regarding the wealth generated by the more successful Indian gaming enterprises. States have opposed tribal gaming on social and religious grounds or have demanded tribal-state revenue sharing agreements.[39] And a primary right granted to tribes by IGRA was struck down in *Seminole Tribe of Florida v. Florida* (1991), as the court ruled in favor of the state, granting it immunity from suit by tribes for failure to negotiate in good faith for gaming rights. Again, tribal sovereignty came under attack.[40]

But *California v. Cabazon* did clear the way for the growth of the Native American gaming industry, and along the way it has generated both tribal revenue and a number of myths. Lingering near IGRA is the notion that the state must keep an eye on Indian prosperity since, in line with a long-standing myth, Indians are incapable of financial responsibility.

Moreover, the success of a few tribal casino operations that have proved transformative, such as those of the Mashantucket Pequot in Connecticut, the Shakopee Mdewakanton Sioux in Minnesota, and the Seminoles' Hollywood Gaming Center on Miami's Gold Coast, has led to the myth that Indians everywhere are benefiting from casino profits. This myth overshadows the experience of the many tribes whose gaming endeavors have proven only marginally profitable. Beyond that, more than two-thirds of 567 federally recognized Indian tribes in the United States do not participate in any form of gaming.[41] In 2014, the U.S. Census Bureau reported that 28.3 percent of Native Americans live in poverty, the highest rate for any racial group, and

---

38. James I. Schaap, "The Growth of the Native American Gaming Industry: What Has the Past Provided, and What Does the Future Hold?" *American Indian Quarterly* 34 (2010): 365–66.

39. Eric S. Lent, "Are the States Beating the House?: The Validity of Tribal-State Revenue Sharing under the Indian Gaming Regulatory Act," *Georgetown Law Journal* 91 (2003): 451.

40. Justin Neel Baucom, "Bringing Down the House: As States Attempt to Curtail Indian Gaming, Have We Forgotten the Foundational Principles of Tribal Sovereignty?" *American Indian Law Review* 30 (2005): 432.

41. Schaap, 369.

compares with a national poverty rate of 15.5%.[42] Put another way, gaming income remains broadly elusive for most Native American communities, where high unemployment and impoverished households remain the norm.

Geography has much to do with the success or failure of Indian gaming ventures. Casinos located near large urban areas have proven successful, but without a concentrated population base from which to draw customers, tribes cannot justify casino investment. The economic prowess of tribes with favorably located gaming enterprises, however, is demonstrated by their creation of more than 636,000 jobs, according to recent statistics, and Indian gaming revenues increased from $7.4 billion in 1997 to $26.7 billion in 2008.[43] Profits have financed schools, hospitals, and housing on reservation land. But too often there prevails resentment and suspicion of tribal wealth generated from the gaming industry. In one of the more notorious attacks against Indian gaming, Donald Trump testified before a House subcommittee in 1993, erroneously claiming that the mafia controlled Native American casinos and that Indians faked their ancestry to cash in on gaming profits.[44] Fearing Native American gaming as competition to his own casinos, he denigrated Indians as unworthy pawns controlled by the underground. Herein lies another myth: that Indians make money only through dishonest means. With no basis in fact, this myth relies on a racist resentment and distrust of Indians. Like so many other myths, this one finds a home in a White privilege worldview and follows the formula, "I'm not prejudiced against Indians, but. . . ."

Sports Teams and Indian Stereotypes

Indian stereotypes have often been enshrined through team names and mascots in high school, college, and professional sports. Most famously (or infamously), five major-league professional sports teams in the United States remain at the center of long-standing attempts to raise awareness of the harm perpetuated by their chosen trademarked identities: the Washington Redskins, Atlanta Braves, Chicago Blackhawks, Cleveland Indians, and Kansas City Chiefs.

Continued defense of the Washington team's name "Redskins," a historically racist slur against Indians, receives support from deep pockets and from a vocal fan base that denies the inherent racism in the name.[45] Conversely, the argument goes, the

---

42. U.S. Census Bureau, https://www.census.gov/newsroom/facts-for-features/2015/cb15-ff22.html (accessed May 13, 2017).

43. Schaap, 370.

44. Shawn Boburg, "Donald Trump's Long History of Clashes with Native Americans," *Washington Post*, July 25, 2016.

45. One summary of the controversy surrounding the team's name is "Media Take Sides on Redskins Name," http://www.pewresearch.org/fact-tank/2013/10/30/media-take-sides-on-redskins-name/ (accessed August 3, 2015).

name actually honors Indians. A range of opinions exists among Indians regarding the team name "Redskins," although most consider it offensive.[46] Similar controversies surround baseball's Cleveland Indians and that team's mascot, Chief Wahoo. Also considered offensive as a racially charged stereotype is the "Tomahawk Chop" perpetuated by fans of Florida State University's Seminoles, the Atlanta Braves, and the Kansas City Chiefs. The University of North Dakota recently changed its team name, "Fighting Sioux" to "Fighting Hawks," but only after years of pressure. It had been one of the thirty college teams currently under notice from the National Collegiate Athletic Association for maintaining racist Indian mascots, nicknames, or logos.[47]

The current policy of the National Congress of American Indians states its unambiguous opposition to the continued Indian stereotyping by sports teams:

> Indian mascots and stereotypes present a misleading image of Indian people and feed the historic myths that have been used to whitewash a history of oppression. Despite decades of work to eliminate the use of discrimination and derogatory images in American sports, the practice has not gone away.[48]

Myths as Tools

Myths about Indians have served as expedient tools to advance political, cultural, and economic agendas for Euro-Canadian and Euro-American westward expansion, and they persist in North America's popularized accounts about the history of its Indigenous Peoples. Unhappily, these myths, and the racism that attends them, continue to manifest themselves in ugly forms.

For example, in the 1997 *Mille Lacs Decision*, the Eighth Circuit U.S. Court of Appeals affirmed the 1837 treaty rights of the Ojibwe, a decision upheld by the U.S. Supreme Court two years later.[49] In short, this meant that the Mille Lacs Band of Ojibwe Indians retained usufructuary rights to spear fishing in Minnesota's Lake Mille Lacs. For decades before, and in some areas continuing today in 2017, White

---

46. See Rachel Johnson, "67 Percent of Native Americans Say 'Redskins' Is Offensive" http://indiancountrytodaymedianetwork.com/2014/06/04/67-percent-native-americans-say-redskins-offensive-155143 (accessed August 3, 2015).

47. For a list of colleges and universities that have recently removed their Indian mascots, nicknames, or logos, see USA Today, "List of Schools That Changed Native American Nicknames," http://www.usatoday.com/story/sports/2013/09/12/native-american-mascot-changes-ncaa/2804337/ (accessed December 7, 2016).

48. National Congress of American Indians, "Anti-Defamation and Mascots," http://www.ncai.org/policy-issues/community-and-culture/anti-defamation-mascots (accessed May 14, 2017).

49. Great Lakes Indian Fish & Wildlife Commission, "Treaty Rights Reserved," http://www.glifwc.org/TreatyRights/treatyrights.html (accessed July 6, 2015).

backlash against the treaty rights stands in full display. One popular slogan proclaims "Save a Walleye. . . . Spear an Indian."[50] Local White citizens formed committees protesting treaty rights, and in public rallies they chanted anti-Indian slogans and carried signs and effigies depicting derogatory stereotypes of Indians. In 1989, members of the Wisconsin House of Representatives introduced a Treaty Abrogation Bill.[51] Elsewhere, anti-Indian groups remain active throughout the United States[52] and in Canada as well, despite the popular image of "Canadian nice." Quebec's 1990 Oka Crisis, which involved a confrontation between Mohawks and the police, led to an emergence of White backlash and increased activity of anti-Indian groups across Canada.[53]

Myths about North American Indians originated as colonial products inherited by North America's nation-states.[54] In part, the popular appeal of myths about Indians speaks to a desire for a simple history driven by heroes and villains; also, the Indian as Other perpetuates the civilization/savage binary that assures the "civilized" individual's sense of superiority. Cultural accretions over half a millennium in the making provide the generation to generation links that have kept these myths alive. This book focuses on seven such myths—myths that have served as convenient tools for persons and groups with various and often conflicting agendas.

These myths include the Myth of the Noble Savage, which conjures images of fierce but chivalrous horse-mounted warriors and virtuous Indian princesses, while the Ignoble Savage myth, to the contrary, portrays Indian men as violent, ignorant, and drunken clowns and Indian women as drudges and sluts. The notion that North America offered only wilderness to be conquered by European colonizers led to the Myth of the Wilderness, in which Indians figured as nonpersons, as part of the landscape. The mythic vanishing Indian faces certain doom as an unsustainable relic of the past who must give way to westward expansion and the advance of civilization. Mythic authentic Indians exist frozen in time in feathers and tomahawks, living in tipis (tepees) surrounded by totem poles. The Myth of the Ecological Indian idealizes each Native American as instinctively at home within the natural world, with inherent gifts for living there in harmonious balance. Finally, the Myth of the Mystical Indian refers to the commercial exploitation of Indian religious practices by non-Indians, a

---

50. Great Lakes Indian Fish & Wildlife Commission, "Protests," http://www.glifwc.org/TreatyRights/protest.html (accessed July 6, 2015).

51. Great Lakes Indian Fish & Wildlife Commission, "Moving beyond Argument Racism & Treaty Rights," http://www.glifwc.org/TreatyRights/MovingBeyondArugment.pdf (accessed July 6, 2015).

52. Gale, "Global Issues In Context," http://find.galegroup.com/gic/infomark.do?&idigest=a1246e 79a84f851714ff24bc5fffc137&type=retrieve&tabID=T001&prodId=GIC&docId=CX28312000 37&source=gale&userGroupName=mtbakerjrhs&version=1.0 (accessed July 6, 2015).

53. Mark Cronlund Anderson and Carmen L. Robertson, *Seeing Red: A History of Natives in Canadian Newspapers* (Winnipeg, Canada: University of Manitoba Press, 2011), 219–42.

54. See David Spurr, "The Colonizer Speaks as Inheritor," in *The Rhetoric of Empire, Colonial Discourse in Journalism, Travel Writing and Imperial Administration* by Spurr (Durham: Duke University Press, 1993), 28.

process that turns the Indian into a static mythologized image of comforting spiritual wisdom.

This book considers post-1492 North American history as a story of interwoven human relationships carried on across half a millennium of contact between North America's Indigenous Peoples and European colonists and Euro-North Americans. Across time, political, religious, and academic institutions, as well as the multiple forms of print and broadcast media, have shaped White North American ideas about Indians. In all areas—race, religion, gender, and class—expectations about North American Indians, past and present, have often been viewed through the distorted lenses of myth and stereotype. The clarifying work of replacing wrongheaded notions about Indians with historical facts remains ongoing, work that the following chapters will now undertake.

1. A Savage Cicero: The Myth of the Noble Savage

In yonder bow'r behold the council meet,
Solemn and grand, without the help of art;
Of justice, commerce, peace, and love, they treat,
Whilst eloquence unlabour'd speaks the heart.
See from the throng a painted warrior rise,
A savage *Cicero*, erect he stands,
Awful, he throws around his piercing eyes,
Whilst native dignity respect commands.
High o'er his brow wantons a plumed crest,
The deep vermilion on his visage glows,
A silver moon beams placid round his breast,
And a loose garment from his shoulders flows.
One nervous arm he holds to naked view,
The chequer'd wampum glitt'ring in his hand;
His speech doth all the attic fire renew,
And nature dictates the sublime and grand.
Untouch'd by art, e'en in the savage breast,
With native lustre, how doth reason shine!
Science ne'er taught him how to argue best,
The schools ne'er strove his language to refine.
What noble thoughts, what noble actions rise
From in-born genius, unrestrain'd and free?[1]

The Myth of the Noble Savage stands amply displayed in this stanza from Francis Hopkinson's 1772 poem, "The Treaty."[2] Set in a forest bower, the scene resumes the poem's primary location as established by Hopkinson's first line, "Mid the deep

---

1. Francis Hopkinson, "The Treaty," in *The Miscellaneous Essays and Occasional Writings of Francis Hopkinson, Esq.* Vol. 1, by Hopkinson (Philadelphia: T. Dobson, 1792), 126. Hopkinson inscribed the poem "to the honourable Thomas and Richard Penn, proprietors of the Province of Pennsylvania" and notes, "This poem was written upon the banks of the river Lehigh in the year 1761, when the author served as secretary in a solemn conference held between the government of Pennsylvania and the chiefs of several Indian nations" (120).

2. See Roy Harvey Pearce's brief explication of Hopkinson's poem in *Savagism and Civilization: A Study of the Indian and the American Mind* (Berkeley: University of California Press, 1988), 179–80.

murmur of luxuriant groves."[3] Although Indians have gathered at the treaty grounds from mountains, valleys, lakes, and plains, the poem's focus remains the forest, the "glitt'ring centre of the pole" to which the chiefs have all been led.[4] This sylvan setting typifies a long-standing landscape equation between the Indian and the woods. Indeed, the early Eurocentric imagination beheld the Noble Savage primarily as an inhabitant of the forest, virtually inseparable from the trees themselves, until, following nineteenth-century trans-Mississippi White settlement, the Indian assumed a new stereotype as strictly a plains dweller.

In Hopkinson's poem, the Indian speaker's nobility in thought and action arises through a natural genius born of an Eden-like land, where he lives in freedom unburdened by the knowledge of science and scholarship. This generic Indian does not exist as an individual person but as a blank slate on which the poet inscribes ideas that resonate with his Euro-American audiences. For example, one denizen of the forest, despite his lack of "art" (read "civilization"), possesses the oratorical eloquence of the Roman statesman and orator Cicero, albeit a "savage" Cicero. By invoking the Roman Republic of the first century BCE, when Cicero lived, Hopkinson relies on a popularized image of that world's noble stature in the Euro-American mind to make his point. The comparison serves to ennoble the Indian speaker, whose own name escapes the poet's notice. Hopkinson also metaphorically identifies the speaker with classical Greece, as "His speech doth all the attic fire renew." "Attic" refers to the Greek dialect spoken in Attica, the peninsula on which Athens is located, but more importantly it connotes an antique era stereotypically characterized by purity and simplicity. Writers, artists, and politicians have long relied on popularized and idealized notions of ancient Rome and Greece to signify power, stateliness, and, of course, nobility. But in the hands of commentators on Native Americans, these notions often extinguish individuality in favor of idealized images in which Indians primarily exist only insofar as they are relevant to a Eurocentric worldview.

Wherefrom the Noble Savage?

A European fantasy inherited by Euro-American and Euro-Canadian cultures, the Myth of the Noble Savage retains its potency down to the present.[5] Indeed, it continues to find lodging in subtle and sometimes surprising corners of both popular and academic cultures. Furthermore, its antiquity positions the Noble Savage as a

---

3. Hopkinson, "The Treaty," 120.

4. Ibid., 125.

5. A current argument questions the thesis that Jean-Jacques Rousseau invented the term "Noble Savage" in the eighteenth century and identifies the term's initial appearance in Marc Lescarbot's 1609 *Histoirie de la Novelle France* (History of New France). For a detailed examination of this argument, see Ter Ellingson, *The Myth of the Noble Savage* (Berkeley: University of California Press, 2001).

foundation myth, so its cultural DNA shows up—to one degree or another—in all other myths covered in this book. In short, the myth freezes Indians in a changeless and primitive state, one untainted by the cares and complexities of civilization as defined by Old World values that prized rigid class structures, written contracts, and private property. In the hands of polemicists the Noble Savage often operated as a tool for criticizing those values. Praised for a perceived simplicity and ease of lifestyle based on wandering freely through nature, the Noble Savage seemed to present an antidote to the urban world's competitive materialism.

Ancient Greek sources show that the Myth of the Noble Savage flourished at least as early as the eighth century BCE. Subsequently, the notion of noble savagery appeared from time to time in a number of European societies, whose educated elites drew many of their ideas from ancient Greco-Roman literature. When sixteenth-century travel writers, and later writers and artists, used classical images to describe North American Indians they did so, in part, to make the strange familiar. By drawing on a traditional stock of idealized images of noble men and women from antiquity, these writers framed their understanding of societies that otherwise appeared inexplicable to their eyes.[6]

Many sixteenth-century European observers transported to the New World the classical myth of a Golden Age, a primordial period of peace and harmony when food grew in such abundance that people did not have to toil and all lived lives of goodness and nobility.[7] Based on such reports, Theodor De Bry's sixteenth-century illustrations often idealized Indians by drawing them in a fashion similar in proportion, stance, and dress to that of ancient Greek statuary, and nudity, which he also depicted, further suggested a purity evocative of Golden Age ideals.[8] According to the thinking of the time, humanity degenerated with the passing of the Golden Age. The virtues of primitivism gave way to the complexities of civilization, a transition indicated in Marc Lescarbot's seventeenth-century record of the eastern Canadian Mi'kmaq in the Bay of Fundy. He did not describe the Indians he met so much as use them to criticize European society. Again, Indians did not exist within their own right; rather they served as tools for examining European society:

> All savages generally do live everywhere in common the most perfect and
> most worthy life of man, seeing that he is a sociable creature, the life of
> the ancient golden age. . . . They are truely noble, not having any action

---

6. Arthur O. Lovejoy and George Boas, *Primitivism and Related Ideas in Antiquity* (Baltimore, MD: Johns Hopkins University Press, 1997), 289–90 and Andrew Fitzmaurice, *Humanism and America: An Intellectual History of English Colonisation, 1500–1625* (Cambridge, UK: Cambridge University Press, 2003), 160.

7. John Dilon, "Plato and the Golden Age," *Hermanthena* 153 (1992): 21.

8. Helen Carr, *Inventing the American Primitive: Politics, Gender, and the Representation of Native American Literary Traditions, 1789–1939* (New York: New York University Press, 1996), 125; Felipe Fernández-Armesto, *Columbus* (New York: Oxford University Press, 1991), 82.

but is generous, whether we consider their hunting, or their employment in the wars, or that one search out their domestical actions, wherein the women do exercise themselves. [But] the most part of the world have lived so from the beginning, and by degrees men have been civilized . . . and have formed commonwealths for to live under certain laws, rule, and policy.[9]

Projected as an image of the European past, Native Americans lived apart from the cultural present of laws, books, judges, and property distinctions, all considered the foundations of "civilized" society. Europeans and North American colonists periodically reinvented the Myth of the Noble Savage in terms recognizable to their own changing worldviews.

Noble Savages and Good Indians: Pocahontas and Squanto Help Build America

Related to the Noble Savage stands the Good Indian, who *becomes* good through placing the interests of White culture above those of his or her own culture. Both the Noble Savage and the Good Indian find expression in the centuries-long process of mythmaking surrounding the story of Pocahontas. In this process, the Pocahontas story changed shape according to the cultural needs of the moment, and as the subject of sculptors, painters, poets, playwrights, and filmmakers, Pocahontas has been politicized at every turn. Perhaps the sparseness of the historical record regarding the life of Pocahontas accounts for the zeal with which her storytellers have rushed to fill in the blanks. To tell only what scholars know as a verifiable account of her life makes for a slim story; therefore, not the *story*, but the *idea* of Pocahontas has been popularized. Tailored to the needs of specific political agendas, whether local, sectional, national, racial, social, or environmental, Pocahontas ceases her historical existence and serves as a malleable artifact shaped to purpose in the hands of the beholder.

Scholars know only the approximate year of her birth, 1595; her so-called rescue of Captain John Smith in 1607; her 1612 abduction by Captain Argall of Jamestown; her 1613 conversion to Christianity; her 1614 marriage to John Rolfe; the 1615 birth of their son, Thomas; her 1616 trip to England, which included a reception at the court of King James I and Queen Anne, attendance at two plays, and sitting for the Simon Van de Passe engraving of her portrait; and her 1617 death and burial at Gravesend in England.[10] Measured elaboration on some of these events can be corroborated through multiple sources; however, the record of her rescue of Captain John

---

9. Marc Lescarbot, *Nova Francia: A Description of Arcadia*, trans. P. Erondelle (London: Routledge, 1928), 227–28.

10. Sharon Larkins, "Using Trade Books to Teach about Pocahontas," *Georgia Social Sciences Journal* 19 (1988): 21–25.

Smith—one of the most mythologized acts in American culture—rests primarily on a single sentence published by Smith in 1624, seventeen years after the event.[11] Note that he refers to himself in the third person, a convention of the time:

> [T]wo great stones were brought before Powhatan: then as many as could laid hands on him, dragged him to them, and thereon laid his head, and being ready with their clubs to beat out his brains, Pocahontas, the king's dearest daughter, when no entreaty could prevail, got his head in her arms, and laid her own upon his to save his from death: whereat the emperor was contented he should live.[12]

In his written introduction of Pocahontas to Queen Anne prior to her royal reception in 1616, Smith glossed the rescue in a single sentence: "[A]t the minute of my execution, she hazarded the beating out of her own brains to save mine [and] so prevailed with her father, that I was safely conducted to Jamestown."[13]

Her marriage to John Rolfe has also achieved prominence in American mythology. A princess,[14] as the daughter of Chief Powhatan, married an Englishman. Before the marriage, Rolfe, a commoner, asked the British Crown for permission to marry a member of Powhatan's royal family. The Crown granted him a knighthood so that he could do so. A challenge for early commentators on the marriage revolved around miscegenation. Some fantasized that the intermarriage between an Indian woman and a White man signaled an end to conflict between Indians and English colonists. The fantasy operated under the assumption that within about three generations only a trace of the desired Indian exoticism would remain, while European traits would dominate and ensure the steady flow of Western values in the blood. Some believed that intermarriage would simplify and expedite colonial land acquisition from Indians, as tribal land would be steadily subsumed under English

---

11. Philip Barbour and Kathleen M. Brown argue that Powhatan, father of Pocahontas, conducted an adoption ritual and not an attempted execution of Smith thwarted by Pocahontas. See Philip Barbour, *The Three Worlds of Captain John Smith* (Boston: Houghton Mifflin, 1964), 167–69; Kathleen M. Brown, *Good Wives, Nasty Wenches, and Anxious Patriarchs: Gender Race and Power in Colonial Virginia* (Chapel Hill: University of North Carolina Press, 1996), 68. Helen C. Rountree and Alden Vaughn argue that lack of evidence regarding Powhatan adoption rituals handicaps any theory involving the rescue. Helen C. Rountree, *Pocahontas's People* (Norman: University of Oklahoma Press, 1990); Alden Vaughn, *American Genesis: Captain John Smith and the Founding of Virginia* (Boston: Little Brown, 1975). For a historiographical survey of the rescue episode, see J. A. Leo Lemay, *Did Pocahontas Save John Smith?* (Atlanta: University of Georgia Press, 2010).

12. Captain John Smith, *Writings with Other Narratives of Roanoke, Jamestown, and the First English Settlement of America*, ed. James Horn (New York: The Library of America, 2007), 321.

13. Robert Beverley, *The History and Present State of Virginia* (Chapel Hill: University of North Carolina Press, 2013), 31. For an insightful analysis of Pocahontas in London, see Brown, *Good Wives*, 42–45.

14. Europeans transferred Old World terms of nobility to the New World; hence proliferated Indian princesses, princes, and kings.

title by rights of inheritance that accumulated through each succeeding generation. At least that was the plan. However, aside from the racist notion of White superiority expressed in the three-generation theory, traditionally Indians did not recognize private ownership of land; rather, the group held land in common. Thus intermarriage by no means entailed a property transfer through inheritance as it did in European tradition.[15]

As race mixing became an increasingly volatile subject, and as antimiscegenation laws spread, targeting unions between Indians and Whites,[16] Pocahontas' marriage became a more socially problematic chapter in her story. Indeed, the marriage made for a lethal propaganda tool in the hands of Northern publishers and politicians during the years leading up the Civil War. Cartoons, editorials, and political orations condemned the marriage as the root of a mongrelized and degenerate Southern aristocracy. At the same time, some abolitionist writers used her marriage as a symbol for peaceful racial coexistence.[17] But Pocahontas, as the original Indian princess, provided Southerners with an origin story separate from the Yankee origin myth based on the Pilgrims of Plymouth Colony. Among other prominent Southern aristocrats, the Randolphs and the Bollings of Virginia pointed with pride to their direct descent from Pocahontas through her son Thomas.[18]

Sectional disputes sharpened competition for pride of place as to which myth best represented the republican ideals of the United States. Southerners tended to champion Pocahontas; Northerners tended to promote Squanto. Both exemplify Good Indians. Pocahontas achieved Good Indian status because she saved a White man from execution and converted to Christianity; Squanto, a Patuxet, achieved Good Indian status because he helped the Pilgrims, and he too supposedly embraced Christianity on his deathbed.

Squanto appears every Thanksgiving as the friendly Indian who saved the Pilgrims from starvation by teaching them how to plant corn. His mythological characterization strips him of any motive other than seeing to their welfare; however, a complex political motivation did indeed stand behind his actions. Enslaved and shipped to Europe in 1614, sold first in Malaga, Spain, and then resold in London, he learned much about European colonial intentions. Purchased in 1617 by John Slany, treasurer of the Newfoundland Company, Squanto learned English, and because of the information he supplied to the company, he made himself increasingly valuable as

---

15. Robert S. Tilton, *Pocahontas: The Evolution of an American Narrative* (New York: Cambridge University Press, 1994), 13–16.

16. In 1691 Virginia amended its 1662 prohibition on interracial marriage to specifically ban unions between Indians and Whites; by 1786 Massachusetts outlawed marriage between Indians and Whites. See Tilton, *Pocahontas*, 14.

17. Ibid., 152–53.

18. Anne Norton, *Alternative Americas: A Reading of Antebellum Political Culture* (Chicago: University of Chicago Press, 1986), 183.

a guide to Europeans voyaging to the Cape Cod region. By 1619, when Sir Ferdinando Gorges employed him in that capacity, Squanto had guaranteed his return home. Because of the London circles in which he worked, he likely knew that an epidemic—the result of contact with Europeans—had decimated the Patuxet and their allies in his absence. Indeed, he found his village completely vacated, its grounds scattered with unburied dead, and its once cultivated fields overgrown. But the Narragansett, long-standing enemies of the Patuxet, mostly survived the epidemic.[19]

A skirmish with another Patuxet enemy, the Pokanoket, drove off the English, and Squanto found himself once again enslaved, this time by the Pokanoket. Again demonstrating his political acumen and sense of self-preservation, he convinced the Pokanoket sachem, Massasoit, that an alliance with the English would strengthen the Pokanoket against their mutual enemy, the Narragansett. An opportunity for cementing this alliance arrived shortly thereafter, in 1620. Squanto and Massasoit watched as the fledgling Plymouth Colony struggled through its first winter in which half of its population died of starvation and disease.

In the spring, Massasoit agreed to free Squanto in order to establish diplomatic relations with the English. This brought Squanto one step closer to his own goal: to establish himself as leader of a reconstituted Patuxet band, as several dozen survivors of the epidemic had taken refuge in other bands throughout the Cape Cod region. Moreover, he sought revenge against the Pokanoket. Massasoit now recognized Squanto's attempt to turn the English against him and set out to kill him. Unable to realize his ambitions, Squanto sought protection with the English, fell sick shortly thereafter, and died. Only by dismissal of Squanto's historical agency can his sanitized myth as helper to the English colonists be invoked every Thanksgiving.[20]

Pocahontas and Squanto have entered American mythology primarily because of their relationship with Anglo-Americans, and both popularly appear within the confines of those relationships. Thus their value depends on their station in the Anglo-American colonial, and later national, enterprise.[21] Once familiarized according to the standards of White American society, they won their place as recognized

---

19. Debate continues among historians and epidemiologists regarding the type of disease responsible for the epidemic. See John S. Marr and John T. Cathey, "New Hypothesis for Cause of Epidemic among Native Americans, New England, 1616–1619," *Historical Review* 16 (2010), https://wwwnc.cdc.gov/eid/article/16/2/09-0276_article (accessed June 26, 2017).

20. Neal N. Salisbury, "Squanto: The Last of the Patuxets," in *Struggle and Survival in Colonial America*, ed. D. G. Sweet and Gary B. Nash (Berkeley: University of California Press, 1989), 228–45. Salisbury summarizes: "The pervasiveness of myth and the paucity of hard evidence have discouraged serious biographies of Squanto." Popular histories often gloss over complexities or exploit gaps in the historical record, tactics that reinforce a mythologized view of the past.

21. Tilton, *Pocahontas*, 164–65; Rayna Green, "The Tribe Called Wannabee: Playing Indian in America and Europe," *American Folklore* 99 (1988): 34; and Maureen Trudelle Schwarz, "Native American Barbie: The Marketing of Euro-American Desires," *American Studies* 46 (2005): 311–12.

John Gadsby Chapman, *The Baptism of Pocahontas* (1840). Photo courtesy of the Architect of the Capitol.

participants—as model Indians—in the nation's history. In 1840 Virginia painter John Gadsby Chapman enshrined Pocahontas' conversion to Christianity on the Capitol rotunda in Washington. *The Baptism of Pocahontas*—bookended by John Trumbull's *Declaration of Independence* and William Henry Powell's *De Soto's Discovery of the Mississippi*—demonstrated a prevailing notion that the survival of American Indians depended on their adoption of America's Christian culture.

By the turn of the nineteenth century, popular writers focused more on the Pocahontas/Smith relationship than the problematically miscegenous Pocahontas/Rolfe relationship.[22] The former relied on a simple and compelling romance that served as a template for the Indian princess myth—after saving the life of a White man, she turns her back on her own culture and embraces Christianity. As a mythologized Indian princess, Pocahontas epitomizes the Noble Savage; as savior of Captain John Smith and Christian convert, she serves as the Good Indian.

The biases of early historians concerning her also colored their accounts. Robert Beverley wrote his 1705 *History and Present State of Virginia* at a time when her marriage to John Rolfe stood relatively equal in importance to her rescue of John Smith. Beverley justified the miscegenation issue because Thomas Rolfe, son of Pocahontas and John Rolfe, became a wealthy Virginia planter, and his descendants flourished as well; therefore, the Pocahontas/Rolfe union stood in "good Repute." However, the

22. Tilton, *Pocahontas*, 32–33.

offspring of other mixed marriages who did not enjoy wealth and privilege fell within his definition of "spurious issue." Class trumped race.[23]

But James Nelson Barker's 1808 play *The Indian Princess*, the first American play performed on an Indian theme,[24] signaled a shift in her mythology by its focus on Pocahontas' relationship with Smith and by dealing with the marriage of Pocahontas and Rolfe without mention of Thomas. As protector, not procreator, she served as a friend to the White man, willing to risk her own life by offering aid, rescue, and comfort and to save White men from "bad" Indians.[25]

The Indian Princess opens with Pocahontas' rescue of Smith and then veers into full departure from the historical record. Miami, the play's Bad Indian, claims Pocahontas as his bride; however, Rolfe's interest in her drives him into a jealous rage. Conspiring with evil Indian priests, Miami attempts to murder both Smith and Rolfe, but Pocahontas somehow brings Lord Delaware to their rescue, and the play ends with an engagement scene between Pocahontas and Rolfe. Significantly, the curtain falls before their mixed-race offspring becomes a dramatic issue.

So-called Indian dramas featuring the archetypal Indian princess multiplied on the Antebellum American stage until John Brougham's 1855 *Po-ca-hon-tas, or The Gentle Savage* lampooned the genre, effectively diminishing its dramatic viability for several decades to come.[26] Brougham turns John Rolfe into a Dutch buffoon. Captain Smith functions as a foil to Rolf, as he also attempts to charm Pocahontas. The play comically works out this historical inaccuracy by banishing historian George Bancroft, whose then popular multivolume *History of the United States* also covered the Pocahontas/John Rolfe marriage.

> POCAHONTAS: Stop! One doubt within my heart arises!
> A great historian before us stands,
> *Bancroft* himself, you know, forbids the *banns*!
>
> SMITH: *Bancroft* be *ban*ished from your memory's shelf,
> For spite of fact, I'll marry you myself.

Brougham recognizes the direction taken by the Pocahontas myth in which Smith, not Rolfe, wins the hand of the Indian Princess. Rolfe complains to Smith about this

---

23. Ibid., 16–18.

24. Walter J. Meserve, *An Emerging Entertainment: The Drama of the American People to 1828* (Bloomington: Indiana University Press, 1977), 181.

25. Rayna Green, "The Only Good Indian: The Image of the Indian in American Vernacular Culture" (Ph.D. diss., Indiana University, 1973), 382.

26. Walter J. Meserve, *An Emerging Entertainment: The Drama of the American People to 1828* (Bloomington: Indiana University Press, 1977), 246.

historical inaccuracy, one that also has Smith winning her hand in a game of cards with Powhatan, called "King" in the play.

> SMITH: Old King of Clubs, you are a jolly trump!
> And don't you be so downcast, you Dutch pump;
> All future history will see you righted,
> With her, in name alone, I'll be united.[27]

A late twentieth-century innovation expanded Pocahontas' mythical potential by positioning her as both environmentalist and international diplomat, as demonstrated in Walt Disney's *Pocahontas* (1995). In the film, the beautiful Indian princess teaches the handsome blonde, blue-eyed Captain John Smith all the marvels of the natural world so that he will learn to be a good steward of the land and live in harmony with all of its creatures. The environmental sentiment does no harm; however, it provides another example of the malleability of Pocahontas as a myth and how far her myth has traveled across the centuries. Sanctified as environmental standard-bearer, Pocahontas has been refashioned in the service of yet another political agenda. Commoditized for its popular appeal, the film's soft and pretty message sells directly to the ecologically minded sensitivities of its intended audience.[28] Here the ease with which Pocahontas has been refashioned to fit the needs of a cultural moment speaks to the disconnection between the mythical and the historical Pocahontas. The distance between a barely documented and less understood incident between an eleven- or twelve-year-old daughter of Powhatan and a self-aggrandizing English soldier makes for a compelling case study of historical myths about Indians and the changes those myths undergo across decades and centuries.

The film also fabricates her role as diplomat and peacemaker between the Powhatan Confederacy and the English, yet another example of the elasticity of Pocahontas as a myth. No historical record supports these environmentalist and diplomatic roles and, of course, no historical record supports the central feature of her myth: her romantic involvement with Captain John Smith. Although Captain John Smith's 1616 letter[29] to Queen Anne claims that Pocahontas saved the colonists from starvation and provided information about Powhatan's intentions regarding the colonists (at best an informant, not an international peace broker), the political motivations of the letter itself undercut its veracity. In short, Smith possibly hoped to leverage his own tenuous position with the queen by using Pocahontas to foreground and augment his *own* role in saving Jamestown. However, taking Smith at his word, the letter values Pocahontas exclusively for her aid to the colonial enterprise as a Good Indian princess. The film's

---

27. John Brougham, *Po-ca-hon-tas, or The Gentle Savage* in *Dramas from the American Theatre, 1762–1909*, ed. Richard Moody (Cleveland: World, 1966), 397–421.

28. The Myth of the Ecological Indian is addressed in Chapter 6.

29. See note 13.

Captain Smith stands distanced from his evil despoiling countrymen and their thirst for gold. Pocahontas appears as a voluptuous beauty—a storybook princess—whose mystic experiences and prophetic dreams even foretell the coming of her true White love. The film relies on a centuries-old Indian Princess Myth in order to sell the love story, without which there would be no Pocahontas story worth marketing.

Russell Means (1939–2012), of Yankton Dakota and Oglala Lakota heritage, provided the voice for Powhatan. One of the founders of the American Indian Movement, Means often went on record disparaging historians and anthropologists, claiming that they only distorted the Indian past.[30] Thus his endorsement of Disney's film as "the single finest work ever done on American Indians by Hollywood"[31] expresses a complex political belief. Disney's depiction of Pocahontas as a beautiful princess whose environmentalism, mystical gifts, and peacemaking skills stand in sharp opposition to the rapacious, violent, and selfish goals of the White man speaks to Means' worldview that, however understandable, requires suspension of Pocahontas' historical record. Again, Pocahontas as a mythical figure becomes very real as a political symbol.

Cultural Nationalism and the Noble Savage

On December 16, 1773, a group of disgruntled American colonists dressed as Mohawk Indians tossed chests full of tea overboard in Boston Harbor. They probably intended to disguise their identities from Crown officials. But in doing so they also likely symbolized their cause in the name of American liberty, in line with the long-standing Eurocentric equation between Indians and freedom. More precisely, these rebels, who took the name Sons of Liberty, appropriated the image of the Indian as Noble Savage—because of the sense of freedom associated with it—to serve as a political tool and to make a political statement.[32]

Following the American Revolution, writers and artists grappled with the creation of a national identity that would distinguish and separate the new nation from the European world. This project of cultural nationalism bred a proliferation of periodicals whose editors urged contributors to submit work that promoted American themes and even to write in an American style. The country had won its political

---

30. For example, Russell Means, "Weekend Update #31: Indigenous Knowledges," October 16, 2009, http://www.russellmeansfreedom.com/tag/anthropology/ (accessed December 11, 2015).

31. Russell Means qtd. in Gary Edgerton and Kathy Merlock Jackson, "Redesigning Pocahontas: Disney, the White Man's Indian, and the Marketing of Dreams," *Journal of Popular Film and Television*, no. 24 (1996): 90, http://ww2.odu.edu/al/knichola/web/pocahontas.html (accessed December 30, 2015).

32. Colin G. Calloway, *New Worlds for All: Indians, Europeans, and the Remaking of Early America* (Baltimore: Johns Hopkins University Press, 2013), 7.

independence from England; it required cultural independence as well. But from what materials would this cultural independence be made?[33]

The new republic's intellectual elite saw the vastness of the land itself as the country's single greatest treasure. In particular, the forests captured their imaginations. Such stands of timber had long ago been felled throughout the Old World. Europe might boast its ancient castles and cathedrals, but America could claim both on an even grander scale: the forests stood in palatial splendor and reached cathedral heights that stretched far beyond the horizon and dwarfed the petty spire, turret, and stained-glass constructions on the other side of the Atlantic. In 1841 American philosopher and poet Ralph Waldo Emerson wrote:

> The Gothic church plainly originated in a rude adaptation of the forest trees. . . . No one can walk in a road cut through pine woods, without being struck with the architectural appearance of the grove, especially in winter, when the bareness of all other trees shows the low arch of the Saxons. In the woods in a winter afternoon one will see as readily the origin of the stained glass window, with which the Gothic cathedrals are adorned, in the colors of the western sky seen through the bare and crossing branches of the forest. Nor can any lover of nature enter the old piles of Oxford and the English cathedrals, without feeling that the forest overpowered the mind of the builder, and that his chisel, his saw, and plane still reproduced its ferns, its spikes of flowers, its locust, elm, oak, pine, fir, and spruce.[34]

Similarly, American author James Fenimore Cooper wrote, "Give me the strong places of the wilderness, which is the trees, and the churches, too, which are arbors raised by the hand of nature."[35]

It did not escape the republic's creative minds that these cathedral forests also contained Indians. And here the mythologized forest wilderness as a dwelling place of the Noble Savage fuses with the Myth of the Wilderness, the myth that is the focus of Chapter 3. This fusion demonstrates the interconnections between historical myths about Indians.

Thus in the White imagination, Noble Savages lived timelessly among deep shades and vernal hues. American cultural independence depended in part on this

---

33. Elise Marienstras, "The Common Man's Indian: The Image of the Indian as a Promoter of National Identity in the Early National Era" in *Native Americans and the Early Republic*, ed. Frederick E. Hoxie, Ronald Hoffman, and Peter J. Albert (Charlottesville: University Press of Virginia, 1999), 261–63.

34. Ralph Waldo Emerson, "History" in *The Selected Writings of Ralph Waldo Emerson* (New York: Modern Library, 1992), 121.

35. James Fenimore Cooper, *The Deerslayer* (Albany: State University of New York Press, 1987), 266.

mythologized image, for Europe did not possess such profoundly exotic beings. Inseparable from the forest, Indians did not belong to civilization but to nature. Most attractive of all, the Noble Savage lived in a sublime, primitive communion with the natural world, as did the distant ancestors of the European past before the light of civilization showed the path out of that darkness. Thus Indians served as living—and coveted—Golden Age relics.

Ironically, American cultural independence depended on a European cultural import for its expression—Romanticism. One European Romanticist in particular served as a model for much of the Antebellum literature produced in the United States—Sir Walter Scott.[36] His stories of ancient Scottish heroes emphasized regional traditions, rugged scenery, and the simple lives of the folkpeople—all models for American Romantics determined to lift both forest and Indian into literary respectability as legitimate themes for American art and literature.[37]

Nineteenth-century Romanticism generally emphasized the power of human emotion and intuition, their often irrational (or suprarational) natures, and the roles they played in shaping people's lives. In the hands of the Romantics, the Noble Savage became emblematic for the program of cultural nationalism in the newly independent nation. The Romantic agenda claimed for America its own Golden Age, rivaling—if not superior to—that of Europe's own mythical past.

An 1819 passage from Washington Irving expresses this Romanticist sentiment at work in his portrayal of noble savagery:

> There is something of the charm of discovery in lighting upon these wild and unexplored tracts of human nature; in witnessing . . . the native growth of moral sentiment, and perceiving those generous and romantic qualities which have been artificially cultivated by society, vegetating in spontaneous hardihood and rude magnificence. [The Indian], free from the restraints and refinements of polished life, and, in a great degree, a solitary and independent being, obeys the impulses of his inclination or the dictates of his judgment; and thus the attributes of his nature, being freely indulged, grow singly great and striking.[38]

American Romantic poet Walt Whitman left a record of his Noble Savage impressions from his brief 1865 employment at the Bureau of Indian Affairs in Washington, D.C. The poet employs the same pattern found in the examples above. Indians appear not as individuated human beings but as part of nature. To Whitman, they are

---

36. Reginald Horsman, *Race and Manifest Destiny: The Origins of American Racial Anglo-Saxonism* (Cambridge, MA: Harvard University Press, 1981), 160–61.

37. Robert F. Berkhofer, Jr., *The White Man's Indian: Images of the American Indian from Columbus to the Present* (New York: Vintage, 1979), 87.

38. Washington Irving, *The Sketchbook of Geoffrey Crayon, Gent.* (Rockville, MD: Serenity Publishers, 2010), 237–38.

"animals" and "specimens." Moreover, he uses Indians as a pivot point to comment on his own unhappiness with certain aspects of White American culture.

> Some of the young fellows were . . . magnificent and beautiful animals, I think the palm of unique picturesqueness, in body, limb, physiognomy, etc. was borne by the old or elderly chiefs, and the wise men. . . . There is something about these aboriginal Americans, . . . something very remote, very lofty, arousing comparisons with our own civilized ideals. . . . I should not apply the word savage (at any rate, in the usual sense) as a leading word in the description of those great aboriginal specimens. [Our] own exemplification of personality, dignity, heroic presentation anyhow (as in the conventions of society, or even in the accepted poems and plays,) seem'd sickly, puny, inferior.[39]

As with other Romantics, in his embracing of the Myth of the Noble Savage, Whitman placed the "aboriginal American" on a pedestal and out of the way of Euro-American political, cultural, and economic interests.

The Noble Savage stood at the center of Henry Wadsworth Longfellow's 1855 *The Song of Hiawatha*, an epic poem that remained popular well into the twentieth century, despite harsh criticism of it as doggerel and the satirical attacks made against it.[40] As a nationalist project intended to contribute to the establishment of a distinct body of American literature, Longfellow reshaped Native American stories to create the image of a Noble Savage acceptable to mid-nineteenth-century Euro-America.

Longfellow fuses Hiawatha, the historical founder of the Iroquois League, with Gichi-manidoo, regarded by the Ojibwe as the greatest of spirit beings. Also, many events in the poem belong to stories associated with Nanabozho, the Ojibwe trickster hare; however, Longfellow considered his name insufficiently melodious, and the trickster figure itself struck him as undignified and lewd.[41] Moreover, the name Longfellow gave Hiawatha's bride, Minnehaha, comes from the Dakota word for waterfall. Thus Longfellow amalgamates stories and characters rooted in traditions from the far eastern edge of the Great Lakes with stories from people living on the far western edge.[42]

Longfellow modeled *The Song of Hiawatha* on *Frithiof's Saga* by Esaias Tegnér, a Swedish poet,[43] but significantly his American epic's structure relied mainly on *The*

---

39. Walt Whitman, *November Boughs* (Mineola, NY: Dover Publications, 2014), 74–75.

40. Carr, *Inventing the American Primitive*, 106.

41. Witgen, *An Infinity of Nations*, 13.

42. Pearce, *Savagism and Civilization*, 194; Alan Trachtenberg, *Shades of Hiawatha: Staging Indians, Making Americans, 1880–1930* (New York: Hill and Wang, 2004), 58–60.

43. Andrew Hilen, *Longfellow and Scandinavia: A Study of the Poet's Relationship with Northern Languages and Literature* (New Haven, CT: Yale University Press, 1947), 62.

Kalevala, a Finnish epic poem compiled in the nineteenth century.[44] Both influences helped Longfellow intersect the Myth of the Noble Savage with American Romantic nationalism, using Native American stories as raw material requiring refinement for his Euro-American audience. He crafted *The Song of Hiawatha* from the Native American stories collected by Henry Rowe Schoolcraft, who regarded them as a "great source of a future poetic fabric, to be erected on the framework of Indian words."[45] Barring the advent of such a poet, "Indian imagery [constitutes] mere allusions, or broken descriptions, like touches on the canvas, without being united. [Without the] skill to connect, it will still remain but a shapeless mass."[46]

Schoolcraft probably lacked a clear understanding of the place that songs and stories held for the Ojibwe people, despite his having married an Ojibwe and lived among them for many years. The material's original significance eluded Longfellow as well.[47] But as Christopher Vecsey notes in his study of Ojibwe religion, "Songs accompanied the administration of medicine and other ceremonial acts to give the ritual potency,"[48] and as Anishinaabe scholar Gerald Vizenor puts it:

> The mythic origins of tribal people are creative expressions, original eruptions in time, not a mere recitation or a recorded narrative in grammatical time. The teller of stories is an artist, a person of wit and imagination, who relumes the diverse memories of the visual past into the experiences and metaphors of the present.[49]

Longfellow attempted to reconstruct Native American material in a poetic form politically and culturally suited to his Euro-American audience's sensibilities while simultaneously assuring that audience of the ethnographic authenticity of his Indians. Thus, his epic's constructed primitivism—especially as conveyed by a monotonous meter that beats along in a tom-tom mimic drone from beginning to end of the poem—says as much about his inability to grasp the meaning of the material within its original Native American context as it does about the Eurocentric construction of the Myth of the Noble Savage as a reliable stereotype.[50]

---

44. Carr, *Inventing the American Primitive,* 127–29.

45. Schoolcraft, *Historical and Statistical Information,* 3:328.

46. Henry Rowe Schoolcraft, *Oneóta, or Characteristics of the Red Race of America* (New York: Wiley and Putnam, 1845), 247.

47. Carr, *Inventing the American Primitive,* 124–25.

48. Christopher Vecsey, *Traditional Ojibwa Religion and Its Historical Changes* (Philadelphia, PA: The American Philosophical Society, 1993), 108.

49. Gerald Vizenor, *The People Named the Chippewa: Narrative Histories* (Minneapolis: University of Minnesota Press, 2002), 7.

50. Though in fairness Longfellow's trochaic tetrameter imitated the Kalevala's metric pattern. Each metric line has four long, or stressed, syllables, each followed by a short, or unstressed, syllable.

A profound influence on both Whitman and Longfellow, and perhaps the most significant American Romantic, James Fenimore Cooper also established the Indian as a literary type. Referred to by his contemporaries as "The American [Sir Walter] Scott,"[51] he wrote eleven novels that featured Indians, although he knew little about them directly and often confused one tribe with another in customs, names, and languages.[52] One of his romantically portrayed forest noblemen—Uncas—stands on display for study by two White protagonists in *The Last of the Mohicans*:

> Graceful and unrestrained in the attitudes and movements of nature . . . there was no concealment to his dark, glancing, fearless eye, alike terrible and calm; the bold outline of his high, haughty features, pure in their native red; or to the dignified elevation of his receding forehead, together with all the finest proportions of a noble head, bared to the generous scalping tuft. . . . The ingenuous Alice gazed at his free air and proud carriage, as she would have looked upon some precious relic of the Grecian chisel . . . while Heyward . . . openly expressed his admiration of such an unblemished specimen of the noblest proportions of man.[53]

Cooper's Noble Savages tend to be found among his fictionalized Delaware Indians and their related Algonquian tribes, especially the Mohicans.[54] For example, Cooper introduces his Mohican chief Chingachgook as "a noble, tall, athletic Indian warrior," whose name "signifies Big Sarpant [sic]: so named for his wisdom and prudence, and cunning."[55]

Cooper often defaults to Indian stereotypes; however, his work also examines the complexities of racial identity and offers significant insight into the nuances of interracial relationships. As with the other American writers discussed above, stereotypes about Indians can accompany strikingly humanized reflections. Regardless, statements in their work are based on assumptions of White superiority; consequently,

51. Kay Seymour House, *Cooper's Americans* (Columbus: Ohio State University Press, 1965), 12.

52. Arthur C. Parker, "Sources and Range of Cooper's Indian Lore," in *James Fenimore Cooper: A Re-Appraisal*, ed. Mary E. Cunningham (Cooperstown: New York State Historical Association, 1954), 449. Parker examines Cooper's primary source, the 1819 *History, Manners and Customs of the Indian Nations Who Once Inhabited Pennsylvania and the Neighboring States*, by Reverend John Gottlieb Ernestus Heckewelder, a Moravian missionary who lived for several years among the Delaware Indians. Heckewelder's bias against the Iroquois—especially the Ononandaga and the Mohawk—and favored treatment of the Delaware may in part explain similar attitudes in Cooper.

53. James Fenimore Cooper, *The Last of the Mohicans* (Albany: State University of New York Press, 1983), 52–53.

54. Paul A. W. Wallace, "Cooper's Indians," in *James Fenimore Cooper: A Re-Appraisal*, ed. Mary E. Cunningham (Cooperstown: New York State Historical Association, 1954), 424.

55. James Fenimore Cooper, *The Deerslayer* (Albany: State University of New York Press, 1987), 152–53.

they make for tough going and speak volumes regarding the degree to which some habits of thinking reinforced (and continue to reinforce) notions of White entitlement and power.

Cooper's work served in part as the formula for paperback Westerns that began to flood the marketplace by the 1860s, especially after the publishing house of Beadle and Adams introduced so-called yellow-backed novels. Cheaply produced, thanks to steam-powered presses, these sensationalized Westerns imprinted upon the popular imagination images of the fully mythologized Indian. Also, fictionalizations of White historical figures—for example, Kit Carson, Wild Bill Hickok, and Buffalo Bill—took their literary cues from the foresters and scouts found in Cooper's work. Indeed, publisher Erastus F. Beadle said that his company's novels "introduced either historical or local characters. They followed right after Cooper's tales, which suggested them."[56]

Hundreds of paperback titles filled the Beadle and Adams catalog, but three examples of yellow-backs that work the Noble Savage angle must suffice for mention: James L. Bowen's *The Red Rider, or the White Queen of the Apache*; Ann S. Stevens' *The Indian Queen*; and Frederick Whittaker's *Weetamora, The Squaw Sachem, or the Earl's Half-Breed Daughter: A Tale of the Old Colony Days*.[57] Bowen's Red Rider "moved among the painted warriors with the air of one aware of her superiority, while the deference of the braves was too marked to escape observation."[58] Stevens' story opens with an Indian council fire, the smoke of which "rolled away over the forest," while "a band of noble, stately-looking men [sat] in a circle of red firelight, grave and dignified as Roman senators."[59] On her part, Whittaker's Weetamora made an entrance with dramatic flair:

> [The] instant this Indian princess made her appearance, the door of several lodges nearby were thrown open simultaneously, as if the occupants had been waiting for the signal. . . . The female chief set to her lips a whistle. . . . Immediately the booming sound of several huge drums was

---

56. Erastus F. Beadle qtd. in Edmund Pearson, *Dime Novels; or, Following an Old Trail in Popular Literature* (Boston: Little, Brown, and Company, 1929), 99.

57. James L. Bowen, *The Red Rider, or the White Queen of the Apache* (New York: Beadle and Company Publishers, 1869), http://dimenovels.lib.niu.edu/islandora/object/dimenovels%3A63#page/7/mode/2up (accessed December 23, 2015); Ann S. Stevens, *The Indian Queen* (New York: Beadle and Adams, 1864), http://dimenovels.lib.niu.edu/islandora/object/dimenovels%3A21760#page/5/mode/2up (accessed December 23, 2015); Frederick Whittaker, *Weetamora, The Squaw Sachem, or the Earl's Half-Breed Daughter: A Tale of the Old Colony Days* (New York: Beadle and Company, 1872), http://dimenovels.lib.niu.edu/islandora/object/dimenovels%3A120#page/5/mode/2up (accessed December 23, 2015).

58. Bowen, *Red Rider*, 17.

59. Stevens, *Indian Queen*, 5.

heard. . . . Every man preserved the usual stolid indifferent aspect peculiar to the Indian.[60]

Dependable Noble Savage stereotypes could always be plugged in as needed to move the plot forward. In the examples above, the majestic Indian princess, the forest setting, a Roman Senate allusion, and stoical, strong and silent Indian warriors all serve as ready-made literary components that had been employed by writers for generations and would continue to be useful for generations to come.

From the Forest to the Plains

The mythologization of the Noble Savage by American writers and artists can also be traced in part to the steady dispossession of Indian land through White settlement. In other words, region by region Indians became safe subjects for rhapsody once White settlement interests eliminated them as military, political, and economic threats. Following Euro-American expansion through the steady dispossession of indigenous territory east of the Mississippi, new landscape backdrops upon which to place the Noble Savage became available. Enter the Western. As a print genre and later in film, the Western placed North American Indians primarily within the majestic High Plains, in picturesque Monument Valley, or in similar rugged and arid settings. The previously timeless Indian of the forest headed west. There, as characterized and commoditized in popular media, the Indian clashed with modernity as manifested by trans-Mississippi nineteenth-century settlers, trappers, and cavalry.

The Wild West opened a range of metaphors that continues to mold the mythical North American Indian. The Noble Savage as forest dweller for the Antebellum Romantics became the plains or (to a lesser extent) high desert dweller for succeeding generations of writers, artists, and filmmakers. Indeed, to this day, the trans-Mississippi West remains the natural habitat most associated with Indians in the popular historical imagination. At the leading edge of the transition stood self-taught American artist George Catlin, who headed west in the 1830s, there to record on canvas images that have since become archetypal of the Noble Savage of the Plains. "Nature has nowhere presented more beautiful and lovely scenes," Catlin proclaimed, "than those of the vast prairies of the West and of *man* and *beast* no nobler specimens than those who inhabit them—the *Indian* and the *buffalo*—joint and original tenants of the soil, and fugitives together from the approach of civilized man."[61] His work tended toward the stereotype of the Noble Savage because he wanted primarily to

---

60. Whittaker, *Weetamora*, 10.

61. Catlin's statement also signifies the proximity between the Myth of the Noble Savage and the Myth of the Vanishing Indian, the latter to be explored in Chapter 4. George Catlin, *North American Indians*, Vol. 1 (Philadelphia, PA: Leary, Stuart, 1913), 293. On the influence of *Gallery Unique*

counter the popular image of the Indian as a drunken beggar. Every Indian, he wrote, "from a beautiful natural precept, studies to keep his body and mind in such a healthy shape and condition as will at times enable him to use his weapons in self-defence [sic], or struggle for the prize in their manly games."[62]

Catlin's traveling exhibition, *Gallery Unique*, presented Noble Savage images to an American public fascinated by his exotic canvases, his lectures, and his collection of Native American artifacts: scalps, pipes, bows and arrows, and sundry other items. Though Catlin's public lectures did at times emphasize historical and cultural differences between Indian nations, sensationalism dominated his orations. Moreover, he distinguished Plains Indians, such as the Crows, for their "noble and lofty bearing" and often measured other Native Americans against standards of noble savagery that he perceived in the American West.[63]

Gallery Unique played to Eastern urban audiences throughout the late 1830s. In 1840 the show opened in London, toured the English provinces for nearly three years, and eventually crossed the channel to play Paris. The popularity of James Fenimore Cooper's novels had whetted French appetites for *Gallery Unique*;[64] moreover, the Iowa Indian performers that he premiered during his English tour proved of particular interest. One French reviewer said the Iowa Indians had been "cast in nature's stateliest mould," and another said they possessed "all the charms of the wildest romance."[65] Romanticism and the Myth of the Noble Savage received a warm homecoming upon returning to their European birthplaces.

Whereto the Myth of the Noble Savage?

The writers and artists examined in this chapter who have relayed the Myth of the Noble Savage across the centuries have simultaneously perpetuated its obverse—the Myth of the Ignoble Savage, as will be explored in the next chapter. Also, the Myth of the Vanishing Indian depends in part on the Myth of the Noble Savage to gain Romantic traction. For example, Longfellow's ennobled Hiawatha departs at the end of *The Song of Hiawatha* as White settlers appear on the horizon.

---

on *Buffalo Bills Wild West Show*, see Paul Reddin, *Wild West Shows* (Urbana: University of Illinois Press, 1999), 1–52.

62. George Catlin, *Letters and Notes on the North American Indians, Two Volumes in One* (North Dighton, MA: JG Press, 1995), 139.

63. Reddin, *Wild West Shows*, 16.

64. Cooper lived in Paris in the 1820s, published several books there, contributed to French journals, and established friendships with some of the great lights of French society, including the Marquise de Lafayette, at whose suggestion Cooper wrote *Notions of the Americans: Picked up by a Travelling Bachelor*.

65. Reviews qtd. in Reddin, *Wild West Shows*, 44.

And the people from the margin
Watched him floating, rising, sinking,
Till the birch canoe seemed lifted
High into that sea of vapors

. . .

And they said, "Farewell forever!"
Said "Farewell, O Hiawatha!"
And the forests, dark and lonely,
Moved through all their depths of darkness,
Sighed, "Farewell, O Hiawatha!"[66]

This sends the message that Indians, however noble, belong only to the past, so they are incapable of surviving in modernity. The Myth of the Authentic Indian often builds on the image of a noble warrior: no feather, no Indian. The Myth of the Ecological Indian freezes Indians in a pre-Industrial era from which they gaze sadly and knowingly upon the postindustrial world. The Myth of the Noble Indian stands built into that gaze, one that condemns White insensitivity to environmental pollution. The Myth of the Mystical Indian stems from White fetishism that automatically ennobles the Indian as a spiritual being who serves primarily as a foil to condemn a perceived spiritual bankruptcy of White society.

Since myths about Native American history originate in Eurocentric worldviews, they remain purpose-built to reinforce those views. By pretending to ennoble Indians, many myths, as noted above, actually segregate and commoditize them. The Myth of the Noble Savage shuts out Native Americans as individuals and dehumanizes them as a frozen type. As a conceptual category that arose in Eurocentric philosophy and fantasy constructions, the Myth of the Noble Savage remains fundamentally detached from the Native American historical record itself.

Stories by Europeans and Euro-Americans that have relied on stereotypes about Indians are best countered by the stories that Indians tell about themselves. In the western Great Lakes region, Ojibwe tales of Nanabozho, the trickster hare, a shape-shifter, express the complexity of human nature and the unpredictability of human relationships, as even the best of intentions can have disastrous consequences. In other words, people remain capable of noble actions and ideas but just as often make mistakes. The ambiguity of the human record militates against the easy stereotyping of groups or individuals. To mythologize Native Americans as Noble Savages strips them of individuality, dispenses with their historical record, and primarily values them relevant to the preconceptions they fulfill in a Eurocentric worldview. European colonizers and later Euro-Americans attempted to freeze Native Americans within European fantasy constructions, one of which idealized Indians as Noble Savages.

---

66. Henry Wadsworth Longfellow, *The Song of Hiawatha* in *Longfellow: Poems and Other Writings*, ed. J. D. McClatchy (New York: Library of America, 2000), 278–79.

But the example of Nanabozho represents the course of history as a matter of shape-shifting, of change over time, with individuals capable of performing any range of destructive, foolish, or wise actions.

Nevertheless, the Myth of the Noble Savage remains very much a part of the cultural landscape and has been commoditized in various ways. Searching "Native American Princess" on the internet generates hundreds of images of White women modeling a wide range of headbands, feather headdresses, and buckskin skirts, and they often hold a tomahawk, or spear, or bow and arrow. The items they wear are all for sale through online merchants, and the clothes are invariably referred to as "costumes," itself a term considered derogatory by Native Americans, for whom traditional clothing is referred to as "regalia." Pocahontas, the original Indian princess, has been widely appropriated by the clothing industry in the form of a "Pocahontas costume," as an internet search demonstrates. Most of the clothing in these images serve the Halloween market. But high fashion also markets the stereotyped Indian princess look. In 2012, Victoria's Secret model Karlie Kloss appeared on the catwalk in a bikini and a flowing feather headdress. Instantaneous outrage and protest by Native American voices led both the model and Victoria's Secret to apologize, however halfheartedly. Sasha Houston Brown, a member of the Santee Sioux Tribe of Nebraska noted:

> The sexual conquest and deliberate dehumanization of Native women has been used as a colonizing tactic for centuries. . . . This type of mentality of domination persists today. Native women, stripped of their humanity, are still objectified as a sexual fetish or exotic other. In fact, these kind of derogatory stereotypes have become a fixture of both American mythology and pop culture. What is different today is that, in the digital age of Instagram and Twitter, you can see a picture of Karlie Kloss donning a feather headdress on your iPhone the moment she starts strutting the runway.[67]

The science fiction film *Avatar* (2009) updates the Noble Savage myth with its idealized forest-dwelling civilization—the Na'vi—that faces the threat of colonization from another planet. Highly principled warriors who fight with bow and arrow, the Na'vi suffer a great number of casualties as they defend their land. Overwhelmed by the noble qualities of the Na'vi, the central character, a White anthropologist, joins them. That is, he "goes native," saves them, and in the end receives their adoration. As Good Indians, they bow before the White man. As Noble Savages they retain their simple primitive lives deep in the forest.

In the twenty-first century, the Noble Savage remains a simple primitive frozen in time.

---

67. Sasha Houston Brown, "Nothing Says Native American Like White Stars in Headresses," *Guernica: A Magazine of Global Arts and Politics*, December 3, 2012, https://www.guernicamag.com/sasha-houston-brown-nothing-says-native-american-like-white-stars-in-headdresses/ (accessed May 30, 2017).

2. Uncivilized and Unwanted: The Myth of the Ignoble Savage

The Goshoots . . . were small, lean, "scrawny" creatures; in complexion a dull black like the ordinary American negro; their faces and hands bearing dirt which they had been hoarding and accumulating for months, years, and even generations, according to the age of the proprietor; a silent, sneaking, treacherous looking race; taking note of everything, covertly, like all the other "Noble Red Men" that we (do not) read about, and betraying no sign in their countenances; indolent, everlastingly patient and tireless, like all other Indians; prideless beggars—for if the beggar instinct were left out of an Indian he would not "go," any more than a clock without a pendulum; hungry, always hungry, and yet never refusing anything that a hog would eat, though often eating what a hog would decline; hunters, but having no higher ambition than to kill and eat jack-ass, rabbits, crickets and grasshoppers, and embezzle carrion from the buzzards and cayotes; savages who, when asked if they have the common Indian belief in a Great Spirit show something which almost amounts to emotion, thinking whiskey is referred to.[1]

This passage from *Roughing It* (1871), one of Mark Twain's most famous books, catalogs nearly every aspect of the Myth of the Ignoble Savage. Twain's disdain for Indians runs throughout his body of work, which might come as a surprise to those who know him merely as a humorist or for the complex examination of slavery in his *Adventures of Huckleberry Finn* (1883). But the villain in his *Adventures of Tom Sawyer* (1876) is Injun Joe. Driven to violence because of his "Indian blood," his extermination comes as a relief to young Tom, who also profits nicely from the Indian's hidden treasure of gold. And regarding his fictionalized Goshoots, Twain's trademark hyperbole—his penchant for the tall tale—goes to work on a portrait that dehumanizes and ridicules Indians for the entertainment of his reading public.

Twain considered Indians a stain that must be obliterated from the land.[2] Fueled in part by his vehement opposition to the notion of a Noble Savage, particularly as

---

1. Mark Twain, *Roughing It* (Berkeley: University of California Press, 1993), 127.

2. Fred Kaplan, *The Singular Mark Twain: A Biography* (New York: Anchor Books, 2003), 90. See also Maxwell Geismar's discussion of Twain's "hatred of all Indians." Maxwell Geismar, *Mark Twain: An American Prophet* (Boston: Houghton Mifflin, 1970), 23.

displayed by James Fenimore Cooper,[3] his contempt for Indians remained unambiguous until one of his last works, *Following the Equator* (1897), offered a measured sympathy for Indigenous Peoples, albeit only for those living outside of the United States.[4] But the Goshoots provided a target upon which he launched one of his most sustained attacks. According to Twain, Indians stood inferior to Whites because of their color, and they lived as dirty and untrustworthy beggars who subsist on the foulest diet imaginable; moreover, they worshiped only the Great Spirit of alcohol. Such observations, he claimed, came from his own personal experience: realistic accounts unlike those of Cooper's idealized armchair fictions.

Twain's views about Indians—often overlooked or excused because of his well-deserved prominence in American literature—do not square with the image of a white-suited wit unleashing caustic insights into the hypocrisies and foibles of American culture.[5] Moreover, he never wavered from his faith in Manifest Destiny, in the God-given right of (White) Americans to expand forever westward at the expense of Indians who did not deserve the land they inhabited; moreover, Manifest Destiny depended on the Myth of the Ignoble Savage for its validation.

Propelled by the political, economic, and social agendas of the federal government and its citizens, the Myth of the Ignoble Savage demonized Indians in order to justify their removal. The myth proclaimed that Indians did not develop the land in accord with American standards of agriculture, which entailed single-crop cultivation, domesticated livestock, fences, and, above all else, private, and titled landownership. Rather, according to the stereotype, Indians merely wandered across the land freely as hunter-gatherers, living a hand-to-mouth existence that contrasted with the settled towns, villages, and farmsteads valued by Euro-Americans. White society often demanded that Indians recognize the sanctity of private landownership if they were ever to achieve a "civilized" state. The myth also identified Indians as sinners lost in wicked religious practices. Far from enjoying the fruits of Christianity, they stood in league with Satan and worshiped him in bizarre rites. Perhaps a few Native souls could be saved through missionary efforts, but Christian salvation could occur only apace with the abandonment of an entire cultural apparatus. Simultaneously, others advocated for the right of Indians to maintain their cultures wholesale, but to enjoy those rights elsewhere.

---

3. For Twain's evisceration of James Fenimore Cooper's Indians see his "Fenimore Cooper's Literary Offenses," http://twain.lib.virginia.edu/projects/rissetto/offense.html (accessed March 11, 2016); for further insight into Twain's ideas about Indians, see his sketch, "The Noble Red Man," http://twain.lib.virginia.edu/projects/rissetto/redman.html (accessed March 11, 2016).

4. Mark Twain, *Following the Equator: A Journey around the World* (Hartford, CT: American, 1897), 214–23.

5. Perhaps overreaching, Leslie Fiedler excoriates Twain, calling him "an absolute Indian hater, consumed by the desire to destroy not merely real Indians, but any image of Indian life which stands between White Americans and a total commitment to genocide." Leslie Fiedler, *The Return of the Vanishing American* (New York: Stein and Day, 1969), 122–23.

Indian removal, ideally to regions far away from White settlements, relied on treaties initiated by the federal government. Meant to guarantee compensation to Indian nations for specific parcels outside of designated settlement boundaries, treaties generally identified a distribution of goods and cash payments to the Indian signatories. But as political winds shifted in Washington, treaties that had originally been written and signed in good faith often did not receive congressional ratification, and ratified treaties often went underfunded or neglected. Further complicating treaty provisions, the complex bureaucracy connecting Washington to the Indian agencies on the ground provided ample opportunity for graft. The nineteenth century saw the removal of many Eastern Indian nations to lands west of the Mississippi. Some thrived; others did not.

The Myth of the Ignoble Savage supports White cultural interests. Constitutionally incapable of surviving in the modern world, dependent on government handouts, Indians know only how to eke out a marginal livelihood as lazy beggars maddened by alcohol. Mark Twain failed—or refused—to recognize the origins of Goshute (not "Goshoot") Shoshone impoverishment, which lay not in the ancient past; rather, it arose as a recent product of U.S. territorial expansion. The colonization of the West by White settlers meant that the Goshute, and other Great Basin and Great Plains Indians, often lost their subsistence lands, which frequently led to starvation, social fragmentation, and desperate poverty.[6] Mark Twain's literary portrait perpetuates the Ignoble Savage Myth but serves as only one example among others in many areas of American culture that persist to the present day. Moreover, the historical roots of the myth predate Twain by many centuries. As with the Myth of the Noble Savage, they lead to the other side of the Atlantic, and to a time long before Columbus set sail.

The Wild Man

The Myth of the Ignoble Savage counts among its many ancestors a figure in European folklore who dates to the Middle Ages—the Wild Man. A cannibal Antichrist who wandered the countryside in the company of bears and devils, he often assaulted women, carried them off to the woods, and there committed unspeakable acts. Largely seen in art, architectural decoration, and literature from the twelfth century onward, this raw product of nature lived in a state of violent unreason.[7] Covered in

---

6. Ned Blackhawk, *Violence over the Land: Indians and Empire in the Early American West* (Cambridge, MA: Harvard University Press, 2006), 11.

7. Richard Bernheimer, *Wild Men in the Middle Ages: A Study in Art, Sentiment, and Demonology* (Cambridge, MA: Harvard University Press, 1952), passim. *The Epic of Gilgamesh*, which originated in Sumer in the third millennium BCE, features the earliest known Wild Man in world literature, Enkidu. More beast than man, he lived only among the animals, although he becomes domesticated in the course of the tale. See William Moran, "*The Gilgamesh Epic*: A Masterpiece," in *The Epic of Gilgamesh*, trans. and ed. Benjamin R. Foster (New York: W. W. Norton, 2001), 171–83. For the

hair from head to foot and wielding a twisted club, he signified the continual threat of savagery to civilized society; however, he might on occasion administer healing herbs to a wounded knight or share his medicinal secrets with peasants.[8]

Carnival participants in fourteenth-century France, and later, sometimes donned animal skins and feathers and paraded as Wild Men. These disguises permitted an outlet for violence and sexual license, and over the centuries masquerading Wild Men became increasingly common cultural fixtures in Western Europe. Thus, in 1501, when Portuguese explorer Gaspar Corte-Real displayed captured Indians—possibly Mi'kmaq—in Lisbon, one observer readily identified them as Wild Men.[9] A 1681 account refers to Newfoundland Beothuk and Labrador Inuit as "the Savages of America, cruel men for no reason, whom our fishermen are obliged to hunt as if they were beasts because, besides showing ferocious traits, their bodies are covered with hair and armed with nails remarkable long and hooked."[10] The details of supposed hairiness, unreason, and violence demonize these Native Americans by invoking a series of Wild Man characteristics.

To many English voyagers, the Indian as wild devil worshiper served as a warning of the fate that awaited fellow European Christians who did not adhere strictly to God's authority. The embodiment of untamed hedonism, the Indian as Other defined everything that Europeans must resist lest they lose their souls to the Devil and suffer eternal damnation. In 1625 Reverend Samuel Purchas declared them:

> more brutish than the beasts they hunt, more wild . . . then that . . . wild Countrey, which they range rather than inhabit; captivated also to Satans tyranny in foolish pieties, mad impieties, wicked idlenesse, busie and bloudy wickednesse; hence have we fit objects of zeale and pitie.[11]

By comparison, the French Jesuits, who ranged far and wide in what is today eastern Canada and the northern United States, tended to regard Indians more favorably than many of the English Protestant lights, who largely inhabited the eastern fringes of the present-day United States. Unlike most seventeenth-century Protestants, they lived among the Indians, learned their languages, and attempted to bridge cultural differences. Moreover, Jesuits served both the Roman Catholic Church and

---

role of the Wild Man in Greco-Roman and Hebrew traditions, see Hayden White, "The Forms of Wildness: Archeology of an Idea," in *The Wild Man within: An Image in Western Thought from the Renaissance to Romanticism*, ed. Edward Dudly and Maximillian E. Novak (Pittsburg, PA: University of Pittsburgh Press, 1972), 3–38.

8. Bernheimer, *Wild Men*, 2.

9. Dickason, *Myth of the Savage*, 77.

10. Ibid.

11. Samuel Purchas, *Hakluytus Posthumus, or Purchas His Pilgrims*, Vol. 19 (Glasgow, UK: University Press, 1906): 231, quoted in Roy Harvey Pearce, *Savagism and Civilization: A Study of the Indian and the American Mind* (Berkeley: University of California Press, 1988), 7–8.

the Crown, often acting as intelligence agents, passing information between Quebec and inland political officials. Commerce, the designs of the French Empire, and Jesuit missionary work in North America intertwined, and the success of all three depended on good relations with Indians.[12] However, this does not mean that Jesuits lacked any measure of disapproval for Native religions and other cultural practices; most Jesuits believed that Indians who did not convert to Christianity remained wild barbarians in the clutches of Satan. Regarding his 1634 encounter with a Huron Indian whom he referred to as "The Sorceror," Father Paul Le Jeune remarked:

> The Sorcerer [is] a very wicked man. . . . Now this wretched man and the smoke were the two greatest trials that I endured among these Barbarians. The cold, heat, annoyance of the dogs, sleeping in the open air and upon the bare ground; the position I had to assume in their cabins, rolling myself up in a ball or crouching down or sitting without a seat or a cushion; hunger, thirst, the poverty and filth of their smoked meats, sickness,—all these things were merely play to me in comparison to the smoke and the malice of the Sorcerer, with whom I have always been on a very bad footing, . . . and judge what treatment I might have received from these Barbarians, who adore this miserable Sorcerer, against whom I was generally in a state of open warfare. . . . He treated me shamefully, . . . but I am astonished that he did not act worse, seeing that he is an idolater of those superstitions which I was fighting with all my might.[13]

Meanwhile, by cultivating fields in accord with English agricultural patterns, and by erecting churches and establishing towns, some Virginia colonists thought to provide models of behavior for Indians, who would then come to understand the benefits of civilization. At least so ran the missionary hope as fortified by the stated design of the English Crown. Indeed, the First Charter of Virginia (1606) expressed a desire to see:

> The Providence of Almighty God, hereafter tend to the Glory of His Divine Majesty, in propagating of Christian Religion to such people, as yet live in darkness, and miserable ignorance of the true knowledge and worship of God, and may in time bring the Infidels and Savages living in those parts, to human civility and to a settled and quiet Government.[14]

---

12. W. J. Eccles, *The Canadian Frontier, 1534–1760* (Albuquerque: University of New Mexico Press, 1983), 7.

13. Paul Le Jeune, "Relation de ce qui s'est passé en La Novvelle France, en l'année 1634," in *The Jesuit Relations and Allied Documents: Travels and Explorations of the Jesuit Missionaries in New France 1610—1791*, http://www.muhlenberg.edu/depts/religion/pearson/Jesuit_Relations_3.htm (accessed April 20, 2016).

14. "The First Charter of Virginia; April 10, 1606," http://avalon.law.yale.edu/17th_century/va01.asp#b1 (accessed April 10, 2016).

By 1622, the English effort to convert Indians to Christianity led to the appointment of a colonial rector to coordinate the work of some fifty missionaries. This fledgling ecclesiastical enterprise had by then accumulated the souls of thirty Algonquian children, most of whom had been forcibly removed from their parents, who remained "wrapped up in the fogge and miserie of their iniquity, and . . . chained under the bond of Deathe unto the Divell."[15] Since its inception in the earliest years of the Jamestown settlement, the missionary project exacerbated growing tensions between English colonists and Powhatan's people. Then when Powhatan died in 1616, his successor, Opechancanough, consolidated a military alliance of Algonquian polities across the region, surrounded the English settlements, and on April 1, 1622 struck in a coordinated attack that killed at least 347 colonists. Opechancanough's attack serves as one example that counters a common question: "Why didn't the Indians just band together and throw out the colonists?" The fact is, Indians led by Opechancanough did unite to throw out the colonists, and they nearly succeeded.

English retaliation came with the conviction that Christian attempts to convert the Indians had proved futile, as noted by a commentator of the time, Edward Waterhouse:

> Because our hands which before were tied with gentlenesse and faire usage, are now set at liberty by the treacherous violence of the Savages, not untying the Knot, but cutting it: So that we, who hitherto have had possession of no more ground then their waste, and our purchase at a valuable consideration to their owne contentment, gained; may now by a right of Warre, and law of Nations, invade the Country, and destroy them who sought to destroy us.[16]

In 1644, Opechancanough launched a second major and unsuccessful offensive; his defeat justified to Virginians their extended land claims from Algonquian territory.

In early seventeenth-century New England, Puritans visualized Indians as agents of the Devil in a cosmic drama of eternal conflict between God and Satan.[17] Accordingly, Indians served as agents of Satan, so they deserved punishment, as exemplified by the actions of the English in the Pequot War (1636–37).[18]

---

15. *Records of the Virginia Company of London*, Vol. 3 (Washington, D.C.: Government Printing Office, 1933), 14–15, quoted in Pearce, *Savagism and Civilization*, 9.

16. Edward Waterhouse, "A Declaration of the State of the Colonie and Affaires in Virginia," *Records of the Virginia Company of London*, 3:556–57, quoted in Pearce, *Savagism and Civilization*, 11.

17. The deeper source of this worldview is found in the Puritan concept of predestination as presented by French theologian John Calvin (1509–64), a belief that often placed Puritans at odds with other Christian sects. For a succinct exploration of these matters, see Charles H. Lippy, Robert Choquette, and Stafford Poole, *Christianity Comes to the Americas, 1492–1776* (New York: Paragon House, 1992), 262–85.

18. Berkhoefer, *White Man's Indian*, 81–3.

In 1636, Puritan authorities attempted to persuade the Pequot to surrender the parties responsible for the deaths of several Englishmen. Furthermore, the English demanded that Pequot chiefs, known as sachems, send a number of children to Boston as hostages to guarantee against future attacks against the colonists. Indian resistance to English demands led to a punitive attack on a Pequot village near the Mystic River. Commanding an alliance of Mohegan, Narragansett, and colonial forces, Captain John Underhill ordered the slaughter of all Pequot villagers. Many women and children were burned to death, their homes aflame. Some survivors faced enslavement to Mohegan and Narragansett sachems; others were sold by the English to Caribbean slave traders. Captain Underhill declared that God required all Pequots to suffer because "sometimes the scripture declareth that women and children must perish with their parents. . . . We had sufficient light from the word of God for our proceedings."[19]

The Wild Woman

While known at times in Greco-Roman antiquity and medieval Europe for her appalling ugliness, hairiness, and gigantic proportions, in other circumstances the Wild Woman tended to shrink and lose much of her hair, except for a long silken mane. Naked cannibal and libidinous hag, the Wild Woman coursed through the European imagination for centuries.[20] Thus it came as no surprise to voyagers from the Old World to find this agent of Satan running wild and free through the New World's forests and plains. The Wild Woman provided a Eurocentric template by which the strange trans-Atlantic females could be understood, as indicated by the sailors from Martin Frobisher's 1577 voyage through the Labrador Sea, who captured an elderly Inuit woman.

> [Her] ugliness was so great that the more ignorant of the Englishmen feared that they had captured a devil or witch who might prove to them an evil possession. They looked carefully all around her for some token of her nativity or an unholy alliance with the powers of darkness; and at last they took off her buskins, to see if she were cloven-footed.[21]

Amerigo Vespucci (1454–1512) claimed that the witchcraft of Indian women led them to use the bite of a poisonous snake to "make the penis of their husbands swell

---

19. Charles Orr, ed. *History of the Pequot War: The Contemporary Accounts of Mason, Underhill, Vincent, and Gardiner* (Cleveland, 1897): 81, quoted in Alfred A. Cave, *The Pequot War* (Amherst: University of Massachusetts Press, 1996), 3.

20. Bernheimer, *Wild Men*, 33–35.

21. Frank Jones, *The Life of Sir Martin Frobisher, Knight* (London: Longman, 1878), 78.

to such size as to as to appear deformed." As a result, the men often "lose their virile organs and remain eunuchs."[22]

Although many colonizers believed that both Indian men and women lived in collusion with the Devil, women generally fell under greater suspicion. This gendered distinction replicated misogynistic stereotypes and folklore about women that permeated European culture. Moreover, notions of women's witchcraft combined in a lethal mix with another apparent aberration in the proper order of the universe: Native American gender roles. To English commentators, they seemed unnatural and barbaric. Indian women performed agricultural work relegated to laboring men in Europe, while Indian men hunted, an activity associated with European aristocracy.[23] Moreover, many English believed that Indian women did not experience pain in childbirth, whereas Christian women, subject to Original Sin, paid for Eve's indiscretion through the pain of childbearing. This distinction underscored the European conception of Indian women as products of savagery and European women as products of civilization.[24] Also skewing European standards of gender identity stood the apparent feminization of Indian men through their fashion of clean-shaven faces. European men generally sported beards at this time, ironically reversing the negative value of hairiness associated with the Wild Man. But this reversal demonstrates the shifting boundary that protected positive European perceptions about themselves against the alien, and therefore dangerous, Native American world.

Because many Native American women appeared scantily clothed in comparison with the multilayered and multiwrapped attire of European women, commentators often described them as naked and therefore sexually available to any passing man. Although some writers might include as an afterthought that women "covered about their middles with a skin,"[25] the idea of female nakedness—or near nakedness—convinced Europeans that Indian women led depraved, immoral, and lewd existences. Moreover, nakedness fit into an equation between Indians and animals that came easily to early colonial observers. Indian women bore the brunt of European condemnation. Their dress signified promiscuity, and their work as field laborers made them mere drudges. Here stood the counterpart to the Indian Princess.

The image of an Indian woman as either a princess or a drudge relies on male perceptions. The Princess aids the White men as a Good Indian, but her sexual desirability

---

22. Louis Montrose, "The Work of Gender in Discourse Discovery," in "The New World," special issue, *Representations* 33 (1991): 5.

23. Brown, *Good Wives*, 58. David D. Smits, "'The Squaw Drudge': A Prime Index of Savagism," in *Native Women's History in Eastern North America Before 1900*, ed. Rebecca Kugel and Lucy Eldersveld Murphy (Lincoln: University of Nebraska Press, 2007), 33.

24. Brown, *Good Wives*, 58. On the notion of Indian women giving birth painlessly, see also Kirsten Fischer, *Suspect Relations: Sex, Race and Resistance in Colonial North Carolina* (Ithaca, NY: Cornell University Press, 2002), 66.

25. Brown, *Good Wives*, 59.

leads to a paradox—what one scholar calls "the Pocahontas Perplex."[26] The paradox stems in part from a pure woman/prostitute binary by which men preserve the purity of their "good" women, made good by marriage, and their use of prostitutes, "bad" women as objects of lust. The racial conflict between White men and Indian women further complicates this paradox.[27] Princess and "squaw" persist as twin images, their stereotypes determined by their function in male fantasies. The Princess cannot share sex with men, but the squaw can. Indian women, in their degraded capacities as squaws, share the same attributes as the ignoble Indian men—drunken thieves exiled to the outskirts.[28]

Gendered divisions of labor among the Algonquians, who were familiar to colonial Virginians, appeared contrary to seventeenth-century European ideals; thus, commentators often regarded Indian men as indolent and Indian women as "squaw drudges." In reality, Algonquian women planted, cultivated, and processed the annual crops of corn, squash, peas, and beans. They made clothing, tools, pots, and baskets. Women taught essential life skills to their children, schooling their sons as hunters and instructing their daughters in agricultural traditions and in the manufacturing of household goods. As agriculturalists, women played central roles in village politics, determining when new fields needed clearing and when old fields needed to go fallow. Men cleared trees and brush to prepare new land for planting. Although men directed the political and religious life of the village, women probably exercised greater power over village affairs than their English counterparts.[29]

Entailing significant political consequences, colonial commentators often compared the sexual powers of European and Native American men and claimed the superiority of the former. In a 1709 account of the Carolina colony, John Lawson boasted:

> *Indian* men are not so vigorous and impatient in their Love as we are. Yet the women are quite contrary, and those *Indian* Girls that have convers'd with the *English* and other Europeans, never care for the Conversation of their own Countrymen afterwards.[30]

26. Rayna Green, "The Pocahontas Perplex: The Image of Indian Women in American Culture," in Kugel and Murphy, 7–26.

27. Ibid., 19.

28. Green writes, "Squaws are shamed for their relationship with white men, and the males who share their beds—the 'squaw men' or 'bucks,' if they are Indian—share their shame. When they live with Indian males, Squaws work for their lazy bucks and bear large numbers of fat 'papooses.' . . . They too are fat, and unlike their Princess sisters, dark and possessed of cruder, more 'Indian' features." Ibid., 22.

29. Brown, *Good Wives*, 50. Smits, "Squaw Drudge," 29.

30. John Lawson, *A New Voyage to Carolina*, ed. Hugh Talmage Lefler (Chapel Hill: University of North Carolina Press, 1984), 46–47.

Colonial notions of Indian male impotency leveraged the English sense of entitlement to Native territory. Characterized as effeminate and lazy, the Indian men did not deserve the land on which they lived. Just as the English claimed easy sexual conquest over Indian women, they justified conquest of the land.[31]

The Captivity Narrative

The first bestseller in American history tells the story of Mary White Rowlandson, the wife of a Puritan minister, and her eleven-week captivity by Narragansett Indians. Published in 1682, Rowlandson's autobiography, *The Sovereignty & Goodness of God*, began the literary genre of the captivity narrative.[32] Hundreds of these narratives appeared in publication over the following centuries. They remained popular well into the nineteenth century, as paperback Westerns sensationalized the genre's dramatic formula, the plot of which first required a virtuous White woman to fall into the clutches of evil Indians. She then encountered both Good Indians and Bad Indians, both Noble Savages and Ignoble Savages, throughout the course of her captivity. Her rescue usually depended on the application of her own wits along with the arrival of White men, who would probably slaughter any number of godless savages before the happy ending. Indeed, Hollywood used the captivity narrative plotline to drive Cowboy and Indian films throughout much of the twentieth century, as discussed below.

Puritans saw the captivity narrative as a religious allegory. That is, on a symbolic plane it told the story of the human soul trapped in a wicked world; however, faith in God's power placed the wandering sinner on the path to salvation. Thus Puritan minsters often wove Rowlandson's story, and many others like it, into their sermons.[33] The demonization of Indians remained fundamental to the allegory.

To New England Puritans, the wilderness started at the edge of their settlements; in it lurked satanic savages. Moreover, Puritans often referred to the wilderness as a "desert," by which they meant a place without people, as in "deserted." Indians did not register as people; like forest animals they belonged to nature. The Massachusetts Bay Colony settlers worried greatly about the eternal fate of their English souls, so the captivity narrative allegory expressed an ongoing spiritual struggle. Indians did not simply *represent* evil; they embodied evil, and its eradication stood foremost on the Puritan agenda.

---

31. Brown, *Good Wives*, 57; Fischer, *Suspect Relations*, 69–70.

32. Neal Salisbury, ed., *The Sovereignty and Goodness of God, Together with the Faithfulness of His Promises Displayed, Being a Narrative of the Captivity and Restoration of Mrs. Mary Rowlandson and Related Documents* (Boston: Bedford/St. Martin's, 1997), vii.

33. Ibid., 44–45.

But Rowlandson's autobiography stood firmly rooted in historical experience, as did many other captivity narratives that followed. "On the tenth of February 1675," her account begins, "Came the Indians with great numbers upon Lancaster."[34] The attackers set fire to her house:

> [The] fire increasing, and coming behind us roaring . . . my brother-in-law (being before wounded, in defending the house, in or near the throat) fell down dead. . . . The bullets flying thick, one went through my side, and the same (as it would seem) through the bowels and hand of my dear child in my arms.[35]

The attack counted as only one of many throughout the Massachusetts Bay Colony in what has become known as King Philip's War (1675–78). Although sparked by the execution of three Wampanoag tribesmen in Plymouth, within the deeper motives for war stood a growing animosity toward the English for their ceaseless intrusion of Wampanoag territory and resources. Thus, in 1675 Metacomet (King Philip) and his Wampanoag warriors burned over 1,200 colonial houses and killed about 600 settlers in a year-long series of raids. The war cost the lives of about 3,000 Indians—although some estimates calculate at least 8,000 Indian deaths—including the life of Metacomet. After the war, colonists captured at least 1,600 Indians, including Metacomet's wife and son, and sold them into slavery in the Caribbean.

Rowlandson's fate belongs within the historical context of Native American warfare, in which captive taking functioned ritually in "raising the dead," a practice that involved the replacement of a family member killed in battle through the capture of another person in some way related to the killer who would then be given to the grieving family. The family might torture to death, enslave, or forcefully adopt the captive as a restored version of the lost relative.[36]

Rowlandson witnesses the ritual torture of one captive and is herself enslaved, although steadily she becomes incorporated into village life. From time to time her narrative comments on acts of kindness shown her by community members. She reports:

> There came an Indian to me and bid me come to his wigwam at night, and he would give me some pork and ground nuts. Which I did eat, and as I was eating, another Indian said to me, he seems to be your good friend, but he killed two Englishmen at Sudbury, and there lie their clothes behind you: I looked behind me, and there I saw the bloody

---

34. The village of Lancaster stood about thirty miles west of Boston and contained about fifty families at the time of Rowlandson's narrative.

35. Salisbury, ed., *Sovereignty and Goodness of God*, 68.

36. Michael Witgen, *An Infinity of Nations: How the Native New World Shaped Early North America* (Philadelphia: University of Pennsylvania Press, 2012), 122.

clothes, with bullet-holes in them. Yet the Lord suffered not this wretch to do me any hurt. Yea, instead of that, he many times refreshed me; five or six times did he and his squaw refresh my feeble carcass. [And] yet they were strangers that I never saw before. . . . So little do we prize common mercies when we have them to the full.[37]

After eleven weeks of captivity, colonial officials arranged a ransom payment of £20 for her release. Barring the ransom, her incorporation into Wampanoag society would likely have deepened. Indeed, of the estimated 1,641 New Englanders taken captive between 1675 and 1763, at least 52 chose not to return to White society, while the length of other captivities ranged from a few days to over two years.[38] Rowlandson's White identity remains intact, and she condemns much of what she sees during her captivity; however, the experience complicates her worldview.

Captivity narratives involving marriages between Indians and Whites raised fears of race mixing, although today scholars understand these marriages as cultural intersections in which distinct racial categories prove irrelevant. For example, Young Bear (Maconaquah), a Miami woman, lived most of her life in Deaf Man's Village, in present-day Indiana. In the late eighteenth century, she had been taken captive from her White family in the Wyoming region of Pennsylvania. In Deaf Man's Village, she married, raised children, and became a respected member of a complexly intercultural community. But when, in 1835, she told a White visitor to her village that she had been born White, the visitor took it upon himself to find her original family. Thus appeared Joseph Slocum, who then traveled to Deaf Man's Village and confirmed that Young Bear was indeed his sister, Frances Slocum.[39]

In Deaf Man's Village, she lived comfortably and happily, and she belonged to an extended family that stretched across generations. To Joseph Slocum's shock, she expressed no desire to return to her White relatives. Her story drew national attention. Newspaper articles often interpreted her as a White woman "gone Indian," thus her refusal to return to "civilization" could be explained in familiar terms. One could be White or Red, civilized or savage; racial lines could not be crossed. Regardless of Young Bear's own self-identity as Native, commentators throughout the nineteenth and early twentieth centuries claimed her as White; after all, any fluidity in racial categories threatened the White worldview. As racially distinct—and racially inferior— to Whites, Indians could not "mix" with Whites; indeed, they must be completely removed from the White world and placed on reservations far away from that world.[40]

---

37. Rowlandson, *Sovereignty and Goodness of God*, 101.

38. Alden T. Vaughan and Daniel K. Richter, "Crossing the Cultural Divide: Indians and New Englanders, 1605–1763," in *Proceedings of the American Antiquarian Society*, 90 (1980): 60.

39. James Joseph Buss, *Winning the West with Words: Language and the Conquest of the Lower Great Lakes* (Norman: University of Oklahoma Press, 2011), 134–36.

40. Ibid., 139–43.

The line between White and Red must be held, regardless of widespread evidence stretching back hundreds of years that marriage between Indians and Whites proved the norm in some places and not the exception, especially in regions thinly populated by White traders who sought Indian women for sexual gratification as well as for companionship, and thus became part of a wider Native American kinship network. The resulting multicultural and multilingual communities flew in the face of easy racial stereotypes. Generally, captivity narratives served to reinforce the stereotype of Indians as irredeemable savages, one repeated in American histories and textbooks for generations.

The Textbook Savage

Historian Francis Parkman (1823–93) wrote off the Pequot as "far worse than wolves or rattlesnakes. . . . A warlike race who had boasted that they would wipe the whites from the face of the earth, but who, by hard marching and fighting, had lately been brought to reason."[41] In other words, they deserved their day of reckoning. Nineteenth-century American histories often featured Indian demonization and degradation, and textbooks—readers and spellers—re-inscribed the Myth of the Ignoble Savage in classrooms throughout the country. Thus generations of Euro-American schoolchildren learned their misconceptions about Indians from their teachers and their texts.

Again concerning the Pequots, an 1831 geography textbook described them as "a savage foe, whose delight was cruelty."[42] The same year, a reader invited students to "see our William Penn, with weaponless hands, sitting down peaceably with his followers in the midst of savage nations whose only occupation was shedding the blood of their fellow men, disarming them by his justice, and teaching them, for the first time, to view a stranger without mistrust."[43]

An 1818 reader tells a Revolutionary War story about the escape of a captured American officer from an unidentified band of Indians: "The savages who had been prevented from glutting their diabolical thirst of blood took every opportunity of manifesting their malevolence for their disappointment, by horrid grimaces and angry gestures."[44] An 1842 reader describes the war as a time when "this great country

---

41. Francis Parkman, *France and England in North America*, ed. David Levin (New York: The Library of America, 1983), 1084.

42. Rev. J. L. Blake, *A Geography for Children* (Boston: Richardson, Lord and Holbrook, 1831), 19.

43. Samuel Putman, *The Analytic Reader* (New York: Jonathan Leavitt, 1831), 76.

44. Rufus W. Adams, *Young Gentleman and Lady's Explanatory Monitor* (Columbus, OH: E. Griswold, Jun., 1818), 60.

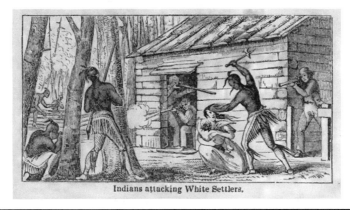

Indians attacking White Settlers.

Indians Attacking White Settlers. Note that the Indians remain mostly within the forest. The settlers defend their prototypical log cabin, made, of course, from the same forest, but "civilized." S. Augustus Mitchell, *An Easy Introduction to the Study of Geography: Designed for the Instruction of Children in Schools and Families* (Philadelphia: Thomas, Cowperthwait and Co., 1847), 51.

was covered with forests, where wild beasts and scarcely less savage Indians roamed in their freedom."[45]

Spellers sometimes used vocabulary words in context to distinguish between homonyms. Thus, "Indians are sometimes very *cruel*. The girls were busily employed in working *crewel*."[46] Another speller gives an example of the word "gory" in the phrase, "A gory scalp."[47]

S. Augustus Mitchell's *An Easy Introduction to the Study of Geography* (1847) consolidates Native American history in a set of images that passed seamlessly from classrooms to paperback Westerns and eventually to movies and comic books.

> Nearly all the Indians in the United States reside in the Western territories. Some of them have good houses and farms, and have been taught to read by missionaries. Others roam over the vast prairies of the far west and hunt the buffalo and other wild beasts. The missionaries are good men, who teach savage nations to read the Bible, worship the true God, and to live like Christians. The first settlers of the western states were exposed to many dangers; their houses were often attacked, and their wives and children murdered by the Indians.[48]

45. Marshman William Hazen, *Hazen's Third Reader* (Philadelphia, PA: E. H. Butler, 1895), 97.

46. Charles Northend, *Dictation Exercises* (New York: A. S. Barnes, 1855), 15.

47. Marcius Wilson, *Wilson's Primary Speller* (New York: Harper and Brothers, 1863), 39.

48. S. Augustus Mitchell, *An Easy Introduction to the Study of Geography: Designed for the Instruction of Children in Schools and Families* (Philadelphia, PA: Thomas, Cowperthwait, 1847), 51. https://archive.org/details/ldpd_11290379_000 (accessed December 8, 2016).

The Pulp Savage and the Silent Savage

Marketed for a mass audience in the period from about 1860 to the early twentieth century, dime Westerns imagined the American West as a mythological frontier. Their literary quality ranged widely, but they generally depended on stereotyped characters and a limited assortment of plots. Regarding the perpetuation of Indian stereotypes, Chapter 1 looked at the dime Western as a vehicle for the Myth of the Noble Savage, but the genre also depended on the Myth of the Ignoble Savage. The economic and political significance of the Myth of the Ignoble Savage cannot be overstated. Mass marketed, the myth forcefully re-inscribed the notion that Indians did not deserve their land; as degenerate, bloodthirsty agents of the Devil they must be extinguished.

In *Job Dean, the Trapper* (1888), a White settler recounts the scene of a recent Indian attack: "When I looked down upon them poor unfortunate creatures, with the blood streaming from them, and them imps of Satan dancing around 'em an' waving their bleeding scalps, my heart turned sick."[49] In *Kent, the Ranger* (1863), another settler also describes Indians in demonic terms: "The building was now one mass of flame. . . . The savages resembled demons dancing and yelling around the ruin which they had caused."[50] Similarly, in a later Indian attack on a settler: "Several savages sprung toward him, setting up their demoniac howls."[51] In *Seth Jones; or, The Captives of the Frontier* (1860), an Indian fighter proclaims: "It seems the devil himself is helping them imps!"[52] And in *The Gray Scalp; or, The Blackfoot Brave* (1870), another Indian fighter asserts: "They steal white men's horses, and thar's no end to an Injun's devilment, nohow."[53] In the West as melodrama, the forces of good and evil—of God and the Devil—continually clashed. Moreover, as summarized in the opening paragraph of *The Doomed Hunter; or, The Tragedy of Forest Valley* (1866):

> It is no extraordinary circumstance in the history of our Western civilization that a howling wilderness—the abode only of wild animals and wilder savages—becomes transformed in a few years to a smiling agricultural district with populous towns and villages. The broad fertile fields . . . present little to mark the scene over which white men and savages fought in relentless warfare, [and] the strategy, the struggles, the daring which wrested those lands from the sullen Indian, and held them against the wiles of his power are passed over and forgotten.[54]

---

49. Ingoldsby North, *Job Dean, the Trapper* (New York: Beadle, 1888), 16.

50. Edward S. Ellis, *Kent, the Ranger* (New York: Beadle, 1863), 16.

51. Ibid., 43.

52. Edward S. Ellis, *Seth Jones; or, The Captives of the Frontier* (New York: Beadle, 1860), 60.

53. Edward Willett, *The Gray Scalp; or, The Blackfoot Brave* (New York: Beadle, 1870), 15.

54. James L. Bowen, *The Doomed Hunter; or, The Tragedy of Forest Valley* (New York: Beadle, 1866), 9.

The erasure of Indians would be so complete as to extinguish even the memory of the wars themselves by which Western civilization secured its triumph over them. But Indians had only themselves to blame for being written out of history, as a settler explains in *Old Crossfire* (1875): "The savage is treacherous; it is his nature and I blame him not. He is murdering those whom he swore should not be harmed." And within a few minutes, "Dark forms, armed and plumed, were rushing through the gate that fronted the mansion. The treachery of the Indian had sprung to the surface."[55] The message here is that Indians cannot be trusted; they, not Whites, broke treaties because betrayal came naturally to them. This view remains current today as some groups, such as the Citizens Equal Rights Alliance, actively litigate to eliminate tribal sovereignty.[56]

Physical descriptions of Indians further identified their ignobility. During a raid on settlers in *Old Zip; or, The Cabin in The Air* (1871), Indian warriors turned a "whole battery of repulsive faces upward against the building; they brandished their guns, tomahawks and knives."[57] Among the Indians listening to a sermon in *The Hunter's Escape: A Tale of the North West in 1862* (1864): "There were brawny and scarred warriors, with coarse, repulsive features, their black, wiry hair falling into their laps as they inclined their heads; . . . there were frowzy squaws scarcely less repellent than their husbands, some with short black pipes inserted between their snaggy teeth." However, the author goes on to note that the same group contained:

> younger and more comely maidens and children—all holding a respectful silence while Father Richter was addressing them. An occasional guttural ejaculation from some of the older ones showed their appreciation of the truths that were uttered in their own highly figurative language. . . . Take the audience as whole, their deportment and interest would compare very favorably with that of any congregation in a civilized country, although their dress and appearance would have suffered from the same comparison.[58]

Giving with one hand and taking with the other, the author appears at first to drop the distinction between savage and civilized audiences; however, Indian "dress and appearance" remain deal breakers.

---

55. Charles Howard, *Old Crossfire* (New York: Beadle and Adams, 1875), 28–29.

56. Terri Hansen, "Anti-Indian CERA Doesn't Like the Law of the Land in United States, or Us, Apparently." *Indian Country Today*, March 28, 2014, https://indiancountrymedianetwork.com/news/politics/anti-indian-cera-doesnt-like-the-law-of-the-land-in-united-states-or-us-apparently/ (accessed June 1, 2017).

57. Bruin Adams, *Old Zip; or, The Cabin in the Air* (New York: Beadle and Adams, 1871), 40.

58. Edward S. Ellis, *The Hunter's Escape: A Tale of the North West in 1862* (New York: Beadle, 1864), 11–12.

Because dime novels were aimed at a working-class audience, critics often branded the genre as lowbrow. This stigma followed into the early years of the film industry inasmuch as turn-of-the-century Cowboy and Indian movies drew on dime novels for their characters, settings, and narratives. Reviewers pointed disparagingly to this relationship. Some filmmakers attempted to appeal to critics, while others ignored them.[59] But Indian stereotypes remained endemic in the Western film genre long after its lowbrow stigma faded, since the dime novel stood only as their most recent cultural ancestor. White American filmmakers, as products of a culture steeped in misconceptions about Indians, inevitably perpetuated stereotypes long predating those in the pages of nineteenth-century pulp fiction. Among these stereotypes, the Ignoble Savage figured prominently on the screen.

D. W. Griffith, one of the most important filmmakers of the silent era, made dozens of Westerns, but *The Battle at Elderbush Gulch* (1913) remains perhaps his most influential work in this genre. Indians make their first appearance in the film during "THE DOG FEAST," according to the intertitle. But "THE CHIEF'S SON [returns] TOO LATE FOR THE FEAST, and with no dogs left to eat, attempts to steal two puppies from settlers who gun him down, an act that "FANS THE EVER READY SPARK OF HATRED TO REVENGE." Warriors descend on the settlers and with sadistic fury smash the brains out of a White child, scalp a settler, set fire to the town, and leave the ground littered with dead Whites. Settlers make their last stand in a besieged cabin and are moments from certain death when the cavalry arrives, kills all the Indians, and saves the family and the puppies too.

Although Whites and Indians kill each other in near equal numbers, the photography of the violence distinguishes between the two groups. The camera looks at most killing from a distance; however, Indians get the close-ups in two scenes shot to convey the greatest degree of horror in the film. The White child's murder scene and the scalping scene both fill the screen. Moreover, the faces of dead Whites get close-ups, while the faces of dead Indians do not. A film tells its stories through sequences edited to move the narrative along and convey a sense of the emotional and psychological realities of its characters. The close-up of a dead or dying settler says, "Savages did this." A film that lacks a similar focus on dead Indians sends the message that their deaths do not have the same level of importance as the death of Whites. As noted in the Introduction and Chapter 1, many films sympathetic to Indians attempt to humanize them, but most Westerns fall into an Indian demonizing routine because the movie industry must make business decisions to stay alive. Stereotypes sell.

This is not to deny that historically Indians committed profound acts of violence and deliberate cruelty against Whites; however, popularized images of this violence generally deny its historical context and represent it as an expression of the inherently

---

59. Andrew Brodie Smith, *Shooting Cowboys and Indians: Silent Western Films, American Culture, and the Birth of Hollywood* (Boulder: University Press of Colorado, 2003), 107–8.

evil nature of a savage race. And when the cinema perpetuates context-free Indian violence, the Myth of the Ignoble Savage continues to masquerade as a cultural fact.

The Indian as Buffoon

In one episode of the newspaper comic strip *Big Chief Wahoo* (1936–47), Wahoo works as a projectionist in a movie theater. The all-Indian audience has come to see *Adventures in Darkest Africa*, and when the film opens with a lion roaring into action, the Indians riot, whip out their bows, and saturate the screen with arrows. Wahoo remarks, "Ugh! Show endum heap sudden!"[60] Another episode features Wahoo and his friend Mooseface in a car on their way to go ice-skating. While Mooseface is at the wheel, Wahoo peers back over his shoulder: "Oh oh! Fun begin now—here come paleface policeman!" The officer stops them, leaps off his motorcycle, and screams: "Hey! Where do you think you're goin'? Didn't you see that sign, 'slow curve?'" Mooseface replies: "Mooseface heap sorry! Couldn't gettum foot on brake—gottum ice skates on!"[61] *Big Chief Wahoo*, which also became a popular comic book series, typifies the Indian as buffoon stereotype that has permeated most areas of popular culture. An aspect of the Myth of the Ignoble Savage, the buffoon stereotype relies on the myth's core degradation of Indians, with their "uncivilized" nature turned into comedy. These goodhearted but slow-witted Indians misread modernity and pepper their limited vocabularies with "ugh," with the "-um" suffix, personal pronoun errors (using "me" instead of "I"), and a number of other grammatical faults intended for comic effects. Moreover, their attempts to fit in with White culture result in failures intended as comedic situations.

Commoditized, the buffoon provided advertisers with a comic angle to sell merchandise and novelty items. In the 1960s, cans of Wigwam Motor Oil displayed a pigeon-toed dancing Indian with his tongue hanging out, panting the slogan: "A buck well spent." A mid-twentieth-century ceramic egg timer displays an Indian woman lounging on an egg with the sandglass pivot in her hand. Instructions on the egg read: "For boilum egg just turnum glass watchum sand go down." A 1966 advertisement for "Injun Brave," a "Roly Poly Punching Toy," claims: "He's the biggest of 'em all. Largest Roly Poly on the market. He's also the funniest to hit. Down he goes, and the weighted bottom brings him back up for more."[62]

---

60. Elmer Woggon and Allen Saunders, *Big Chief Wahoo Collection* (Atlantic Mine, MI: Keri Therrian, 2016), 23.

61. Ibid., 28.

62. For images of "Wigwam Motor Oil," "Egg Timer," and "Roly Poly Punching Toy," and similar items, see http://www.authentichistory.com/diversity/native/is3-buffoon/ (accessed March 26, 2016).

For decades, animated cartoons depended on a steady infusion of the Indian as buffoon to drive their storylines. "Big Chief Ugh-Amugh-Ugh"[63] (1938), a Popeye cartoon, opens with the chief singing, "Me Big Chief Ugh-Amugh-Ugh gotta have a squaw." His bride turns out to be Olive Oyl. "Me makum squaw beautiful," he says. But Popeye soon stumbles on the scene, and in a spinach-enhanced fury defeats the chief, takes his warbonnet, and lords it over the chastised Indian, who then grovels in obeisance at his feet. One Bugs Bunny cartoon, "A Feather in His Hare"[64] (1948), concerns an Indian character who wants "to cacthum rabbit." Bugs Bunny, in a ploy typical of his character, easily sends him down a dead-end trail while the Indian happily responds, "Me thankum you much, ugh." The Indian buffoon consistently falls prey to Bugs Bunny's antics. Of course, this same plot construction propels all of the rabbit's cartoons. He outsmarts every adversary who comes his way. However, a number of Indian stereotypes come to his assistance in "A Feather in His Hare." After a slapstick scalping routine in a "hare cut" teepee, Bugs turns the hunter into a cigar store Indian. Next, the Indian tells him, "Me last Mohican." Bugs replies, "Well, look, Geronimo. . ." This dim-witted and easily confused buffoon stereotype is of course no Geronimo. The use of Mohicans for comic effect also appears in "Oily American" (1954), which features an Indian named Moe Hican made wealthy through the discovery of oil on his land; however, he lives in a teepee inside of his mansion, which signals his buffoon status.[65]

Among the Indian buffoons who have frequented American cinema, the Ma and Pa Kettle comedies popular in the 1940s and 1950s feature two: Crowbar and Geoduck (pronounced Gooey-duck). Although buffoonery also drives the comic situations of the White characters in the series—as stereotyped hillbillies, the backward Kettles do not quite fit in with the changing world around them—the comedy driving Crowbar and Geoduck generally arises from racist assumptions. Crowbar never utters a word, underscoring the stereotype of the Indian stoic; Geoduck speaks in a chopped nongrammatical monotone, or "Tontospeak."

Films in both the silent and the sound eras used Indian buffoonery for comic effect. Most gags in Buster Keaton's *The Paleface*[66] (1922) build on stereotyped depictions of Indians as dim-witted, easily duped, and childishly sentimental primitives.

---

63. "Big Chief Ugh-Amugh-Ugh," directed by Dave Fleischer (Paramount, April 25, 1938). https://www.youtube.com/watch?v=5CIoELlqrMc (accessed March 24, 2016).

64. "A Feather in His Hare," directed by Charles M. Jones (Warner Brothers, February 7, 1948). http://www.dailymotion.com/video/xbu9uy_fethry-in-his-hare_shortfilms (accessed March 24, 2016).

65. "The Oily American," directed by Robert McKimson (Warner Brothers, July 10, 1954). http://www.dailymotion.com/video/x3bobkq (accessed March 24, 2016).

66. Buster Keaton, *The Paleface*, written and directed by Buster Keaton and Edward F. Kline (January 1922, Joseph M. Schenck), https://www.youtube.com/watch?v=GqwDpfWJWyQ (accessed March 27, 2016).

The film abounds in scalping jokes and slapstick war dances. The Three Stooges in *Whoops, I'm an Indian*[67] (1936) derive their intended comedy by donning warbonnets, painting their faces, and communicating in mere grunts. *Go West*[68] (1940) gives the Marx Brothers an opportunity to run through a series of gags premised on Indian buffoon characteristics of gullibility and ignorance.

As with film, some television series made ample use of the Indian as buffoon. *F Troop* (1965–67) lampoons both Whites and Indians. The soldiers of Fort Courage and the Indians—the Hekawi tribe—share comic situations. However, Hekawi comedy relies on broken English delivered in stoical monotone; moreover, some episodes carry subtle reminders of their inferior status to the Whites. Much of the comedy in the series stems from Sergeant O'Rourke's personally lucrative arrangement with the Hekawis, who sell him trinkets and beadwork for tourists and alcohol for the soldiers and settlers. In "The Return of Bald Eagle,"[69] the sergeant reminds the Indians that if they disobey his orders, he will send them "back to hunting and fishing" and "weaving your own blankets." Although intended comedically, the scene demonstrates the White prerogative that underlines the series, regardless of episodes in which the Indians appear to best the Whites.

In the examples above, White actors in redface play the Indians. This tends to ensure that the comedy relies on Indian stereotypes. However, in recent years, films and television series written, produced, directed, and acted by Native Americans express comedic situations based on indigenous experiences. *Mixed Blessings* (2007–10), set in present-day Fort McMurray, Alberta, and aired on the Aboriginal Peoples Television Network, explores the comedic conflicts that arise in a mixed family of Cree and Ukrainian-Canadian backgrounds. The series' co-creator Ron E. Scott, a member of the Métis nation of Alberta, states, "The message is simply that people are people. But especially in the native culture, there's a great sense of humour which helps us deal with the conflicts, which are typical to what we all go through in our relationships."[70] Similarly, the comic situations in the Native American feature film *Smoke Signals* (1998) proceed directly from an indigenous point of view. The film turns the stereotyped Hollywood Indian on its head. *Smoke Signals* takes ownership and claims sovereignty over indigenous comedy.[71]

---

67. Moe Howard, Larry Fine, and Curly Howard, *Whoops, I'm an Indian*, directed by Del Lord (September 1936: Columbia), https://www.youtube.com/watch?v=p3rHDEuvMds (accessed March 27, 2016).

68. *Go West*, directed by Edward Buzzell (Burbank, CA: Warner Home Video, 2004), DVD.

69. "The Return of Bald Eagle," *F Troop*, ABC, October 12, 1965.

70. Ron E. Scott. Quoted in Dustin Tahmahkera, *Tribal Television: Viewing Native People in Sitcoms* (Chapel Hill: University of North Carolina Press, 2014), 142.

71. For an extensive analysis of *Smoke Signals*, see Amada J. Cobb, "This Is What It Means to Say *Smoke Signals*: Native American Cultural Sovereignty," in *Hollywood's Indian: The Portrayal of the*

Controversy during the production of *The Ridiculous Six* (2015) led several Navajo actors to walk off the set, protesting the film's Indian stereotypes and misrepresentation of Apache culture. One of the film's Native actors, John Gates, noted Hollywood's long-standing practice of casting stereotyped Indians:

> I've been told that local New Mexico casting companies will not cast Native people, almost 100% of the time, unless we're cast as 19th-century characters. And that's just not right. I've worked as an attorney and I've worked in higher education both at the undergraduate and the graduate level for the past 17 years, I could play those roles easily. As could many of my colleagues who were out there.[72]

Indian Hating: *The Searchers*

Indian hating depends on the Myth of the Ignoble Savage to justify itself; therefore, it is effectively as old as the myth itself. Undifferentiated as individuals, all Indians deserve disdain for their mere existence and must be treated as enemies. The racism that fuels Indian hating demands that all Indians be exterminated or, at the very least, driven far into the wastelands.[73] Indeed, in 1825 President James Monroe requested Congress to enact "a well-digested plan" for Indian removal west of the Mississippi because "experience has shown" that Indians could "never be incorporated into our system in any form whatever." Monroe disapproved of forcible removal; if Indians only consented to their displacement voluntarily, Whites would "become in reality their benefactors."[74] The notion of Indian removal as an act of White largesse allowed cultural room for some Americans to see themselves as carriers of Christian charity.

One Hollywood film examines the archetypal Indian hater. Director John Ford's *The Searchers* (1956) tells the story of Ethan Edwards, played by John Wayne, who returns to his west Texas family in 1868. Soon thereafter, Comanche raiders kill his brother and sister-in-law and take his two nieces captive. Consumed by vengeance,

---

Native American in Film, ed. Peter C. Rollins and John E. O'Connor (Lexington: University Press of Kentucky, 2003), 206–28.

72. John Gates, quoted in "The Story about Adam Sandler's 'Ridiculous Six' You Didn't Hear: Four Natives Speak," *Indian Country Today*, June 4, 2015, https://indiancountrymedianetwork.com/culture/arts-entertainment/the-story-about-adam-sandlers-ridiculous-six-you-didnt-hear-four-natives-speak/ (accessed June 1, 2017).

73. For an exhaustive theory-centered examination of Indian hating, see Richard Drinnon, *Facing West: The Metaphysics of Indian-Hating and Empire-Building* (Norman: University of Oklahoma Press, 1997).

74. James Monroe, *American State Papers, Documents Legislative and Executive of the Congress of the United States*, Vol. 5 (Washington, D.C.: Gales and Seaton, 1858): 358, quoted in Drinnon, *Facing West*, 115.

Ethan spends the next five years tracking down Scar, the Nawyecka band chief who led the attack and abducted his nieces, Debbie and Lucy. Ethan intends not to bring the girls back but to eradicate the dishonor of their captivity by killing them. Contaminated through rape by Indians, a certainty implied throughout the film, Debbie and Lucy can no longer return to the White world and are better off dead.

Although ambiguity and character depth distinguish *The Searchers* from most Hollywood Westerns, stereotypes about Indians persist throughout the film. While several White characters pursue love interests, represent compassion, and demonstrate racial tolerance, Indians range only within the confines of Ignoble Savage attributes as evil killers or as simpleminded buffoons. However, the film does manage to interrogate the stereotype of Indians as savages destined for extinction.

Ethan's hatred leads him to shoot the eyes out of a dead Indian, eternally damning him to "wander forever between the winds." Later he fires his rifle repeatedly into a buffalo herd, figuring that "Killin' buffalo's as good as killin' Injuns in this country." His quest leads him to an encounter with a White woman and two girls recovered from Indian captivity during a U.S. cavalry attack on a Comanche village. All three have been driven into deep insanity through their captive experiences. A soldier comments to Ethan: "It's hard to believe they're White." Ethan glowers, "They ain't White. Not anymore. They're Comanch."

Ethan travels with Martin Pawley, a part-Indian adopted into his brother's family as a child. Martin demands his right to join the search to prevent Ethan from killing the girls. Ethan intends to carry out a sentence condoned by the White world, as demonstrated in an exchange between Martin and his love interest, Laurie Jorgensen. Laurie insists that Martin give up the search for Debbie (Lucy had already been found dead). But Martin demands, "I gotta fetch her home." To which she replies, "Fetch what home? The leavings a Comanche buck sold time and again to the highest bidder, with savage brats of her own? . . . Do you know what Ethan will do if he has a chance? He'll put a bullet in her brain. I tell you, Martha [Ethan's sister-in-law killed by Scar] would want him to."

Ethan finds Debbie but ultimately decides not to kill her and takes her home, and in the film's final scene, the White community welcomes her back with open arms. But after the Jorgensen family takes her into their cabin, Ethan remains isolated outside. Framed by the cabin door he pauses, then turns and disappears into the distance. Still conflicted, he cannot see himself joining a world populated by people of mixed blood like Martin or people like Debbie, who suggests a troubling Indianization.

The film's ambiguity does not allow a tidy ending in which Indian hating disappears with Ethan over the horizon of history. In that cabin, Laurie Jorgensen hates Indians as much as Ethan, regardless of her impending marriage to Martin. However, Martin represents the Good Indian, one completely absorbed into White society, and one who rejects every aspect of Native American culture. The Bad Indian, like Scar, represents the enemy of the White world. Most Indians in *The Searchers* are Bad Indians—Ignoble Savages. The road to Indian hating runs straight through their territory.

The dictates of westward expansion demand that Indians who refuse to accept the obsolescence of their (savage) world must suffer the consequences.

Manifest Destiny, the Ignoble Savage, and the Power of the Popular Press

Coined in 1845 by newspaperman John O'Sullivan, the term summarized an already long-standing belief that America's destiny—its westward expansion as a nation—moved forward with God's blessing. The belief in Manifest Destiny permeated nineteenth-century America, carried well into the twentieth century, and, some would argue, continues to inform U.S. foreign policy. Hollywood Westerns drove home the message that Indians (however unfortunately) stood in the way of progress—of the nation's Manifest Destiny—so they must be removed, one way or another. Westerns could be said to sooth an uneasy conscience of a White audience that might be troubled by atrocities against Indians. Fortunately for that audience, the movies perpetuated the myth of Indians as incompatible with progress: their primitive lifestyles and superstitious beliefs made them unfit for modern civilization. According to this rationale, the Indians remained responsible for their own purported demise. They had only themselves to blame. The logic absolved White historical responsibility.

As Euro-American populations expanded, agricultural, mineral, transportation, and industrial interests worked in tandem with federal agencies to secure land rights through treaties with Indian nations. The spread of White settlement, and the many treaties broken by the federal government across time, sought justification within the principles of Manifest Destiny. As O'Sullivan proclaimed, "It is by the right of our manifest destiny to overspread and to possess the whole of the continent which Providence has given us for the development of the great experiment of liberty and federated self-government entrusted to us."[75] O'Sullivan identified a principle implied by President James Monroe's 1823 Monroe Doctrine that warned European nations that any interference in the affairs of either North or South America would trigger intervention by the United States.[76] The term struck a chord, and "Manifest Destiny" became a battle cry for nineteenth- and twentieth-century expansionists. The phrase, and the ideology behind it, justified the ongoing displacement of Indians so that Euro-Americans could "possess the whole of the continent." Expansionists thus wielded Divine Providence as a political instrument in the service of their cause.

---

75. See "Manifest Destiny—A Philosophy That Created a Nation," http://www.let.rug.nl/usa/essays/1801-1900/manifest-destiny/manifest-destiny—-the-philosophy-that-created-a-nation.php (accessed April 12, 2016).

76. "The Monroe Doctrine," http://www.ushistory.org/documents/monroe.htm (accessed April 12, 2016).

The rise of mass-circulation newspapers in the nineteenth century provided an influential forum for the spread of Manifest Destiny as a national ideology. In part to promote the interests of powerful expansionists, the press relied on long-standing negative stereotypes about Indians. Indeed, editors, industrialists, railroad tycoons, and land speculators often shared the same political, economic, and social ideas. These mutual interests fueled the highly partisan nature of the press at this time. Journalism as a profession with rigorous standards of fact checking and objectivity had yet to evolve.

One of the most influential newspapermen of the nineteenth century, Horace Greely, gained fame as a tireless advocate for westward expansion. Indeed, the phrase generally attributed to him, "Go west, young man,"[77] rings with the enthusiastic boosterism at the heart of Manifest Destiny. Moreover, as Greely reported from Denver in 1859, Indians did not deserve the land because

> the Indians are children. Their arts, wars, treaties, alliances, habitations, crafts, properties, commerce, comforts, all belong to the rudest ages of human existence. [They] are utterly incompetent to cope in any way with the European or Caucasian race. . . . It needs but little familiarity with the actual, palpable aborigines to convince anyone that the poetic Indian—the Indian of Cooper and Longfellow—is only visible to the poet's eye. To the prosaic observer, the average Indian of the woods and prairies is a being who does little credit to human nature—a slave of appetite and sloth, never emancipated from the tyranny of one animal passion save by the more ravenous demands of another.[78]

Greeley went on to describe Indian women as "degraded and filthy, . . . neither too proud nor too indolent to work." While women did all the work—they pitched the tents, chopped the firewood, dressed and cooked the game, sewed, and more—the men stood immune from daily toil. "Squalid and conceited, proud and worthless, lazy and lousy, they will strut out or drink out their miserable existence."[79]

These evaluations reveal more than Greeley's prejudice. They expressed prevailing notions about Indians commonly held by most Euro-Americans throughout the country. He re-affirmed national anti-Indian prejudices, and his position as one of the nation's most popular and powerful newspaper editors placed the stamp of approval on those prejudices.

Canadian westward expansion interests also relied on the Myth of the Ignoble Savage, and newspapers used it freely to justify White violence against Indians and Indian

---

77. For a discussion regarding the murky origins of this famous phrase, see Robert C. Williams, *Horace Greeley: Champion of American Freedom* (New York: New York University Press, 2006), 308.

78. Horace Greely, *An Overland Journey from New York to San Francisco in the Summer of 1859*, ed. Charles T. Duncan (New York: Alfred A. Knopf, 1964), 119.

79. Ibid., 121.

removal. Following the 1869 acquisition by the Crown of Rupert's Land, the territory of the Hudson's Bay drainage that vastly expanded Canada's western domain, the press consistently condemned the region's Indians. The Toronto *Globe* claimed, "The Indian . . . is almost useless. He is inert and uncleanly. He is driven to the chase by the direct extremity of hunger. He walks about in stately indolence."[80] In 1873, the Montreal *Gazette* claimed that "a material force of disciplined men will be necessary to enforce law and order" in the Indian nations of western Canada. "Bred as [the Indian] has been to consider the country his own, he can never be made to understand that he should be dispossessed of it."[81] Seven years later, the *Gazette* declared, "Fear or expectation of favor keep the red-skins in subjection, but [they easily] become the reckless, murderous devils which nature has made them in their native condition."[82] The same year, the Calgary *Herald* advised:

> Let any eastern man, no matter how enthusiastic on the Indian question, live for six months among them, see them beg, see them steal, sell their women and lie around, too lazy and shiftless to make an effort to earn the slightest part of their own living. . . . This may sound like strong language, but it is the absolute truth.[83]

The project of westward expansion in the United States and Canada, and its attendant ideological justifications, gained traction through rapid developments in print technology and in the news-gathering process. By the 1830s, steam-driven presses reduced production costs and assured mass distribution of major newspapers. Advertisers who wanted to get their messages in front of as many readers as possible provided lucrative revenue streams for publishers. Thus evolved the "penny press." By massively increasing circulation, and by charging a mere penny per issue, publishers provided unprecedented exposure for businesses eager to advertise their wares and services. By 1835 the *New York Herald*'s circulation topped 20,000. Founded in 1841, Horace Greeley's *New-York Tribune* boasted 40,000 readers by 1860. By 1890, the United States had over 1,600 newspapers with a combined circulation of nearly 8.4 million, and almost every town had its own weekly paper—almost 9,000 in 1880.[84] Moreover, by the 1870s an estimated 4,295 inexpensive weekly magazines circulated among 10.5 million readers at a time when the U.S. population stood at only

---

80. *Globe*, August 17, 1869. Quoted in Mark Cronlund Anderson and Carmen L. Robertson, *Seeing Red: A History of Natives in Canadian Newspapers* (Winnipeg, Canada: University of Manitoba Press, 2011), 38.

81. *Gazette*, June 4, 1873. Quoted in Anderson and Robertson, *Seeing Red*, 40.

82. *Gazette*, April 13, 1885. Quoted in Anderson and Robertson, *Seeing Red*, 67.

83. *Herald*, March 12, 1885. Quoted in Anderson and Robertson, *Seeing Red*, 70.

84. John M. Coward, *The Newspaper Indian: Native American Identity in the Press, 1820–90* (Urbana: University of Illinois Press, 1999), 13.

30 million.[85] To captivate readers, papers and magazines featured stories of drama and conflict with headlines sensationalizing crime, scandal, and war. Because of the scale of newsprint distribution and readership, the ideological power of the press crossed into a new historical era.

Early Antebellum papers depended on a network through which editors in different parts of the United States and its territories exchanged news by mail; participating papers thus acquired national and international news. But the mid-nineteenth-century advent of telegraphy made the old system obsolete. Although the telegraph relayed news instantly, it did so at a very high cost, so in 1846 six publishers established the New York Associated Press, a cooperative arrangement that defrayed costs and geographically enlarged the news network.[86]

Because of their wide distribution to hundreds of papers every day, Associated Press reports possessed tremendous influence over a wide range of topics, including Indian news. Reporters often shared the same anti-Indian prejudice, as did their editors and readers, so their dispatches perpetuated the Myth of the Ignoble Savage, but now they did so in the era of mass communication. The stories fed the economic interests of the press. Newspapers, aligned with government and business interests, saw Indians as obstacles to the nationalist project of westward expansion, and they needed to please both advertisers and readers with stories that confirmed the righteousness of that project.[87]

Most Indian Wars reporters traveled with the army and often empathized with its goals, even to the point of fighting Indians along with the soldiers. Moreover, Indian Wars reporters took it upon themselves to embellish their writing in order to produce colorful adventure stories. Accurate reporting seemed less important than did the creation of melodramatic battlefield scenarios that relied on a stereotyped clash between the forces of good and evil, between the cavalry and the Indians. *Chicago Times* correspondent Charles Sanford Diehl reasoned, "Journalism and the army have a certain relationship. They both represent action."[88]

Stories of cooperation and mutual respect did not make headlines. Editors and journalists focused on drama and violence, which ensured an inflammatory tone of most Indian news. An 1866 New Orleans *Picayune* editorial summarized, "We cannot open a paper from any of our exposed States or Territories, without reading frightful accounts of Indian massacres and Indian maraudings."[89] Some newspapers

---

85. Susan Belasco Smith and Kenneth M. Price, "Introduction: Periodical Literature in Social and Historical Context," in *Periodical Literature in Nineteenth-Century America*, ed. Kenneth M. Price and Susan Belasco Smith (Charlottesville: University Press of Virginia, 1995), 5.

86. John M. Coward, *Newspaper Indian*, 16–17.

87. Ibid., 39.

88. Charles Sanford Diehl, *The Staff Correspondent* (San Antonio, TX: Clegg, 1931), 89.

89. Editorial, *Evening Picayune* (New Orleans), December 31, 1866. Quoted in Coward, *Newspaper Indian*, 5.

advocated profound vengeance against Indians. In 1864 the *Daily Rocky Mountain News* declared that "Self preservation demands decisive action, and the only way to secure it is to fight them their own way. A few months of active extermination against the red devils will bring quiet, and nothing else will."[90]

Earlier, the Second Seminole War (1835–43) had given the U.S. press an opportunity to present Indians as creatures of violence and cruelty; their evil nature disqualified their claims to the land that only Whites could properly develop.

The Seminoles as a distinct historical people date to the early eighteenth century when Creek, Alabama, Choctaw, Yamasse, Yuchi, and other bands moved into the Florida panhandle and over time established an identity separate from their original nations. The name "Seminole" is a corruption of the Spanish collective name for these groups, *cimarrón* ("wild one" or "runaway").[91]

Amid Florida boundary disputes with Spain, the United States claimed the panhandle region of the present-day state, and in 1817 Andrew Jackson led an invasion force against the Seminoles—beginning the First Seminole War—in order to protect the interests of White settlers. Following the 1821 Adams-Onís Treaty, by which the United States acquired Florida from Spain, the growing number of the Euro-American settlers in the panhandle region demanded federal removal of all Seminoles. The 1823 Treaty of Moultrie established a reservation near present-day Ocala, Florida, and by 1827 most Seminoles had resettled on it. However, settlers continued their demands for full removal of the Indians from the territory to areas west of the Mississippi River. The 1830 Indian Removal Act further threatened the Seminoles. Two years later, seven Seminole chiefs signed the Treaty of Payne's Landing, which called for the Seminoles to move west. However, most Seminoles did not recognize the treaty, charging that it misrepresented their interests and that the chiefs signed it under duress.[92]

The U.S. Senate ratified the treaty in April 1834, and the federal government expected the Seminoles to complete their removal from the Florida Territory by 1835.[93] Continued Seminole resistance infuriated White settlers, who often struck out on their own with attacks that ensured escalating violence until federal troops stepped in. The most famous initial military action by Seminole forces against U.S. forces came in December 1835. The Seminoles attacked the command of Major Francis Dade and killed most of his soldiers, an act that immediately became known as the Dade Massacre in the popular press.[94]

---

90. Editorial, *Daily Rocky Mountain News* (Denver), August 10, 1864. Quoted in Coward, *Newspaper Indian*, 105.

91. John Missall and Mary Lou Missall, *The Seminole Wars, America's Longest Indian Conflict* (Gainesville: University Press of Florida, 2004), 7.

92. Ibid., 1–31.

93. Ibid., 83–87.

94. Ibid., 95–97; Coward, *Newspaper Indian*, 56–58.

Headlines decried the attack as an act of brutal Indian savagery. "Horrid Massacre" blared *The United States Gazette*. "We do not remember the history of a butchery more horrid, and it stands without an example in the annals of Indian warfare. Our citizens we are sure, will meet together and send some relief to the suffering and defenceless inhabitants of Florida."[95]

The term "massacre" had long been used to describe any military action taken by Indians against Whites. But the conjunction of the Second Seminole War with the growing power of the press, as discussed above, stigmatized all Indian victories against Whites as massacres, and did so for a reading audience of an increasing mass scale. Day after day, repeated vilification of Indians in newspapers throughout the country denied the Native American perspective in the war. Moreover, by a call to aid the "defenceless inhabitants of Florida," the *Gazette* implied that the Seminoles attacked settlers unable to protect themselves, not fully armed professional soldiers in a war zone.[96]

Significantly, "massacre" appeared only rarely when Whites killed Indians. The Seminole attack on Dade's men stood as a massacre because the Indians won. If Dade had successfully destroyed the attacking Seminoles, no newspaper would have called it a massacre. By using language in this way, papers protected the interests of its readers—the White population—reporting the battle in highly emotional terms and repeatedly stereotyping Indians as dangerous savages.[97]

In 1837, the New Orleans *Picayune* explained that the removal of the Seminoles was necessary because they could not be trusted: "Their fate seems to be a hard one, but their treachery, and the safety of our white population require it." Then the paper explained the main flaw in the Native character: "When once the Indian is aroused to revenge and war, his spirit will never be subdued. They cannot—must not be trusted." An editorial in the *Picayune* echoed this judgment when discussing Seminole chief Osceola: "This fellow is possessed of great daring—and we shall not be surprised to hear further of his tricks and treachery."[98]

Indians were the enemy, and the enemy was evil by definition. Under such circumstances, it is not surprising to find anti-Indian themes in the papers. But such reporting served a more important ideological function as well. News from the Second Seminole War reinforced the identity of these Indians as subhuman savages resistant to progress and incapable of civilization.

In 1864, Colonel John Chivington, stationed in Denver with seven hundred troops under his command, faced mounting local pressure to attack the region's Cheyenne Dog Soldiers. They refused to recognize a land exchange treaty recently signed by

95. *The United States Gazette* (Philadelphia), January 23, 1836. Quoted in Coward, *Newspaper Indian*, 57.

96. Coward, *Newspaper Indian*, 58.

97. Ibid., 59.

98. Editorial, *Picayune* (New Orleans), March 24, 1837. Quoted in Coward, *Newspaper Indian*, 59.

Black Kettle and other Cheyenne chiefs, and they frequently attacked White settlers whom they considered as trespassers on their land.[99] Chivington desired battlefield glory,[100] but not in battle against the Dog Soldiers, whose military prowess would have meant heavy casualties for his command. Instead, he led his troops against Black Kettle's peaceful Cheyenne camp near Sand Creek, Colorado. Ignoring both the American flag and the White flag flying over the camp, the soldiers opened fire. By the time they finished their work, about 150 Cheyenne lay dead in the snow. Soldiers raped the women before murdering and mutilating them. The army attempted to prosecute Chivington, but he resigned and the court dropped the issue.[101]

The facts of the massacre would eventually emerge; however, the *Daily Rocky Mountain News* controlled the narrative for months following the attack, using the telegraph to manage the eastward flow of information. *News* editor William N. Byers maintained close alliances with Chivington and with territorial governor John Evans, all ardent supporters of economic growth in Denver and of Colorado statehood, positions threatened by Indians, who, by defending their land and its resources, were invariably termed "hostiles." Thus, according to the *News*, the soldiers had won "for themselves and their commanders, from Colonel down to corporal, the eternal gratitude of dwellers on these plains."[102]

Weeks later, however, another story emerged in the Eastern press. Leaked by political enemies of Evans, Chivington, and Byers, letters claimed that soldiers massacred and mutilated peaceful Indian men, women, and children. The *News* counterattacked, singling out the "humanitarian" Eastern papers as anti-Western and too sympathetic to the Indians at Sand Creek. Most papers followed Byers lead, and his defense of Chivington typified a narrative pattern in which Western correspondents, armed with a narrow range of Ignoble Savage imagery, distorted Indian-White encounters. They

---

99. The February 1861 Treaty of Fort Wise was signed by the Cheyenne chiefs Black Kettle and White Antelope and Arapahoe Chief Little Raven, among other chiefs. They agreed to exchange land received under the 1851 Treaty of Fort Laramie for a significantly smaller parcel of reservation land in eastern Colorado. The Dog Soldiers refused to acknowledge the authority of the chiefs who signed the treaty and militantly resisted its implementation. See Francis Paul Prucha, *American Indian Treaties: The History of a Political Anomaly* (Berkeley: University of California Press, 1997), 269–70.

100. Colonel Patrick Connor, who gained recent fame for his role in the Bear River Massacre, happened to be in Denver at the time, supervising military protection for mail routes. Connor's stories about his "victory" at Bear River galled Chivington and may, in part, have provoked him to action.

101. See "Massacre of the Cheyenne Indians" in *Report of the Joint Committee on the Conduct of the War* (Washington, D.C.: Government Printing Office, 1865), 4–108. Also available online, http://quod.lib.umich.edu/m/moa/aby3709.0003.001/5?view=image&size=100 (accessed August 21, 2105).

102. Editorial, *Daily Rocky Mountain News* (Denver), December 8, 1864. Quoted in Coward, *Newspaper Indian*, 98.

reported Indians as hostile, motivated only by their inherent savagery, and promoted military action against them.[103]

Byers' *Daily Rocky Mountain News* played a role that made Chivington's attack on Black Kettle's camp inevitable. With the discovery of gold near Pike's Peak in the late 1850s, a flood of prospectors and settlers swept into the region and infringed on Indian lands. In an 1864 editorial "Fortunes for the Taking," Byers proclaimed, "No country in the world offers greater inducements for the influx of immigration than does Colorado today."[104] The same year, the *News* published Governor Evans' "Appeal to the People." Evans called for Colorado citizens to "organize for the defense of their homes and families against the merciless savages." Citizens would be

> entitled to all the property belonging to hostile Indians that they cap-
> ture. . . . Any man who kills a hostile Indian is a patriot; but there are
> Indians who are friendly, and to kill one of these will involve us in a
> greater difficulty. It is important therefore to fight only the hostile, and
> no one has been or will be restrained from this.[105]

In August 1864 Governor Evans' call for a militia appeared in Washington's *National Intelligencer*, a call in which Evans warned that "unless authority is given [for the militia], the Whites will be destroyed."[106]

That same August the *News* claimed that Indians planned a simultaneous attack on several frontier posts and that Denver military officials were investigating an Indian attack at nearby Cherry Creek: "There is one thing certain, however, that Running creek, Cherry creek and Plum creek are at the mercy of those thieving, scalping sons of butchery."[107] Byers opposed "anything which looks like a treaty of peace with the Indians who have been actively engaged in the recent hostilities. The season is near at hand when they can be chastised and it should be done with no gentle hand."[108] A few months later, on November 29, Chivington launched his chastisement against the Cheyenne, to which Byers responded:

> Our people may rest easy in the belief that outrages by small bands are at
> an end, on routes where troops are stationed. Having tasted of the "bitter

---

103. Coward, *Newspaper Indian*, 105–7.

104. Editorial, *Daily Rocky Mountain News* (Denver), March 25, 1864. Quoted in Coward, *Newspaper Indian*, 103.

105. John Evans, "Appeal to the People," *Daily Rocky Mountain News* (Denver), August 10, 1864. Quoted in Coward, *Newspaper Indian*, 105.

106. John Evans, "Appeal to the People," *National Intelligencer* (Washington D.C.), August 15, 1864. Quoted in Coward, *Newspaper Indian*, 106.

107. Editorial, *Daily Rocky Mountain News* (Denver), August 18, 1864. Quoted in Coward, *Newspaper Indian*, 108.

108. Editorial, *Daily Rocky Mountain News* (Denver), September 27, 1864. Quoted in Coward, *Newspaper Indian*, 108.

end," the news of which will quickly be dispatched among the others, the supremacy of our power will be seriously considered, and a surrender or a sueing for peace be perhaps very soon proclaimed.[109]

Foundation Myths

The Myth of the Noble Savage and the Myth of the Ignoble Savage possess distinct characteristics. Separating them in order to analyze these characteristics runs the risk of presenting an artificial view of the multilayered societies that produced them; these myths nearly always operate simultaneously. After all, any society contains simultaneous and contradictory ideas and impulses; the complexity of human nature makes it so.

These myths possess deep historical roots. As demonstrated in the first two chapters, the roots reach back to antiquity. They later flourished in certain areas of the medieval European world and found fertile ground again in the New World. Then, as centuries passed and new historical conditions arose, the Myths of the Noble and Ignoble Savage branched out.

As will be explored in the following chapters, the Myths of the Noble and Ignoble Savage provided the foundation for other myths of Native American history that (mis)informed Euro-American culture. Westward expansion, industrialization, new and expanding forms of mass communication, and the interests of so-called countercultural movements of hippies and new agers assured ongoing opportunities for White culture to misrepresent Indians and to read into them a variety of fantasies that suited White political and social agendas.

---

109. Editorial, *Daily Rocky Mountain News* (Denver), December 8, 1864. Quoted in Coward, *Newspaper Indian*, 110.

3. An Empty Land: The Myth of the Wilderness

The forest which I see in the western horizon stretches uninterruptedly towards the setting sun, [and the sun] is the Great Western Pioneer whom the nations follow. . . . The West . . . is but another name for the Wild, [and] in Wildness is the preservation of the world. . . . Our ancestors were savages. The story of Romulus and Remus being suckled by a wolf is not a meaningless fable.[1] The founders of every state which has risen to eminence, have drawn their nourishment and vigor from a similar wild source. . . . One who pressed forward incessantly . . . would always find himself in a new country or wilderness [and climb] over the prostrate stems of primitive forest trees. [The] task of the American [is] "to work the virgin soil." [The] farmer displaces the Indian even because he redeems the meadow, and so makes himself stronger and in some respects more natural. . . . The very winds blew the Indian's corn-field into the meadow, and pointed out the way which he had not the skill to follow. He had no better implement with which to intrench himself in the land than a clam-shell. But the farmer is armed with plow and spade. . . . The wildness of the savage is but a faint symbol of the awful ferity [wildness] with which good men and lovers meet.[2]

In his essay "Walking," American writer Henry David Thoreau (1817–62) envisions an imaginary land. Here a wilderness of virgin soil, only lightly scratched by the "clamshell" tools of Indians, awaits the (White) pioneer, a rugged figure whose plow redeemed the earth from the alleged agricultural ignorance of Native Americans.

Quite poetic, but was it true? In point of fact, Native Americans did not think of their homelands as wilderness. As Omaha Nation member Francis La Flesche, America's first Native American ethnologist, noted in 1901:

The white people speak of the country at this [mid-nineteenth century] period as "a wilderness," as though it was an empty tract without human interest or history. To us Indians it was as clearly defined then as it is

---

1. Twin brothers, who were key actors in ancient Rome's foundation myth, they had been abandoned and left to die in the wilderness but were nourished by a she-wolf.

2. Henry David Thoreau, "Walking," in *Henry David Thoreau: Collected Essays and Poems*, ed. Elizabeth Hall Witherell (New York: Library of America, 2001), 235.

to-day; we knew the boundaries of tribal lands, those of our friends and those of our foes; we were familiar with every stream, the countour [sic] of every hill, and each peculiar feature of the landscape had its tradition. It was our home, the scene of our history, and we loved it as our country.[3]

Although neither the first nor the last to envision zones of prehistorical primitiveness stretching across the North American continent, essentially devoid of human habitation and impact, Thoreau did stand at a pivotal moment in the history of the wilderness myth. Seventeenth-century Puritans had feared the wilderness as Satan's abode; however, by the mid-nineteenth century—Thoreau's time—gentler notions of the wilderness arose. By the end of the century, national parks began to institutionalize the wilderness. The 1964 Wilderness Act enshrined an already long-standing definition:

> A wilderness, in contrast with those areas where man and his own works dominate the landscape, is hereby recognized as an area where the earth and its community of life are "untrammeled by man," where man himself is a visitor who does not remain. An area of wilderness is further defined to mean in this Act an area of undeveloped Federal land retaining its primeval character and influence.[4]

But the wilderness, whether feared, romanticized, or federally defined, had first to be invented, and then reinvented, and then invented again. Moreover, Eurocentric worldviews that at one time equated Indians with the wilderness steadily removed them from it. For wilderness to be a landscape untrammeled by man required the erasure of Native American history from that landscape and the physical removal of the Indians themselves. At best, in accord with the stereotypical image of Indians as nomadic hunter-gathers, they registered merely as visitors who do not remain.

Canonized by conservationists and preservationists, Thoreau's body of work concerning his contemplations on nature continues to influence popular notions of the human relationship with the environment. *Walden* (1854), his most famous book, champions simplicity, solitude, and reflection as virtues derived from living a self-sufficient lifestyle in the woods. "Walking" expresses a similar philosophy but manages to frame it in the language of Manifest Destiny.

Although the term "Manifest Destiny" had not yet arisen, its germination as a nationalist project can be traced at least to the cultural, economic, and political consequences of the Louisiana Purchase (1803), through which France sold its trans-Mississippi land to the United States, doubling the size of the young republic. The term's coinage coincided—and its implications matured—with the Mexican-American War (1846–48). Following Mexico's defeat, the United States took

---

3. Francis La Flesche, *The Middle Five: Indian Boys at School* (Boston: Small, Maynard, 1901), xvii.

4. 1964 Wilderness Act, http://www.wilderness.net/nwps/legisact (accessed April 10, 2016).

possession of present-day Colorado, Nevada, Utah, California, and most of Arizona and New Mexico; acquisition of southern New Mexico and southern Arizona awaited the Gadsden Purchase (signed in 1853) by which the United States secured Mexico's sale of the region, primarily for the construction of a southern transcontinental railroad. Within a half century, the borders of the United States leapt to the edge of the continent. The "Great Western Pioneer" strode confidentially all the way to the Pacific Ocean. Of course, that pioneer image as the embodiment of American and Canadian ideals also tends to erase the facts inherent in the continent's transregional, transnational, and transcultural history, particularly in the borderlands regions of the North American West.

Another European import, along with the Myths of the Noble and Ignoble Savage, the Myth of the Wilderness flourished in its new land. Thoreau's invocation of Romulus and Remus, the legendary twins of Roman antiquity, reflects the wilderness myth's historic hold on the Euro-American mind. Moreover, the wildness that figures so prominently in the fable about the founding of the Roman state serves as an allegory for the founding of the United States and the "destiny" awaiting it; its national westward mission will draw "nourishment and vigor from a similar wild source." By climbing "over the prostrate stems of primitive forest trees," the American pioneer enters a virgin land on which to build a new country, a latter-day Roman Republic. Wildness preserves the world by testing the mettle of its conquerors. Only the hardiest pioneers need apply. The rigors of the West weed out any weakness. The process preserves the world through regeneration by the strongest. The Indian survives merely as a "faint symbol" for the wildness of the *emotional* landscape "with which good men and lovers meet."

Errand into the Wilderness

The word "wilderness" traces one of its origins to the Old English poem *Beowulf*, in which "wilde" combines with "dēor" (beast) to make "wildēor."[5] From this came the Middle English "wilderne" (wild, savage, deserted), and thence arose one modern notion of wilderness as a place of wild beasts.[6] The term gained prominence with the early sixteenth-century compilation of a literary masterpiece, the King James Bible, in which it makes 294 appearances.[7] Finally, Samuel Johnson's 1755 *Dictionary of the*

---

5. *Beowulf*, line 1430 reads: "wyrmas ond wildēor" (serpents and wild beasts), http://www.perseus. tufts.edu/hopper/text?doc=Perseus%3Atext%3A2003.01.0001%3Acard%3D1383 (accessed May 14, 2016).

6. Eric Partridge, *Origins: A Short Etymological Dictionary of Modern English* (New York: Random House, 1988), 805–6.

7. "King James Bible Online," http://www.kingjamesbibleonline.org/wilderness/ (accessed April 10, 2016).

English Language defined wilderness as "a desert; a tract of solitude and savageness."[8] However, long before Johnson, and in militant denial of the King James Bible's Anglican authority, early seventeenth-century Puritan settlers in North America relied on their Geneva Bible for evidence enough to define the New World as both a spiritual and a physical wilderness.[9] William Bradford, reflecting on the dire condition of his fellow Plymouth Colony Puritans, declared:

> What could they see but a hideous and desolate wilderness, full of wild beasts and wild men—and what multitudes there might be of them they knew not? Neither could they . . . go up to the top of Pisgah[10] to view from this wilderness a more goodly country to feed their hopes. . . . The whole country, full of woods and thickets, represented a wild and savage hue. . . . What could now sustain them but the Spirit of God and his Grace? May not and ought not the children of these fathers rightly say: "Our fathers . . . were ready to perish in this wilderness; but they cried unto the Lord, and he heard their voice. . . . He hath delivered them from the hand of the oppressor. When they wandered in the desert wilderness out of the way, and found no city to dwell in, . . . their soul was overwhelmed in them."[11]

In his 1670 sermon, "A Brief Recognition of New England's Errand into the Wilderness," Reverend Samuel Danforth exhorted his congregation to remember that John the Baptist did not begin his ministry in Jerusalem or in any other city, but in the wilderness, "in a wooded, retired and solitary place, thereby withdrawing himself from the envy and preposterous zeal of [those] addicted to their old Traditions." He then asked:

> To what purpose did the Children of Israel leave their Cities and Houses in Egypt, and go forth into the Wilderness? Was it not to hold a feast to the Lord, and to sacrifice to the God of their fathers? . . . But how soon did they forget their Errand into the Wilderness, and corrupt themselves in their own Inventions?

---

8. For a succinct discussion of the term "wilderness" and its many applications, see Roderick Frazier Nash, *Wilderness and the American Mind* (New Haven, CT: Yale University Press, 2014), 1–7.

9. For insight into the theological and political controversies surrounding the King James and the Geneva Bibles, see Alister McGrath, *In the Beginning: The Story of the King James Bible and How It Changed a Nation, a Language, and a Culture* (New York: Anchor, 2002).

10. According to Deuteronomy 34:1–4, Pisgah is the mountain from which Moses views the Promised Land. Significantly, God tells him that Canaan would belong to his descendants, but Moses would not live to enter it.

11. William Bradford, *Of Plymouth Plantation, 1620–1647*, ed. Samuel Eliot Morison (New York: Knopf, 1998), 62–63.

Thus Danforth proclaims his mission "to excite and stir us all up to attend and prosecute our Errand into the Wilderness" and asks his fellow Puritans: "To what purpose then came we into the Wilderness? . . . Was it not the expectation of the pure and faithful Dispensation of the Gospel and Kingdome of God?"[12]

Wilderness as a metaphor for a spiritual state of confusion and wandering remains foremost in Danforth's sermon. However, mounting doctrinal and political differences between New England Puritans and the Puritans who remained back home on English soil appeared to Danforth, and to other New England Puritan religious leaders, as evidence of corruption among their trans-Atlantic brethren; New England Puritans alone must carry on the message, must fulfill their errand in the North American wilderness. They must not lose their way, as did the followers of Moses in the desert wilderness.

Danforth's sermon recognizes the wilderness as both a physical and a metaphysical space, and as notions of the American wilderness develop across the centuries, its definitions tend to fuse this secular/sacred binary; moreover, the sense of mission, or errand, into the wilderness eventually becomes retooled in the language of Manifest Destiny. By proclaiming the right of the United States "to overspread and to possess the whole of the continent which Providence has given us," journalist John L. O'Sullivan channeled his inner Moses in 1845 and pointed the way through the wilderness for Americans to follow as their Manifest Destiny.[13]

Determining Historical Changes in Native American Populations

The illusions of an "empty land" and of a coast-to-coast wilderness can be sustained only through the willful and politically motivated exclusion of Native American populations. These populations have fluctuated over time in regions throughout the North American continent, but the historical record often demonstrates gradual though extensive recovery from population downturns caused by warfare or infectious diseases.

Beginning with the turn of the sixteenth century, an unintended consequence of European contact with the Americas proved devastating for many of the continent's Indigenous Peoples.[14] The introduction of European, Asian, and African pathogens,

---

12. Samuel Danforth, "A Brief Recognition of New England's Errand into the Wilderness" (Lincoln: University of Nebraska Digital Commons, 2006), http://digitalcommons.unl.edu/cgi/viewcontent. cgi?article=1038&context=libraryscience (accessed April 11, 2016). For an extensive examination of Danforth's sermon and of Puritan origins of American political and social doctrines, see Perry Miller, *Errand into the Wilderness* (Cambridge, MA: Harvard University Press, 1996).

13. And I Quote, "John L. O'Sullivan Quotes," http://www.andiquote.co.za/authors/John_L_ OSullivan.html (accessed May 19, 2016).

14. For a description of the sixteenth-century spread of contagious diseases in the Americas, see Alfred W. Crosby, Jr., "Conquistador y Pestilencia," in *The Columbian Exchange: Biological and Cultural Consequences of 1492* (Westport, CT: Praeger, 2003), 35–63.

against which Native populations possessed no immunity, proved fatal throughout the Americas. Smallpox and measles, both highly contagious, spread faster than did the European colonizers themselves. However darkly, the speed of contagion demonstrates the extensive trade and communication networks—the water- and roadways—that linked the First Peoples across thousands of miles. Areas of contagion varied widely. Europeans often interpreted the deaths they witnessed as signs of the innate weakness of uncivilized savages. They also attributed the die-offs to God's will, as a sign of His displeasure with the heathens of the New World.

To determine the precontact population of North America stands as the first essential step for estimating the number of North American First Peoples who died of European-borne contagious diseases in the sixteenth century. But the challenge of estimating Indigenous populations before Europeans made contact with the Americas is matched only by the challenge of estimating postcontact populations. Historical demographers—scholars who study past population numbers—generally fall into one of two camps: the low counters and the high counters. For the North American continent above the Rio Grande, low counters generally claim a pre-1492 population of about one million, give or take a few hundred thousand. High counters claim about eighteen million. Anthropologist Russell Thornton argues for a middle figure of about seven million.[15]

Heated debate, often fueled by social, cultural, and political agendas, continues regarding the number of deaths, but most scholars dismiss arguments of a continent-wide pandemic, or Indian Holocaust. The new diseases struck some regions but left others untouched.[16] Within a few generations, populations in stricken areas often became re-established as natural immunity and resistance increased.[17] Regardless, historians cannot skate over the day-to-day trauma wrought by the new diseases as they tore through villages and regions. The experience changed the lives of the First Peoples in perhaps unprecedented ways.

The Spaniards, as the first Europeans to make landfall in the Caribbean and mainland Americas, initiated the spread of contagious diseases. In 1519, the first major smallpox epidemic started in the Caribbean, continued through Mexico, and then headed south through Central America and probably struck regions of Peru as well.[18] Smallpox arrived in the lower Mississippi region with Hernando De Soto's 1539–42 expedition. Beginning in the 1580s, Indians residing in today's Southwestern United States probably contracted the disease.[19]

---

15. Russell Thornton, "The Demography of Colonialism," in *Studying Native America: Problems and Prospects* (Madison: University of Wisconsin Press, 1998), 17–39, 18.

16. Ibid., 21.

17. Crosby, *Columbian Exchange*, 39.

18. Ibid., 39.

19. John Aberth, *The First Horseman: Disease in Human History* (Upper Saddle River, NJ: Pearson, 2007), 50–57.

Early sixteenth-century expansion of the European cod-fishing industry off New-foundland led to the establishment of coastal processing stations to preserve the fish for shipment back across the ocean. Through contact with sailors, Indians contracted smallpox, measles, and other contagious diseases. For example, a smallpox epidemic between 1616 and 1619 decimated Indian villages throughout New England. In 1620, Plymouth Colony built on the site of the deserted Wampanoag village of Pahtuksut, its inhabitants wiped out by smallpox. Twenty colonists died during a 1633 epidemic, but the number of Indian deaths in that epidemic dwarfed the number of English deaths. Here the Puritan minister Increase Mather saw the Hand of God at work:

> The Indians began to be quarrelsome concerning the bounds of the land they had sold to the English; but God ended the controversy by sending the smallpox amongst the Indians at Saugust, who were before that time exceeding numerous. Whole towns of them were swept away, in some of them not so much as one Soul escaping the destruction.[20]

The righteousness of God appeared visibly and indisputably at work in Mather's worldview. Moreover, as we saw in Chapter 2, White violence against Indians has been justified historically on theological grounds since the earliest days of European contact with North America's First Peoples.

Sometimes the spread of contagious diseases among Indians has been called genocidal.[21] But the introduction of deadly pathogens came as an unintended (and unknown) consequence of European contact with the Americas. It did not arise out of a state policy calling for the extermination of Indians. Despite claims to the contrary, smallpox, measles, and other infectious diseases probably did not spread through deliberate actions by Europeans or by Euro-Americans.[22] Indeed, some have combined the centuries-long record of White violence against Indians with Indian deaths from contagious diseases and compared the net effect with the Jewish Holocaust in Nazi Germany, a comparison that works best to contrast the events; an equation only distorts both of them.[23]

---

20. Increase Mather, *A Relation of the Troubles That Have Happen in New England by Reason of the Indians There* (Boston: John Foster, 1677), 110.

21. The term "genocide" was coined in 1944 by war refugee Raphael Lemkin to describe Nazi policies for the systematic murder of European Jews. He combined *genos/gens* (Greek and Latin for "race" or "family") with *cide* (Latin for "killing").

22. For an examination of the controversy surrounding Lord Jeffry Amherst's attempt to use infected blankets to spread smallpox to Indians in 1763, see Elizabeth A. Fenn, "Biological Warfare in Eighteenth-Century North America: Beyond Jeffery Amherst," *The Journal of American History* 86(2000):1552–1580; Adrienne Mayor, "The Nessus Shirt in the New World: Smallpox Blankets in History and Legend," *The Journal of American Folklore* 108 (1995): 54–77.

23. See the now discredited polemicist Ward Churchill, *A Little Matter of Genocide: Holocaust and Denial in the Americas, 1492 to Present* (San Francisco: City Lights, 2001), 4–7; David E. Stannard, *American Holocaust: The Conquest of the New World* (New York: Oxford University Press, 1993).

Creating the Wilderness through Indian Removal

The nineteenth century saw displacement of over sixty Native American nations in acts of ethnic cleansing known corporately as Indian Removal.[24] Beginning with the administration of Thomas Jefferson (1801–9), a policy took shape for removing Indians who lived east of the Mississippi to land on the western side of the river in order to clear the way for White settlement, particularly in the Ohio River Valley and in the Southeast. But with each passing year, increasing numbers of White settlers crowded into the western land on which the displaced Indians attempted to establish new homes. The legal foundation for Indian Removal solidified with *Johnson v. M'Intosh* (1823), in which Chief Justice John Marshall ruled that the title of land, which had been "discovered and conquered," belongs to the conquering nation and the Indigenous Peoples of the land had only "a right of occupancy," which could be abrogated. The court based the ruling on the late fifteenth-century Doctrine of Discovery that permitted Europeans to exploit non-Christians in lands that they "discovered."[25]

The Cherokee Nation's Trail of Tears stands as the most famous example of the removal experience. The nation's original homeland once stretched throughout southern Appalachia with villages and fields in regions of present-day South Carolina, North Carolina, Tennessee, Alabama, and Georgia. Today, most Cherokees live in eastern Oklahoma. Their original homeland remained intact during the mid-eighteenth century through alliances with the English government: the English needed the Cherokee as military allies in a series of wars against the Tuscaroras and the Shawnee. However, when backcountry Virginia colonials killed several Cherokee warriors, and the Cherokees replied in kind, the alliance spun out of control, the political terrain shifted, and in 1760 the English destroyed towns, fields, and granaries throughout Cherokee territory.[26]

They conflate the spread of epidemic diseases with acts of violence against Indians, overtly claiming that the spread of smallpox and measles was as deliberate as direct physical violence. This blurs two distinctly different consequences of European contact.

24. The term "ethnic cleansing" entered common usage around 1992, with the Bosnian War. It has been criticized as a euphemism for genocide. See Norman M. Naimark, *Fires of Hatred: Ethnic Cleansing in Twentieth Century Europe* (Cambridge, MA: Harvard University Press, 2002), 3. Also, regarding the Trail of Tears, Theda Perdue and Michael D. Green state, "In the twentieth century similar government policies of expelling one people to make room for another have been called 'ethnic cleansing.'" *The Cherokee Nation and the Trail of Tears* (New York: Penguin, 2007), 42.

25. The opinion on *Johnson v. M'Intosh* delivered by Chief Justice Marshall is at http://press-pubs.uchicago.edu/founders/documents/a1_8_3_indianss9.html (accessed June 26, 2017).

26. For a description of the events leading up to dissolution of the alliance and the English attack on the Cherokee, see Tom Hatley, "Anatomy of a Conflict," in *The Dividing Paths: Cherokees and South Carolinians through the Revolutionary Era* (New York: Oxford University Press, 1995), 119–40.

The United States and the Cherokee Nation signed the Treaty of Hopewell in 1785, an attempt to establish mutual coexistence with a promise to work for political solutions to conflicts between the two nations. Secretary of War Henry Knox defended the territorial rights of the Cherokee, believing that their sovereignty had to be respected by the federal government and by the states. But White citizens of Georgia and North Carolina did not recognize the authority of the federal government,[27] and certainly did not recognize Cherokee sovereignty. They confiscated Cherokee land, knowing that the federal government simply did not have the resources to stop them. Through violence and the threat of violence against the Cherokee, these illegal settlers defended their claims. They played a waiting game, confident that they would wear down both the Cherokee and the government.

Knox decided that the best solution for easing friction between Whites and Indians required the spread of "civilization" to the Cherokee. They must embrace the values of White America. The Cherokee must convert to Protestant Christianity, learn to read and write English, and become farmers. They must cease being Indians and become Americans. Although some Cherokee feared that their own culture would be lost, many others believed that their survival depended on making significant economic and social changes. They wrote a constitution, drew up a code of laws, built their own schools, created their own alphabet for the Cherokee language, and established their own printing presses to publish books, pamphlets, and a weekly newspaper in both Cherokee and English. The nation grew increasingly prosperous. The wealthiest Cherokee owned Black slaves, farmed hundreds of acres, and lived in stately houses that fully expressed the ideal of the gentleman farmer.

But to the chagrin of federal advocates for "civilization," most Cherokee retained traditional communal land ownership. The tradition proved lucrative and produced capital for further investment in the nation's infrastructure. They built toll roads, operated ferries, and established inns for travelers. Moreover, the Cherokee transformed the traditionally localized government structure into a centralized system, further enhancing a sense of Cherokee national identity.

Ironically, federal advocates of "civilization" considered the Cherokee Nation a failure. After all, the purpose had been to assimilate the Cherokee into American culture, not to create a rival nation within the borders of the United States.[28] Above all else, communal land ownership vastly complicated the primary goal: convince the Cherokee to cede their territory in exchange for land west of the Mississippi River.[29]

---

27. Nor did they have to until 1789. The Treaty of Hopewell was written while the government operated under the Articles of Confederation, which recognized the authority of states over Indians within their borders. The Constitution superseded the Articles in 1789, and it gave Congress authority over the states in all issues regarding Indians. Still the power of the Constitution did not stop Georgian settlers from continued encroachment on Cherokee land.

28. Unallowable by the U.S. Constitution in the first place.

29. Perdue and Green, *Cherokee Nation*, 41.

The nation held nearly five million acres in the state of Georgia and refused to sell. Georgia demanded the land.[30] The demand set the stage for the Trail of Tears.

Principal chief from 1828 to 1866, John Ross led the nation throughout the removal process, a period in which conflicts between pro-removal and anti-removal factions led to political assassinations and to a heated divisiveness that would mark the Cherokee Nation's history for generations to come. Ross' wealth and property made him a typical member of the Cherokee elite. He ran a ferry service, raised tobacco and other crops on 170 acres, and owned twenty Black slaves.[31] Ross also established powerful political relationships in Washington, making him a known quantity in both the Indian and White worlds. Tirelessly, he and his political allies lobbied Congress for recognition of Cherokee sovereignty—the right to control their own destiny as a nation—and demanded redress for border violations made by Georgia.

Contention between Georgia, the federal government, and the Cherokee Nation led to two landmark decisions handed down by Chief Justice John Marshall. The question in the 1831 *Cherokee Nation v. Georgia* case asked whether the Cherokee Nation constituted a foreign state. Marshall said no; rather, he defined it as a "domestic dependent nation." This prompted the question: Since nations exist with inherent autonomy, how could one nation be dependent on another? However contradictory, the statement continues to inform the legal relationship between the federal government and Indians. Marshall went on to write that tribes existed in a "state of pupilage [that] resembles that of a ward to his guardian." In effect, the decision infantilized Indians. It said that they lacked adult skills to control their own destiny. However, Marshall's 1832 decision in *Worcester v. Georgia* refined the earlier decision. "The Cherokee Nation," he wrote, "is a distinct community, occupying its own territory, with boundaries accurately described, in which the laws of Georgia can have no force." The decision affirmed Cherokee sovereignty.[32]

Elation in the Cherokee Nation stood in stark contrast to disgust in Georgia and in the White House. President Andrew Jackson responded to the Supreme Court's *Worcester v. Georgia* decision by ignoring it. Following a series of duplicitous and illegal power plays against the Cherokee Nation, he declared that removal to Indian Territory in the West would commence on May 23, 1838. Thus began the Trail of Tears.

---

30. By U.S. Constitutional law, the Cherokee could sell land only to the federal government, not to states or to individuals. Indian land purchased by the government would then be opened to White settlement. Georgians would thus receive legal claim and title to land formerly occupied by the Cherokee Nation.

31. Gary E. Moulton, *John Ross, Cherokee Chief* (Athens: University of Georgia Press, 2004), 30–31.

32. *Cherokee Nation v. Georgia*, https://scholar.google.com/scholar_case?q=cherokee+nation+v.+georgia+(1831)&hl=en&as_sdt=6,24&as_vis=1&case=6481524100903611909&scilh=0 (accessed August 1, 2015); *Worcester v. Georgia*, https://scholar.google.com/scholar_case?q=cherokee+nation+v.+georgia+(1831)&hl=en&as_sdt=6,24&as_vis=1&case=6938475705816460383&scilh=0 (accessed August 1, 2015).

Although several thousand Cherokee had voluntarily relocated to the West from 1794 to 1819 under relatively good conditions, over thirteen thousand reluctant Cherokee deportees who endured the Trail of Tears made the journey under military escort. Most soldiers treated them like prisoners and abused them for sport. Throughout 1838, the Cherokee left Georgia in groups numbering from several hundred to several thousand, covering most of the distance to Oklahoma in flatboats and riverboats. But they also walked hundreds of miles to their final destination, one never reached by about four thousand exiles. Measles, cholera, starvation, drowning, cold, and assorted accidents left nearly one-fourth of the total Cherokee population in graves scattered along the trail from Georgia to Oklahoma.[33]

But the Trail of Tears has overshadowed the removal experience of many other Native Americans with land originally located east of the Mississippi. For example, Indian nations of the Old Northwest—the present-day states of Ohio, Indiana, Illinois, Michigan, and Wisconsin—underwent removal on a smaller, but no less traumatic, scale, than the Southeastern Indians. Old Northwest removal history involves the Potawatomi, Delaware, Seneca, Cayuga, Miami, Shawnee, Wyandot, Odawa, and Ojibwe Indian nations. That history must also take into account the experiences of tribes that successfully resisted removal.[34]

Whereas the Cherokee attempted to maintain their homeland by developing legal and economic structures of a sovereign nation recognizable by the U.S. government, the tribes of the lower Great Lakes region originally had an often mutually beneficial relationship with Europeans and Americans thanks to the region's lucrative fur trade. Over generations, the fur trade led to a social and political blending between Indians and Whites. Then as settler interests led to land cession treaties with tribes, the annuities received for the ceded land made their way into the hands of merchants and land speculators. That money, in turn, financed road and canal building, infrastructure that attracted growing numbers of settlers, and this led to the region's increasing reliance on a market economy based on agriculture, which superseded the earlier exchange economy. Hence, ironically, many lower Great Lakes tribes financed their own removal. Moreover, many of these tribes faced a series of trans-Mississippi removals that forced them to repeatedly rebuild their lives as White settlers expanded their own westward interests. The removal experience for Native Americans preceded the 1830 Indian Removal Act passed during the Andrew Jackson administration and continued throughout the nineteenth century.[35] Thus, as one historian notes, we need to reconfigure our understanding of Indian Removal history, recognize "the pure relentless power of the removal and dispossession that framed the lives of Indian men

---

33. Perdue and Green, *Cherokee Nation*, 139.

34. John P. Bowes, *Land Too Good for Indians: Northern Indian Removal* (Norman: University of Oklahoma Press, 2016), 6–13.

35. Ibid., 4.

and women," and move their stories from the periphery to the center of our histories of White settlement.[36]

Not a Wilderness: Look at the Maps and Chronicles

If Euro-American notions of wilderness suggest an unmapped region, maps and other historical documents produced by North American Indians tell a different story. Moreover, Native American historical accounts are often rooted in a perspective in which both individual and group identities stand inseparable from the land itself. Any chronicle—as well as any history—stands on the assumption that the people and events it records exist within a defined space. A sense of history presupposes a sense of permanence as well as change.

For example, the Lakota winter count uses pictographs in conjunction with an orally transmitted historical account. The Lakota term *waniyetu* refers to an annual timespan or season as measured from first snow to first snow. The Lakota term *wówapi* indicates anything that is marked or drawn so that it can be read. Thus *waniyetu wówapi* translates as "winter count." Pictographic calendars known as "winter counts"—with each year indicated by a single significant event—were kept by each Lakota band and probably maintained by an individual tribal historian in consultation with community elders. Each pictograph served as a mnemonic device; read sequentially the calendars provided key data for oral histories that often spanned a century or more with the narratives passed down from generation to generation.[37]

Chronicles drawn on hide, cloth, or paper, winter counts recorded floods, fires, epidemics, astronomical events, battles, peace treaties, the deaths of famous leaders, and other important events. Sometimes a single band maintained multiple copies of winter counts, and winter counts circulated among closely allied bands. Corroboration of major events in Lakota history can be made by comparing winter counts kept by different bands. The tradition of keeping winter counts as physical documents probably developed in the early nineteenth century, although they often recorded older events maintained previously as oral histories unaccompanied by pictographs. By the 1930s, the practice of keeping winter counts dissipated, and the few maintained today serve not as community records but as individual family histories. The change occurred in tandem with the development of the Dakota dialect of the Sioux language family as a written language, its alphabet developed by Protestant missionaries working in Minnesota in the 1830s and 1840s, and the subsequent development as a written language of Lakota, another Sioux dialect. By the end of the nineteenth

---

36. Ibid., 225.

37. Candace S. Greene and Russell Thornton, eds. *The Year the Stars Fell: Lakota Winter Counts at the Smithsonian* (Lincoln: University of Nebraska Press, 2007), 1–2.

century, text replaced pictographs on some winter counts, and some of these texts appeared in native-language newspapers.[38]

As records of change over time, winter counts demonstrate the historical relationship of the Lakota people to a region radiating from the Black Hills in western South Dakota and extending into neighboring regions of Nebraska, Wyoming, and North Dakota. The Lakota immigrated into these areas from the western Great Lakes region by the turn of the nineteenth century. In their new homelands, they increasingly depended on the acquisition of horses, and as horse-mounted hunters, they became gradually more dependent on buffalo.

These nineteenth-century economic and cultural changes in the Lakota world have since entered the popular historical imagination of White Americans as fixed and timeless images. Together with other western Indian nations who eventually developed horse cultures, the Lakota merged into a stereotype as nomadic hunters forever drifting across the land in search of game. The stereotype gained traction at the same time that the White notion of wilderness shifted, and the trans-Mississippi West became defined as a region in which the dual goals of conquest and preservation could be realized.

Those Native American nations who did follow nomadic patterns did *not* conform in any way to the popular stereotype that has them wandering aimlessly across the land in search of food. In fact, North American nomadism stemmed from the need of some Native groups to periodically travel from place to place along regular routes in order to hunt game as it moved across its grazing range and to harvest plant products as they ripened across different seasons. However, Indigenous economies across the continent varied widely, and many nations established sedentary livelihoods. For example, northwest coastal Indians with access to plentiful fishing grounds had little reason to travel beyond their own region.

But as White settlement expanded across the continent, the Eurocentric perspective that came with it valued permanent settlement and devalued Native American economic structures that required seasonal migration. As the trans-Mississippi West became increasingly romanticized in popular culture, the stereotype of the Plains Indian solidified to represent all Native Americans.[39] That stereotype viewed nomadism as wasteful, irresponsible, and primitive—prejudices that date to the earliest European appraisals of Native Americans but that became keenly focused on Plains Indians. Manifest Destiny matured as a national idea at about the same time that stereotypical images of Plains Indians began to proliferate. Further consequences of this conjunction will be discussed below.

Ledger art, another narrative genre of the Plains Indians, proliferated with the mid-nineteenth-century westward migration of White settlers, railroad construction,

---

38. Ibid., 3.

39. This issue will be explored in Chapter 5, "The Myth of the Authentic Indian."

Likely a self-portrait by Arrow, a Southern Cheyenne warrior, this example of ledger art tells the story of a skirmish with soldiers of the 7th U.S. Cavalry on June 26, 1867—nine years before the Battle of the Little Big-horn—near Fort Wallace, Kansas. Arrow gallops over the first soldier and rides directly into the others, who may be too stunned by Arrow's charge to fire, as indicated by the absence of muzzle blasts. Note the paper itself—a page from a ledger book. From *Arrow's Elk Society Ledger*, Plate 4, page 5. Courtesy of Morning Star Gallery, Santa Fe. Plains Indian Ledger Art Publishing Project, U.C. San Diego, La Jolla, California. View the complete book at plainsledgerart.org.

and the conflicts that often arose between White interests and Indians. Using pencils and crayons, ledger artists most often worked in readily available ledger books, hence the genre's name, although artists also painted on animal hides. The drawings communicated multiple narratives, prompting oral histories of famous warriors, heroic battles, and horse raids. But most often ledger artists told the stories of Indian cultures undergoing wrenching transitions to reservation life and to federal policies of assimilation that attempted to erase traditional Native American identities.[40]

Moreover, the shifting political landscape of the Great Plains during the nineteenth century led to increasing competition among Native American nations who had transitioned to a horse culture, which in turn led to greater access to buffalo and a greater reliance on grasslands for grazing. Intertribal competition for horses, buffalo, and grasslands elevated significantly by the mid-nineteenth century. Lakota expansion into the central plains led to conflicts with the Pawnee, Arikara, and Crow. Meanwhile, the Comanche and Kiowa, who moved into western regions of Oklahoma and Texas, met resistance from the Apache, Osage, and Caddo.[41] Shifting alliances and rivalries between Western Indian nations and the military operations of the United States further complicated all levels of Indian life on the Great Plains. The turmoil

---

40. Colin G. Calloway, ed., *Ledger Narratives: The Plains Indian Drawings of the Lansburgh Collection at Dartmouth College* (Norman: University of Oklahoma Press, 2012), 3–4.
41. Ibid.

of these years filled the ledger books of Indian artists. As historical documents, their pictures record an era of great political, economic, and cultural upheaval; they tell the stories not of some nomad-crossed wilderness but of complex politically charged issues and relationships that permeated nineteenth-century Native American history throughout the Great Plains.

The land itself serves as a document. In central Arizona, Western Apache "place-makers"—tribal historians—describe past events as if personally witnessing them as they occurred on a specific point in the landscape. These stories are narrated in the present tense, which suggests that the past never stops happening; it remains fused to the present. Ancestors continue to express their thoughts and feelings in the place-maker's narrations, and their actions continue to occur. Place names proliferate in this spatial and atemporal concept of history. Specific features in canyons, mountains, and arroyos, single rocks or rock formations, points along lakeshores and riverbanks as well as lakes and river themselves, and seemingly vacant stretches of open plain—all lie embedded with the past. The landscape contains multiple levels of historical significance, and knowledge of place remains linked to knowledge of oneself.[42] This Western Apache worldview understands a sameness between people and their landscape; they not only inhabit the land but are inhabited by it.[43] Thus wilderness could not be a more alien concept in this sense of history; the land remains everywhere inhabited by the past, and without it the present ceases to exist.

In another type of historical documentation, Native American maps depended on pictographic traditions to convey information about the landscape. But they often provided more than mere geographic records; they wove history, mythology, and spiritual beliefs into multidimensional documents, the full expression of which required the skills of oral interpreters. Inscribed on birch bark, animal skins, rocks, and—following European contact—paper, they impart meaning to the land in terms of its human investment across time. Generally not intended as permanent documents, the few that survived over the centuries include those collected or copied by White explorers or commissioned by surveyors or anthropologists.[44]

Birch bark served multiple purposes for Native Americans throughout the Great Lakes region and the Northeastern woodlands. Used to construct canoes, houses, and a wide range of food containers, birch bark also served as a medium for recording both messages and maps. Likewise, animal skin maps have been located and preserved in areas across North America, and petroglyphs also display complexly mapped regions, as with Map Rock, located near the Snake River in Idaho. Etched in about one hundred square feet of basalt, this array of petroglyphs might have been

---

42. Keith H. Basso, *Wisdom Sits in Places: Landscape and Language among the Western Apache* (Albuquerque: University of New Mexico Press, 2000), 32–34.

43. Ibid., 102.

44. Mark Warhus, *Another America: Native American Maps and the History of Our Land* (New York: St. Martin's Press, 1997), 8–9.

Map Rock, Canyon County, Idaho. Courtesy Map Rock Commissioners, https://www.canyonco.org.

made by the Shoshone, who entered the region in the fifteenth century. The carvings represent animals they hunted along the Snake and Salmon rivers. Within a wider historical context, Map Rock's location in an extensive field of petroglyphs southeast of present-day Boise coincides with archeological evidence of winter lodges in the region that date to about 2000 BCE. This suggests that the rock could mark an ancient crossing point. Moreover, the buffalo, deer, mountain sheep, elk, antelope, and human figures strung along the mapped rivers might also express the close historical relationship experienced by those who carved the rock and their surrounding landscape.[45]

Not a wilderness, but a populous world with deep historical roots, a landscape long familiar and transregionally connected by complex routes well known by the Indigenous Peoples who used them. Europeans traders in Indian Country used these routes as well, as did the increasing numbers of White settlers.

The Wilderness Road

Daniel Boone (1734–1820) owes much of his folk hero status to John Filson's *The Discovery, Settlement and Present State of Kentucke* (1784) and to Timothy Flint's *Biographical Memoir of Daniel Boone, the First Settler of Kentucky* (1833).[46] On thin foundations of historical accuracy, these authors mythologized the prototypical American frontiersman, an image expanded through dime novels such as Joseph E. Badger's *The Wood King, or, Daniel Boone's Last Trail: A Romance of the Osage Country* (1873):

> Steadily Boone pressed on through the tangled forest with the yells of the Osage warriors ringing clearly in his ears, and something of the fire of his younger days gleamed in his blue eyes and brought a flush to his bronzed cheek, as he felt himself once more pitted against the dusky heathen who had dealt him so many bitter blows.[47]

---

45. Ibid., 21.

46. For further discussion regarding the influence of these books, see Michael A. Lofaro, *Daniel Boone: An American Life* (Lexington: University Press of Kentucky, 2012), passim.

47. Joseph E. Badger, *The Wood King, or, Daniel Boone's Last Trail: A Romance of the Osage Country* (New York: Beadle and Adams, 1873), 62.

Through films and a popular television series that ran from 1964 to 1970, Daniel Boone and the American wilderness became synonymous.

Hired by the Transylvania Company in 1775, Boone led thirty woodsmen into the Appalachian Mountains to cut a road from western Virginia into central Kentucky. The company aimed to entice settlers onto Kentucky land that it had purchased through a treaty with several Cherokee bands. However, both the legality of the treaty and the conflicting land claims made by the multiple bands of Indian nations who did not sign the treaty ensured ongoing conflict and bloodshed between White settlers and Indians.

What came to be known as the Wilderness Road served as the conduit for generations of Virginians heading west through the Cumberland Gap to settle in Kentucky. Ironically, much of the road followed routes established by Indians who had lived in the region for centuries. Working with detailed mental maps, they had long domesticated certain areas of the country through agricultural practices and through methods of game management.[48] The road's name sidesteps all of this. The ascription of "wilderness" to this long-inhabited region effectively delegitimized Indigenous knowledge of and claims to the land. The land awaited White settlement and legitimation through lines drawn by surveyors and then mapped into plat books.

Yellowstone: A Case Study of Institutionalized Wilderness

Many current ideas about wilderness in North America solidified with the creation of the federal park system. Regarded as pristine and uninhabited national treasures, Yosemite, Yellowstone, Glacier, and nearly seven hundred other federally designated wilderness areas attract millions of visitors annually.[49] Moreover, as they gaze upon geysers, giant sequoias, rugged mountains, and waterfalls, visitors partake in a carefully staged wilderness myth.

Generally, romantic notions of national parks as primordial landscapes tend to ignore the significance of Native American history on those landscapes. The Wilderness Myth also glosses over the dispossession of Native Americans that often accompanied the establishment of national parks. When President Grant designated Yellowstone as the United States' first national park in 1872, the Indian eviction process from "the people's national park lands" began.[50]

---

48. William E. Doolittle, *Cultivated Landscapes of Native North America* (New York: Oxford University Press, 2001), 63 and 141–44.

49. Michael Lewis, "American Wilderness: An Introduction" in *American Wilderness: A New History*, ed. Michael Lewis (New York: Oxford University Press, 2007), 3.

50. Mark David Spence, *Dispossessing the Wilderness: Indian Removal and the Making of the National Parks* (New York: Oxford University Press, 1999), 57–59.

In Canada, the park as pristine wilderness myth gained traction when, with the establishment of Banff as the first Canadian national park in 1885, the government evicted the Stoney Indians from park boundaries, although they had been living on that land for centuries. However, the Canadian exclusion policy has been gradually eliminated over the past fifty years. Parks Canada, the arm of the government that manages Canadian national parks, now generally collaborates with First Nations in park management decisions.[51] The story is somewhat the same in the United States. Until passage of the National Historic Preservation Act in 1992, which established the National Tribal Preservation Program, the United States Department of the Interior often restricted or denied Native American rights regarding use of park lands, and park histories often ignored or discounted the many centuries of Indian presence on those lands.[52] Recent efforts by the National Park Service to develop programs concerning Native American history attempt to undo the many years of institutional neglect.[53] But much work remains to undo ideas about wilderness as inherently uninhabited or as a place where Indians merely passed through without leaving a trace, ideas that have been centuries in the making.

The Crow, Shoshone, and Bannock have deep historical connections to the area now occupied by Yellowstone National Park, as have the Blackfeet in Glacier and the Yosemite Indians in Yosemite. Native American claims to resources and to traditional sites of religious importance located on parklands challenge preservationist idealizations of a historically unpeopled wilderness through which Indians merely wandered or that they avoided altogether.[54]

In 1870 Henry Washburn, surveyor general of Montana, led an expedition into the region that would soon become Yellowstone National Park. The party noted significant Indian presence. It encountered a group of about one hundred Crow, followed extensive trails that had been blazed by Indians, and found seasonal campsites with stacks of lodge poles ready for reuse. Yet the explorers regarded the group of Crow Indians as refugees from the plains who sought temporary shelter in the mountains, and they believed that the campsites stood as ancient artifacts of a vanished people. The Washburn expedition journals established the template for subsequent

---

51. "Many of Canada's National Parks Now Honor First Nations," Indian Country Today Media Network.com, http://indiancountrytodaymedianetwork.com/2012/07/13/many-canadas-national-parks-now-honor-first-nations-peoples-123279 (accessed April 28, 2016).

52. For more information regarding recent efforts by the National Park Service to work with Native American interests, see "Working with Native Americans," https://www.nps.gov/history/tribes/ (accessed May 25, 2016).

53. For more information on the programs that have been developed by the National Park Service regarding Native American History, see https://www.nps.gov/americanindian/ (accessed May 25, 2016).

54. Spence, *Dispossessing the Wilderness*, 6–7.

evaluations of Indian history in Yellowstone. Indeed, one journal entry interpreted the country as a primeval wilderness "never trodden by human footsteps."[55]

However, for thousands of years people had been harvesting resources from the land that became Yellowstone Park.[56] The region's fish, birds, deer, elk, mountain sheep, antelope, and bison, along with crops of seeds and legumes, ensured a varied and substantial diet. The Yellowstone region also possessed rich deposits of obsidian, a highly desirable trade item. Shaped into knife blades, arrowheads, and jewelry, Yellowstone obsidian has been found in Hopewell Indian sites in the Ohio River Valley that are more than 1,500 years old;[57] conversely, pottery manufactured by the somewhat later Mississippian peoples turns up in archeological sites in Yellowstone.[58] This range of evidence implies the existence of a long-distance trade and communication network active for hundreds of years in which the Yellowstone region played a significant role, especially as proof of numerous Native American quarries lies scattered throughout Obsidian Cliff in the park's northwest corner.[59]

A folk belief passed down from White fur trappers claimed that Indians avoided the geysers and fumaroles because they feared the wrath of the "evil spirit" who supposedly resided among them; the Washburn expedition repeated this fallacious notion, and continued repetition in park literature further enhanced its credibility as a long-accepted fact.[60] However, the Crow, who know the geysers as *Bide-Mahpe* (sacred or powerful water), record a tradition that associates them with benevolent, *not* malevolent, spirits.[61] Moreover, evidence of campsites in the geyser basin indicates a history of Native American habitation, countering the notion that Indians avoided the region.[62] The Kiowa know Yellowstone's Dragon's Mouth Spring as *Tujg Sa'u Dah*

---

55. Ibid., 42–43.

56. For one overview of this, see http://indiancountrytodaymedianetwork.com/2014/03/01/native-history-yellowstone-national-park-created-sacred-land-153807 (accessed May 25, 2016).

57. The Hopewell culture dates from approximately 200 BCE to 500 CE. See James B. Griffith, A. A. Gordus, and G. A. Wright, "Identification of Hopewellian Obsidian in the Middle West," *American Antiquity* 34 (1969): 1–14.

58. The Mississippians, also known as the Mound Builders, flourished in the Mississippi River Valley and throughout the Southeast from approximately 800 to about 1600 CE.

59. Spence, *Dispossessing the Wilderness*, 45.

60. Lee H. Whittlesey, "Native Americans, the Earliest Interpreters: What Is Known about Their Legends and Stories of Yellowstone National Park and the Complexities of Interpreting Them," *The George Wright Forum* 19, no. 3 (2002): 40–41. For a glimpse into the National Park Service's mid-twentieth-century perpetuation of erroneous folk beliefs regarding Native American history in regions that became national parks, see Horace Marden Albright and Frank J. Taylor, "Look! Real Indians!" in *Oh Ranger!* by Albright and Taylor (New York: Chatham Press, 1972), https://www.nps.gov/parkhistory/online_books/albright3/chap6.htm (accessed May 25, 2016).

61. Lee H. Whittlesey, *Storytelling in Yellowstone: Horse and Buggy Tour Guides* (Albuquerque: University of New Mexico Press, 2007), 16.

62. Spence, *Dispossessing the Wilderness*, 43.

(the place of hot water) and trace their mythical origin to it, although they eventually migrated southward. According to the story, the benevolent spirit Doh Ki promised the Kiowa a beautiful homeland if they dove into *Tujg Sa'u Dah*. Fearful of the boiling pool, all ran away except for one, and when he emerged, the former barren landscape was transformed by Doh Ki into rich forests, meadows, and streams.[63]

In line with the Myth of the Wilderness stands a persistent claim that Indians left no mark on Yellowstone except for a few scattered campsites. But in Yellowstone, as in regions throughout North America, Native Americans across time significantly altered the land on which they lived, particularly through the use of fire.[64] By deliberately setting fires, Indians created and maintained Yellowstone's plant and animal habitats. Fires opened up savannahs for animals to graze. Fires cleared underbrush in forests and kept trails open for travel. By manipulating the environment to control the selection of animals for hunting and to encourage the growth of certain crops, Indians continually altered Yellowstone's landscape in accord with the needs of their communities.[65]

Across the centuries, game, fish, and other wild foods (nuts, berries, and tubers) attracted multiple Native American nations to Yellowstone. By the nineteenth century, Shoshone bands in the eastern foothills of the Rocky Mountains hunted elk and deer in the fall, and in the spring they hunted bison on the plains south of Yellowstone River. In the 1820s and 1830s intertribal fur trade gatherings during the so-called Mountain Man Rendezvous Era brought the Shoshone into contact with other Native American nations that lived throughout the Rockies.[66] Nez Perce, Salish, Kalispel, and Coeur d'Alene bands often traveled through Yellowstone on their way to buffalo grounds near the Missouri River. By the early nineteenth century, Crow bands wintered on the eastern and northern edges of Yellowstone's current boundaries and regularly hunted throughout the future park. On occasion, Blackfeet bands also hunted the same land.[67]

In two 1868 treaties with the United States, the Crow and the Shoshone ceded lands both within and adjacent to the current boundaries of Yellowstone National Park, although leaders of both nations negotiated continued hunting and harvesting rights—usufruct rights—in the ceded territory. The treaties also established Shoshone and Crow reservations on or near the park's borders. One Shoshone band, the Tukudeka, did not take part in negotiations, so it did not feel bound by treaty obligations. Approximately two hundred band members remained in Yellowstone throughout the

---

63. Peter Nabokov and Lawrence Loendorf, *Restoring a Presence: American Indians and Yellowstone National Park* (Norman: University of Oklahoma Press, 2016), 67–75.

64. Chapter 6, "The Myth of the Ecological Indian" examines these alterations in detail.

65. Spence, *Dispossessing the Wilderness*, 44–45.

66. Virginia Cole Trenholm and Maurine Carley, *The Shoshinis: Sentinels of the Rockies* (Norman: University of Oklahoma Press, 1964), 56–73.

67. Spence, *Dispossessing the Wilderness*, 45.

1870s. Meanwhile, the Crow, Shoshone, and other Indian nations exercised their treaty rights to hunt and to harvest food within the park. By the 1880s, however, the Crow faced significant threats from the encroachment of gold miners on the western edge of their reservation. By treaty, the Crow permitted industrial development on their land; however, mining operations depleted game stocks and destroyed food-gathering sites on the reservation and in neighboring areas of the park. Moreover, the combination of commercial and Native American hunting decimated deer and elk populations and led to the near extinction of buffalo in the Lower Yellowstone Valley. The depletion of food sources meant that the Crow increasingly depended on agency rations. With dwindling prospects in the Yellowstone region, the Crow agreed to another removal. By 1884, they relocated to an agency nearly two hundred miles east of the park. During the Crow removal period, the Tukudeka finally agreed to their own permanent removal from the park and to settlement on reservations in present-day Idaho and Wyoming. However, along with other Shoshone bands, they continued hunting and harvesting in Yellowstone on a regular basis until Congress—owing to the efforts of General Philip H. Sheridan—implemented military control of the park in 1886.[68]

Starting in the early 1880s, Sheridan vigorously lobbied Washington officials for the military management of Yellowstone National Park, and by mustering the support of preservationists, sportsmen's groups, and key senators,[69] he convinced Congress to pass an act that authorized the secretary of war to dispatch "the necessary detail of troops to prevent trespassers or intruders from entering the park for the purpose of destroying the game or objects of curiosity therein, . . . and to remove such persons from the park if found therein."[70] The "trespassers or intruders" included White hide hunters, but the act also effectively denied all usufruct rights previously granted to Native Americans.

Preservationists generally advocated Indian removal from wilderness areas, arguing that wilderness required protection from Indians who damaged it through allegedly reckless hunting.[71] Their ideas found support in government policy. One letter written by commissioner of Indian Affairs E. A. Hyatt in 1879 illustrates this common ground. He wrote in response to a Wyoming Indian agent who reported the

---

68. Ibid., 49–53.

69. Paul Andrew Hutton, *Phil Sheridan and His Army* (Norman: University of Oklahoma Press, 1999), 354–58.

70. 47th Congress, Session II, Chapter 143, 1883, http://uscode.house.gov/statviewer.htm?volume=22&page=627 (accessed May 5, 2016).

71. For an example of the ambivalence and the changes in perception among preservationists regarding Native Americans, see Richard F. Fleck, "John Muir's Evolving Attitudes toward Native American Cultures," *American Indian Quarterly* 4 (1978): 19–31. Also instructive is Fleck's own presentation, which depends heavily on Noble Savage tropes.

successful removal of Ute Indians from a section of the park. The agent stated that Indians

> had no appreciation of the value of forests, and in order to obtain dry fuel for winter use, or to drive the deer to one place where they might be easily killed, fires were lighted, by which large tracts of valuable timber were burned over, to the great exasperation of settlers.

The commissioner replied:

> I am in receipt of your letter . . . relative to the departure of the Indians from the Middle Park, their destruction of grass, timber, etc. [As noted in my previous telegram] "Take a decided stand with your Indians to prevent further depredations." . . . Complaints of a serious character have been made to the office in regard to the fires which have been set by Indians . . . and these heedless and lawless acts, unless checked, will lead to collisions between the whites and the Indians. . . . If possible, ascertain what Indians committed the depredations [and subject them] to some adequate punishment. . . . You are directed to adopt decisive measures to put a stop to these roaming habits of your Indians. [They are to be regarded] as hostile Indians and liable to arrest if they are found outside of their reservations without passes.[72]

Captain Moses A. Harris served as Yellowstone's first military superintendent (1886–89), and preventing Indians from entering the park became his primary duty. He wrote that one Native American hunting party worked "more destruction during a summer's hunt than all of the [White] hunters put together."[73] But Harris commanded only thirty troops, so Shoshone and Bannock hunting parties easily evaded the superintendent's meager military patrols and continued using customary camps, maintaining them with seasonal fires. He regarded these traditional burns as dangerous vandalism. He berated Indian agents who seemed to him unwilling to enforce laws that regulated the movement of Indians and who failed to restrict Indians to their reservations and prevent them from entering the park. An exasperated Harris turned to his friend George Bird Grinnell, editor of the influential magazine *Forest and Stream*. In one of many similar articles, Grinnel wrote:

---

72. E. A. Hyatt, *Annual Report of the Commissioner of Indian Affairs* (Washington, D.C.: Government Printing Office, 1879), xxvi, http://digicoll.library.wisc.edu/cgi-bin/History/History-idx?type=turn&entity=History.AnnRep79.p0030&id=History.AnnRep79&isize=M (accessed May 4, 2016).

73. Moses A. Harris, *Report of the Superintendent of the Yellowstone National Park, 1889* (Washington, D.C.: Government Printing Office, 1889), 15–16. Quoted in Spence, *Dispossessing the Wilderness*, 63.

A serious danger menaces the game and the forests of a portion of the Yellowstone National Park. The danger arises from the invasion of the country to the south and west . . . by Indian hunting parties, principally Bannocks and Shoshones from the agencies at Fort Hall, Lemki and Washaki. These Indians leave their reservations and proceed toward the borders of the Park, where they destroy great numbers of elk, drying the meat for winter use, and carrying it and the hides to their home. A far more serious injury . . . is caused by the forest fires which these Indians kindle to drive the game. . . . Captain Harris has . . . done everything in his power to keep the Indians away from the Park. He has repeatedly notified the Interior Department of these depredations, but the agents in charge of these Indians have met his remonstrances with denials of facts which are perfectly well known. . . . We propose shortly to furnish some facts connected with this topic which will be interesting reading for those who have visited or may contemplate visiting the Park.[74]

However, official records filed with the secretary of the interior indicated that bison and elk populations in the park region noted by Grinnell actually increased over the decade preceding his article.[75] Whether Grinnell ignored or had not been made aware of these statistics remains unknown.

In summary, manufacturing a safe wilderness experience for park tourists required the full removal of all Indians and the complete elimination of all Indian activity within park boundaries. As Yellowstone became increasingly institutionalized as a park, it also tended to promote conceptions of wilderness as historically unpopulated regions.[76] However, as we have seen, Yellowstone's geography remained well known to multiple Native American nations, who for centuries harvested its many resources and who lived on its land.

Consistently, White authorities willfully refused to recognize the benefits of seasonal burning in forest environments, benefits long known to Native Peoples. Burning underbrush opens areas for wildlife to graze and stimulates germination of certain tree species. Moreover, seasonal burns clear deadwood, so they actually prevent larger fires that could destroy entire forests. Today, the rationale driving these resource management measures practiced by Native Americans is finally understood. Fire control

---

74. George Bird Grinnell, "Indian Marauders," *Forest and Stream: A Weekly Journal of the Rod and Gun* 32 (April 4, 1889): 209, http://ia800501.us.archive.org/32/items/ForeststreamXXXIA/ForeststreamXXXIA.pdf (accessed May 5, 2016).

75. Aubrey L. Haines, *The Yellowstone Story*, Vol. 2 (Boulder: Colorado Associate University Press, 1977), 483–89.

76. Spence, *Dispossessing the Wilderness*, 69.

authorities now follow similar measures through what they call "prescribed burning," where the absence of human settlement allows.[77]

Find the Indian in the Picture

Thomas Moran (1830–1902) painted his seven-by-twelve-foot canvas, *The Grand Cañon of the Yellowstone* (1872), in his Newark, New Jersey studio. Although based on extensive notes and sketches he made while traveling with an 1871 geological survey team, Moran said of his canvas, "I place no value upon literal transcripts from Nature. My general scope is not realistic; all my tendencies are toward idealization. . . . Topography in art is valueless."[78] *The Grand Cañon of the Yellowstone* combines multiple angles of the canyon itself and creates the illusion that the canvas represents a single stationary perspective. In effect, Moran presents a controlled and edited idea of wilderness.[79]

By the mid-nineteenth century, not only did aesthetically transformed portrayals of the North American wilderness—particularly the land that stretched from the Great Plains westward—hang on gallery walls, they also proliferated in magazines, popular prints, and through paintings commissioned by railroad companies advertising the opportunities and splendors that awaited settlers and travelers. Landscape art served well as a nationalist project, in part because it often wrote Indians out of that project. By the nature of the genre, scenes formulated from great panoramic distances diminished Indians into tiny specks somewhere within the frame. Of course, all human presence—Indian or White—appeared in miniature against the grand vistas. But the all-White audience for the paintings likely understood their fellow Whites as hearty adventurers exploring a land nearly emptied of human habitation.

---

77. Rachel G. Schneider and Deborah Breedlove, "Prescribed Burning" in *Fire Management Study Unit*, U.S. Department of Agriculture and Georgia Forestry Commission, 30–37, https://www.fs.usda.gov/Internet/FSE_DOCUMENTS/fsm9_028958.pdf (accessed June 3, 2017).

78. Thomas Moran, quoted in Nancy K. Anderson, "Curious Historical Data" in *Discovered Lands, Invented Pasts: Transforming Visions of the American West*, ed. Jules Prown et al. (New Haven, CT: Yale University Press, 1992), 1–36. Similar aims inform landscape aesthetics in general. See Joni Louise Kinsey, *Thomas Moran and the Surveying of the American West* (Washington, D.C.: Smithsonian Institution Press, 1992), 11–40.

79. Kinsey, *Thomas Moran*, 57. Moran produced scores of landscapes, and his name is often associated with the Hudson River School, a group of mid-nineteenth-century American artists. These artists romanticized landscapes as wilderness; at times the wilderness bore evidence of White encroachment, but most often it stood as an unpeopled expanse that expressed endless possibilities with room enough for both reverence and settlement. For a study of the Hudson River School in a historical context, see Barbara Babcock Millhouse, *American Wilderness: The Story of the Hudson River School of Painting* (Hensonville, NY: Black Dome Press, 2007).

Thomas Moran, *The Grand Cañon of the Yellowstone* (1872). The humans, barely seen here, are dwarfed by the mighty splendor of the canyon. Smithsonian American Art Museum lent by the Department of the Interior Museum.

The one Indian man in Moran's picture stands accompanied by three equally small White men. The Indian stands next to Ferdinand Vandiveer Hayden, the survey team's leader. Hayden faces the valley; the Indian faces the viewer. The former wears a hat and gestures toward the valley; the latter, according to some scholars, wears a medal similar to the type presented to Indian signatories by White diplomats to acknowledge the completion of land transfer treaties.[80]

Because the conventions of the genre delimit human presence and emphasize the land itself, the resulting illusion of an empty land stirred nationalist notions of the unlimited development available across the Western wilderness. Leading these development interests, railroads thrived through advertising the scenic qualities and the economic potentials of the land. Jay Cooke and Company, the financial agents of the Northern Pacific Railroad, advertised Yellowstone as Wonderland and hoped that rail passengers would begin flocking to its wilderness attractions. The first mass circulation of Yellowstone images appeared in 1871 in *Scribner's Monthly*, the engravings produced by the magazine's main landscape illustrator, Thomas Moran.[81] Moran understood the relationship between landscape art and nationalism:

---

80. Angela Miller, "The Fate of Wilderness in American Landscape Art: The Dilemmas of 'Nature's Nation,'" in *American Wilderness: A New History*, ed. Michael L. Lewis (New York: Oxford University Press, 2007), 107.

81. Sue Rainey, *Creating Picturesque America: Monument to the Natural and Cultural Landscape* (Nashville, TN: Vanderbilt University Press, 1994), 163–64.

Before America can pretend to a position in the world of art it will have to prove it through a characteristic nationality in its art, and our artists can only do this by painting their own country, making use of all the technical skill and knowledge they may have acquired in the schools of Europe and the study of the art of the past.[82]

Indeed, underscoring the inherent nationalism of his masterpiece, the federal government purchased *The Grand Cañon of the Yellowstone* for $10,000, an enormous sum at the time—approximately $188,000 in today's money. Displayed in the Senate lobby, it became the first landscape painting to join the mostly historical canvases in the congressional collection.[83]

In 1880 Moran went to Quebec to make arrangements for contributing to an enormous two-volume work, *Picturesque Canada*, designed as a counterpart to the already successful and similarly ambitious *Picturesque America* (1872). Both publications were intended to entice tourists into wilderness destinations and to define the land itself in terms of nationalist interests. The term "picturesque" refers to a type of painting meant to arouse curiosity and delight in the viewer. In the United States, picturesque landscape paintings grew increasingly popular following the Civil War as people attempted to move beyond the years of national carnage. Magazines and newspapers hired prominent artists who traveled the country, and the images they produced proved a boon to the nascent tourism industry. Indians had for some time been depicted as picturesque subjects. In 1859, landscape artist Albert Bierstadt commented while traveling through the Rocky Mountains:

We do not venture a great distance from the camp alone, although tempted to do so by distant objects, which, of course, appear more charming than those nearby; also by the figures of Indians so enticing, travelling about with their long poles trailing along the ground, and their picturesque dress, that renders them such appropriate adjuncts to the scenery.[84]

Bierstadt produced numerous paintings that depicted Native Americans, and his interest in them as picturesque subjects who blended into the scenery continued a long-standing Eurocentric notion, one that remains influential to this day. But during his career, Bierstadt gained his greatest fame from his panoramas.

The first of Bierstadt's "Great Pictures," *The Rocky Mountains, Lander's Peak* (1863), presented the American West as a theatrical experience for ticket-paying audiences. The

82. Thomas Moran, "American Art and American and American Scenery," in *The Grand Canyon of Arizona*, ed. C. A. Higgins and J. W. Powell (Santa Fe, NM: Passenger Department of the Santa Fe Railway, 1902), 86.

83. Thurman Wilkins, *Thomas Moran: Artist of the Mountains* (Norman: University of Oklahoma Press, 1998), 5.

84. Albert Bierstadt, "Letter," *The Crayon: A Journal Devoted to the Graphic Arts and the Literature Related to Them* (September 1859): 287.

Albert Bierstadt, *The Rocky Mountains, Lander's Peak*, 1863.

six-foot-by-ten-foot canvas toured Eastern cities accompanied by a sophisticated advertising campaign, not unlike that of touring theatrical companies.[85] An Indian camp
stretches across the foreground, but thematically it merely echoes the implied timelessness of a landscape dominated by Lander's Peak, a summit in the Wyoming Range
named for General Frederick W. Lander. Lander accompanied Bierstadt on an expedition into the West. Following the general's death in the Civil War, Bierstadt appropriated
his name for the landmark, effectively claiming and monumentalizing the landscape as a
distinctly American treasure. The unidentified Indians camp lies in the shadow of Bierstadt's monument. Moreover, despite Bierstadt's appeal to the painting's authenticity
and his claim that the canvas possessed "a geographical and historical value such as few
works by modern artists have obtained," he freely rearranged the region's geography for
dramatic effect and added the Indian camp as a picturesque touch.[86]

Poster Indians, Totem Poles, and the Tourist Trade

Art commissioned for posters by the Canadian Pacific Railway (CPR) vividly expressed
the taming of the Canadian wilderness through iron rails and White settlement, with

85. Nancy K. Anderson and Linda S. Ferber, *Albert Bierstadt: Art and Enterprise* (New York: Hudson
Hills Press, 1990), 25.
86. Robert V. Hine and John Mack Faragher, *The American West: A New Interpretive History* (New
Haven, CT: Yale University Press, 2000), 489–90.

Indians exoticized into mere landscape elements. In 1885, the CPR finished a line that connected eastern Canada with British Columbia, making it Canada's first transcontinental railroad. The CPR promoted agricultural settlement in the Canadian west because it meant revenue through grain and machinery shipments.

These promotions bypassed the thorny issues of Indian claims to the land. Images of Indians remained limited to smiling figures with arms open in welcome to trains, visitors, and settlers. Saturating the marketplace by being distributed freely throughout eastern Canada and the British Isles, CPR posters conveyed images of unfettered settlement opportunities. With the advent of Canadian Pacific steamships, posters for ocean cruises to Alaska nearly always included totem poles.[87] Historically indigenous to Northwest coastal Indian nations, totem poles became increasingly commoditized by the CPR and by other tourist interests, implying perhaps that Indians passively condoned White settlement.

Totem poles probably originated on Haida Gwaii (until 2010 known as the Queen Charlotte Islands) or in nearby Tsimshian territory and began spreading north and south by the mid-eighteenth century. Images on poles include animals, plants, geological formations, celestial events, ancestors, and supernatural beings.[88] The poles do not express a hierarchy of images, so the cliché "low man on the totem pole" rests only on a misconception.[89]

Myths about totem poles originated with the English explorers who first ventured into the Northwest coastal region, beginning with Captain James Cook (1728–79), who sailed along the Pacific coast in 1778 in search of the fabled Northwest Passage—a waterway supposedly linking the Atlantic and Pacific Oceans. Cook and his crew spent several weeks with the Mowachaht, a band of Nuu-chah-nulth. The captain recorded the hospitality of Maquianna, the village leader, and documented his impressions of the people he met, the houses in the village, and the *klumma*—presumably the Mowachaht term for what would become known as totem poles. Because of language barriers between the English and their Mowachaht hosts, Cook acknowledged his inability to understand much of what he saw; however, he suggested that the poles might represent idols or possibly ancestors.[90] Although his inference regarding the presence of ancestral images remains astute, the poles never served as idols—as objects of worship. However, this would become one of the most persistent misconceptions about totem poles.[91]

---

87. Marc H. Choco, *Canadian Pacific: Creating a Brand, Building a Nation* (Berlin: Calisto, 2015), 160–62.

88. Aldona Jonaitis and Aaron Glass, *The Totem Pole: An Intercultural History* (Seattle: University of Washington Press, 2010), 17–18.

89. Ibid., 5.

90. Ibid., 15–16.

91. Ibid., 5.

Generally, a pole portrays the interaction of supernatural beings with ancestors, and the episodes comprise a family history. The totem pole played a particularly important role for families with an elite status. In the hierarchical Northwest Coast societies, individuals ranged from commoners to chiefs, with relative status based on inherited position and wealth. A highly ranked family maintained its position by hosting potlatches—celebrations during which the family lavished food and valuables on its guests. The potlatch also celebrated the erection of a totem pole, linking both in a mechanism that validated rank and maintained the owner's social status.[92]

In 1891 the Pacific Coast Steamship Company published John Muir's *All about Alaska*, in which the famous conservationist gushed, "To the lover of pure wilderness Alaska is one of the most wonderful countries in the world. No excursion that I know of may be made into any other American wilderness where so marvelous an abundance of noble, newborn scenery is so charmingly brought to view." Regarding totem poles, he remarks:

> The colorful lichens and mosses gave them a venerable air, while the layer of vegetation often found on such as were most decayed produced a picturesque effect. . . . The completeness of form, finish and proportion of these timbers suggest a skill of a wild and positive kind, like that which guides the woodpecker in drilling round holes, and the bee in making its cells.[93]

His depiction of totem poles as vanishing picturesque ruins and his metaphors that suggest Indians belong to the animal world of the wilderness assisted the company's commercial agenda; its 1908 brochure *Alaska via Totem Pole Route* stressed the significance of totem poles for the wilderness experience: "The totem-poles of Alaska are as different from everything else in the world as the scenery surpasses all other scenery; nowhere else such a combination of magnificent mountains, glaciers, and picturesque fiords as in the land of the totem-pole."[94] Here, the totem pole appears as part of the natural world, divorced from human agency.

As the Northwest Coast tourist trade gained momentum, souvenirs bearing images of totem poles proliferated. Today, tourist shops throughout Alaska, British Columbia, Washington State, and elsewhere market totem pole replicas and totem-pole-emblazoned merchandise. The wilderness experience of the Northwest Coast would not be complete without the purchase of totem pole memorabilia.[95]

---

92. Ibid., 4.

93. John Muir, *All about Alaska*, quoted in Jonaitis and Glass, *Totem Pole*, 59–61.

94. Pacific Coast Steamship Company, 1908, quoted in Jonaitis and Glass, *Totem Pole*, 62.

95. For an excellent exploration of the tourist shop industry, see Kate C. Duncan, *1001 Curious Things: Ye Olde Curiosity Shop and Native American Art* (Seattle: University of Washington Press, 2000).

John Gast, *American Progress*, 1872. Lithograph, Library of Congress.

John Gast's *American Progress*: From the Myth of the Wilderness to the Myth of the Vanishing Indian

The same year that Thomas Moran painted *The Grand Cañon of the Yellowstone*, John Gast's *American Progress* (1872) made its first appearance in magazines and in guide-books for tourists. Whereas the nationalism of Moran's canvas appears abstract and relatively nuanced, Gast presents a concrete nationalist allegory with a direct and unambiguous message: American progress brings light to the wilderness, and Indians have no place in the coming new order. *American Progress* claims the wilderness as an American birthright and declares the righteousness of Manifest Destiny.

A towering feminine figure crowned with "The Star of Empire" bears a science textbook in one hand and strings a telegraph wire with the other. In the distance, ships ply the Mississippi waters; trains steam westward. Stagecoach, covered wagon, horseback rider, hunter, and miner all move determinably into the receding dark of the western wilderness. A log cabin stands surrounded by a fenced field worked by two farmers plowing the land with a team of oxen.

In the farthest western reaches at the darkened left edge of the canvas, Indians and buffalo flee the procession of American Progress. One Indian wields a tomahawk, one runs with a bow and arrow in hand; leading them, a horse-drawn travois bears a mother and child. A bare-chested woman leads the horse. A stampeding bison herd parallels the flight of the Indians. The sky above both Indians and buffalo looms dark, yet the clouds part and lighten in the wake of the rushing westward advance of American progress. Progress tames the wilderness.

American Progress affirms the wilderness as a zone of opportunity; the colossal White angelic woman with her flowing fair locks symbolizes the cultural purity of the westward-rushing pioneers. The procession brushes away the last of the Indians, and here intersect the Myth of the Wilderness and the Myth of the Vanishing Indian. The Myth of the Wilderness excludes, diminishes, corrupts, or attempts to erase Native American history on the land, as does the Myth of the Vanishing Indian. Yet, as will be seen in the next chapter, the latter myth emphasizes the notion that Native Americans had always been undeserving of the vast wilderness and are destined to disappear; moreover, their racial inferiority to Whites makes them incapable of surviving in the modern world that is busily transforming the "empty wilderness" into something considered useful by the expanding republic as an expanse open for Whites to settle and to enjoy.

4. THE END OF THE TRAIL: THE MYTH
OF THE VANISHING INDIAN

Roll back the tide of time. . . . Here lived and loved another race of beings.
Beneath the same sun that rolls over your heads, the Indian hunter pursued the panting deer; gazing on the same moon that smiles for you, the
Indian lover wooed his dusky mate. Here the wigwam blaze beamed on
the tender and helpless, the council-fire glared on the wise and daring. . . .
Here they warred; the echoing whoop; the bloody grapple, the defying
death-song, all were here. Here too, they worshipped; and from many
a dark bosom went up a pure prayer to the Great Spirit. The poor child
of nature knew not the God of revelation, but the God of the universe
he acknowledged in everything around. . . . And all this has passed away.
Across the ocean came a pilgrim bark, bearing the seeds of life and death.
The former were sown for you, the latter sprang up in the path of the simple native. Two hundred years have changed the character of a great continent, and blotted forever from its face a whole, peculiar people. . . . Here
and there a stricken few remain; but how unlike their bold, untamed,
untamable progenitors! The Indian of falcon dance, and lion bearing, the
theme of the touching ballad, the hero of the pathetic tale, is gone! And
his degraded offspring crawl upon the soil where he walked in majesty,
to remind us how miserable is man when the foot of the conqueror is on
his neck. As a race they have withered from the land. [Their] war-cry is
fast dying away to the untrodden west. Slowly and sadly they climb the
distant mountains, and read their doom in the setting sun.[1]

This excerpt from the 1825 Independence Day address by the popular nineteenth-
century poet and orator Charles Sprague (1791–1875) encapsulates the Myth of the
Vanishing Indian. After bidding his Boston audience to think back to a time when
the noble Indian race once thrived, Sprague reverently invokes images of a proud and
simple people. Sadly, the course of empire doomed the continent's children of nature.
The orator measures out a modicum of sorrow that he and his audience must feel for
that dying race, but he simultaneously administers the antidote. After all, two hundred years earlier the Pilgrims—understood as instruments of God—cast the "seeds of

---

1. Charles Sprague, *The Poetical and Prose Writings of Charles Sprague* (Boston: Ticknor, Reed, and
Fields, 1850), 150–53.

life and death." As benefactors of God's plan, Christian America must also recognize His wisdom at work in the extinction of the "simple native."

Sprague expressed sentiments already long-held by his 1825 audience. Moreover, the fusion of piety and progress that together destined Indians to "climb the distant mountains, and read their doom in the setting sun" served as forgone conclusions for generations to come. Although his Independence Day address typifies countless other works regarding the preordained demise of Native Americans, his "Roll Back the Tide of Time" lived on for a century or more as a popularly anthologized piece in numerous textbooks and readers.[2]

Stereotypes of both Noble and Ignoble Savages crowd Sprague's oration. The Myth of the Vanishing Indian depends on them. So noble a race could not survive the complexities of modernity, and the few who continue to "crawl" over the land only prove by their ignoble "degraded" state that Indians overcome by progress naturally "withered" to the level of vermin. The images of nobility belong to a bygone era remembered only by "touching ballad" and "pathetic tale." The present lot of Indians deserved no such treatment. Apparently contradictory, noble and ignoble stereotypes actually complement each other in racist harmony.

The Myth of the Vanishing Indian crystallizes long-standing notions of a racially structured world. For more than a millennium, Europeans divided humankind between Christians and infidels. In more modern times, Europeans and Euro-Americans built on these categories to include differences in skin color. A complex cultural process that evolved over centuries, "color coding" attempted to demonize people not of European origin.[3] Both Native Americans and the growing numbers of enslaved Africans—Red and Black—thus ranked below White Americans.[4] Because both Africans and Indians could be—and often were—converted to Christianity, other distinctions, however specious, maintained the color lines. By the nineteenth century, a "science" based on the assumed superiority of White to non-White largely replaced or supplemented the older Christian/non-Christian dichotomy. Skin color served as an explanatory foundation—and justification—for advancing White Eurocentric cultural values often at the expense of both African American and Native American

---

2. To name only a few anthologies in which Sprague's "Roll Back the Tide of Time" (or variations of this title) appeared: Noble Butler, *The Common School Speaker* (Louisville, KY: Morton and Griswold, 1856), 47–48; Ainsworth R. Spofford and Charles Gibbon, eds., *The Library of Choice Literature and Encyclopedia of Universal Authorship*, Vol. 6 (Philadelphia, PA: Gebbie, 1893), 302–3; *Noble Lives of a Noble Race* (Minneapolis, MN: Brooks Press, 1909), 174–75; *The Republican*, Vol. 12 (London: R. Carlile, 1825), 612–14.

3. For a discussion that frames ideas of racial extinction in a world historical context, see Patrick Brant Linger, *Dark Vanishings: Discourses on the Extinction of Primitive Races, 1800–1930* (Ithaca, NY: Cornell University Press, 2003).

4. Although, for some, the "apelike," uncivilized Irish were the exception. Many, such as political cartoonist Thomas Nast, placed Indians above the Irish, who, starting in the mid-nineteenth century, began flooding the cities of the Northeast.

cultures. Furthermore, the Myth of the Vanishing Indian relies (and relied) on problematic population estimates for Native Americans, as discussed in the previous chapter. Population decline across time—however real—presumably indicated the inherent racial weakness of Indians. Their complete extinction could happen any day. Their passing could be mourned, but Indians must die away into "the untrodden West" as White civilization took its racially superior place on the continent.

Two popular poems by American writer William Cullen Bryant (1794–1878) imagine a continent covered with Indian graves. Although thematically his "Thanatopsis"[5] (1821) and "The Prairies" (1834) concern the mutability of all life, with the *entire* earth serving as "one mighty sepulcher," Bryant chose Indians as an example for the passing away of one race when confronted by a superior race. For with the westward advance of White settlers, "the red man . . . left the blooming wilds he ranged so long." But long before that, the "warlike and fierce Indians" destroyed the Mound Builders, "a disciplined and populous race." So the threat of unchecked savagery remained constant throughout time. Here Bryant subscribed to the popular notion that saw the ancient Mound Builders as members of a great race with no relationship to the "The red man. . . . The roaming hunter tribes." The Mound Builders "vanished from the earth."[6] In turn, the Indians themselves now faced the same destiny.

Early in James Fenimore Cooper's novel *The Last of the Mohicans* (1826), Chingachgook laments:

> Fallen, one by one: so all my family departed, each in his turn, to the land of the spirits. I am on the hilltop, and must go down into the valley; and when Uncas [his son] follows in my footsteps, there will no longer be any of the blood of the Sagamores, for my boy is the last of the Mohicans.[7]

After Uncas dies in battle with the Huron, Chingachgook cries out, "I am a blazed pine, in a clearing of the palefaces. My race has gone from the shores of the salt lake, and the hills of the Delaware."[8] As understood by Cooper's audience, and by readers for generations to come, Chingachgook stands emblematic of the fate awaiting all Indians.

---

5. "Thanatopsis" is a Greek word meaning "meditation on death."

6. Several studies that discuss the origin of the myth that the Mound Builders were from a now-extinct, non-Indian civilization are Donald J. Blakeslee, "John Rowzée Peyton and the Myth of the Mound Builders," *American Antiquity* 52 (1987): 784–92; and contra, Jeffrey K. Yelton, "A Comment on John Rowzée Peyton and the Mound Builders: The Elevation of a Nineteenth-Century Fraud to a Twentieth-Century Myth," *American Antiquity* 54 (1989): 161–65. See below, pp. 94–96, for a fuller discussion of the Mound Peoples and this myth.

7. James Fenimore Cooper, *The Last of the Mohicans* (Albany: State University of New York Press, 1983), 33.

8. Ibid., 349.

Cooper named Uncas after a Mohegan sachem (chief), an English ally in seventeenth-century Connecticut. Cooper merged the names of the Mohegan and Mahican tribes into "Mohican," initiating a popular confusion between the two peoples that continues to the present day. The Mohegan live today as a federally recognized tribe in Connecticut. The Mahican, originally based in the Hudson River Valley, currently live as a federally recognized tribe, the Stockbridge-Munsee Community, in Wisconsin.

Self-taught Philadelphia portrait painter George Catlin (1796–1872), whom we saw in Chapter 1, desired to leave "a monument to a dying race"[9] in his hundreds of paintings of Indians whom he met throughout the American West. Also a famed showman, Catlin toured North America and Europe with an exhibition that combined his paintings, extensive program notes, and dramatic lectures on Native American history and culture. He believed that his growing collection of canvases constituted a national treasure, and current scholarship concurs. Unfortunately, in his own time, harsh criticism, neglect by galleries, disinterest by the Smithsonian, and his own penchant for poor business decisions conspired to postpone his well-deserved acclaim until long after his death.

He ventured west in 1830. Over the next six years, he visited—by his own account—forty-eight tribes to "[Lend] a hand to a dying nation [and snatch] from a hasty oblivion what could be saved for the benefit of posterity."[10] He produced nearly five hundred sketches and portraits of individual Indians and drawings of the multiple facets of village life such as hunting, various ceremonies, and feasts. He defended the often unfinished or roughly sketched portraits that he displayed as evidence of the state of emergency under which he worked to record "wild Indians" before they "[melted] away at the approach of civilization."[11]

Catlin's motivations often appear contradictory. What part mercenary, what part dedicated artist, what part sympathetic friend of the Indian account for his work? In 1838, his father wrote about the Mandan smallpox epidemic: "[He] mourns the dreadful destiny of the Indian Tribes by the small pox . . . but unquestionably that shocking calamity will greatly increase the value of his enterprize [sic] & his works."[12] His son remarked:

> So have perished the friendly and hospitable Mandans, from the best accounts I could get; and although it may be *possible* that some few individuals may yet be remaining, I think it not probable; and one thing is

---

9. George Catlin, *The Letters of George Catlin and His Family: A Chronicle of the American West*, ed. Marjorie Catlin Roehm (Berkeley: University of California Press, 1966), 442.

10. George Catlin, *Letters and Notes on the Manners, Customs, and Condition of the North American Indian*, Vol. 2 (New York: Wiley and Putnam, 1844), 3.

11. Ibid., 17.

12. Catlin, *Letters of George Catlin*, 127.

certain, even if such be the case, that, as a nation the Mandans are extinct, having no longer an existence.[13]

He miscalculated. Today the Mandan, Hidatsa, and Arikara nations form the Three Affiliated Tribes in western North Dakota.[14]

Remove the Myth of the Vanishing Indian and the main articulated object of Catlin's mission crumbles. He hoped to gain fame as the artist who set out to salvage the last days of a dying race. So long as Indians agreed to disappear, his mission retained its urgency. Fortunately for Catlin, the myth far outlived him.

In photography, Edward S. Curtis (1868–1952) provided the myth with a perceived documentary realism often associated with the camera. Published from 1907 to 1930, his forty-volume work *The North American Indian* demonstrates his artistic prowess; scholars continue to study his facility with the camera and his eye for composition. Curtis established his theme for the series in the first volume's opening photograph, *The Vanishing Race—Navajo*. Silhouettes fading away anonymously in soft focus, several Indians on horseback ride off into a blurred distance. His caption states: "The thought which this picture is meant to convey is that the Indians as a race, already shorn in their tribal strength and stripped of their primitive dress, are passing into the darkness of an unknown future."[15] But he complicates the vanishing race theme subtly throughout the series. Indeed, near the end of his first volume, *Out of the Darkness*, he depicts Navajo riders emerging from Tesakod Canyon into bright sunlight. Such counterweights conveying survival and open futures for Indians appear to contradict Curtis' salvage rationale. Consistently, however, Curtis invoked statistics of Indian population decline to accentuate his governing refrain of the vanishing race.

Even when the 1910 U.S. Census indicated a nationwide Indian population increase, Curtis adhered to a race-based argument and claimed that numbers alone could not prevent the dissolution of Indian "characteristics."

> The final answer to the rise or fall of a race is not had in a census report. . . . Careful study will show that hundreds of tribes or bands existing four hundred years ago are extinct. Let any one of those who proclaims the Indian race is not a dying one, give even a month to a careful study of the subject, and he will forever cease to write in that strain. The serious student of the Indian is constantly face to face with the fact that he is dealing with a life of yesterday—not today or tomorrow.[16]

---

13. Catlin, *Letters and Notes*, 2:258.

14. MHA Nation, http://www.mhanation.com (accessed June 26, 2016).

15. Edward S. Curtis, *The North American Indian: The Complete Portfolios* (Cologne, Germany: Taschen, 2016), 36.

16. Edward S. Curtis, quoted in *Edward S. Curtis and the North American Indian Project in the Field*, ed. Mick Gidley (Lincoln: University of Nebraska Press, 2003), 135.

Reflecting a common notion of his time, Curtis regarded culture as a genetic inheritance; the disappearing "racial characteristics" of "tradition, lore, life and manners" meant that the race of Indians stood "almost at the vanishing point."[17] Curtis and many of his fellow Euro-Americans disregarded the historical agency of Indians and their ability to adapt to new circumstances. Narrowly and erroneously defined as "primitives," Indians could not belong to modernity; therefore, extinction loomed imminently before them. Indians belonged only to the past, "not today or tomorrow."[18]

The Vanishing American (1925), a novel by American writer Zane Grey (1872–1939), depicts White settlers, government officials, and missionaries as culprits who steal Indian land and forcefully convert Indians to Christianity. Originally serialized in *Ladies Home Journal,* the story elicited harsh criticism from religious groups and from the Bureau of Indian Affairs.[19] To deflect similar controversy, the novel's 1925 film adaptation minimalized White aggression to the action of only a few corrupt individuals, sidestepping any larger indictment of institutional culpability in the mismanagement of Indian affairs.[20] Moreover, the film explains the Vanishing American as a product of Social Darwinism, opening with the statement: "We have unmistakable proof that throughout all past time there has been a ceaseless devouring of the weak by the strong . . . the survival of the fittest." Next, fleeting images of presumably primitive peoples appear and disappear across the screen with the title card: "How many races?" The film concludes with the death of its Indian hero, Nophaie, signaling the fate of all Indians as a vanishing race.

Grey's novel ends with Marian, the White heroine and Nophaie's love interest, watching a group of Navaho ride away into

> a magnificent, far-flung sunset. . . . It was an austere and sad pageant. [The] dark forms, silhouetted against the pure gold of the horizon, began to vanish, as if indeed they had ridden into that beautiful prophetic sky. "It is—symbolic—" said Marian. "They are vanishing—vanishing! . . . My Nophaie—the warrior—gone before them." At last only one Indian was left on the darkening horizon . . . bent in his saddle, a melancholy figure . . . diminishing, fading, vanishing—vanishing.[21]

Grey's description invokes Curtis' photograph *The Vanishing Race—Navajo* and James Earle Fraser's statue *End of the Trail.* Modeled in 1894, displayed in plaster to wide acclaim in 1915, and first cast in bronze in 1918, the statue depicts a generic

---

17. Ibid., 134.

18. The notion that Indians belong only to the past raises issues that belong to the Myth of the Authentic Indian, to be discussed in the next chapter.

19. Thomas Pauly, *Zane Grey: His Life, His Adventures, His Women* (Urbana: University of Illinois Press, 2005), 51.

20. Frank Gruber, *Zane Grey* (New York: Word, 1970), passim.

21. Zane Grey, *The Vanishing American* (New York: Harper and Brothers, 1925), 308.

Indian slumped forward in his saddle as if drawn wearily earthward. His spear hangs down, as does his horse's head. "Diminishing, fading, vanishing—vanishing," the Indian rides into the grave.

Fraser's statue, included in this book's epilogue, has become a highly popular image of the American Indian. Reproduced and commercialized in almost every conceivable form as, for example, *End of the Trail* belt buckles, bookends, fine art desk ornaments, cremation urns, and iron-on patches, it sustains the Myth of the Vanishing Indian through its proliferation in the marketplace. Indeed, Fraser intended the statue to represent the Indian as a dying race, and there appears little room for ambiguity here. At the same time, however, he hoped that the statue might suggest a sustaining sense of the Indian's spiritual strength as symbolized by a strong wind—evidenced by the horse's tail whisking between its legs— and by the muscular body of the mounted rider. Admirable as these touches might be— and apologizers take pains to point them out—they appear overruled by the sculpture's name itself, *End of the Trail*, and by the overriding gravitational pull that plunges both horse and rider downward in defeat, although some commentators read the pose as a warrior at rest, steeling himself for the next battle.[22]

The Invention of the Anglo-Saxon Race

Seventeenth-century English colonials crossed the Atlantic with a firm belief in the purity of their Anglo-Saxon heritage. Whatever religious or political differences existed or eventually arose between colonials and Mother England, each side gloried in Anglo-Saxonism, in a myth that exalted the history, culture, and "race" of the Angles and the Saxons, two Germanic tribes that migrated to England in the fifth and sixth centuries. The result was a sense of English uniqueness as a "chosen people."[23]

By the revolutionary era, interpretations of the Anglo-Saxons as freedom-loving yeoman farmers generated significant political consequences. In *A Summary View of the Rights of British America* (1775), Thomas Jefferson recalled his Saxon ancestors,

---

22. For a succinct overview of Fraser and *End of the Trail*, see the National Cowboy and Western Heritage Museum, "End of the Trail: Introduction." The museum houses Fraser's massive original statue. The display is sensitively curated and interpreted, and the museum's current and ongoing work in addressing the Vanishing Indian Myth models resistance to censorship, the impulse toward which would have historically problematic artifacts—and the traumas sometimes evoked by them— hidden away or destroyed, effectively denying the complexities of the historical record. http://nationalcowboymuseum.org/learn-discover/online-unit-studies/end-of-the-trail-introduction/ (accessed December 12, 2016). For current controversy regarding *End of the Trail*, see Kim Schneider, "New Lesson for 'End of the Trail.'" *Winona Post*, January 7, 2015. http://www.winonapost.com/News/ArticleID/42195/New-lesson-for-'End-of-the-Trail' (accessed December 12, 2016).

23. Reginald Horsman, *Race and Manifest Destiny: The Origins of American Racial Anglo-Saxonism* (Cambridge, MA: Harvard University Press, 1981), 10.

who "left their native wilds and woods in the North of Europe [and] had possessed themselves of the island of Britain." From their Germanic homeland they (supposedly) brought customs of political democracy and established "that system of laws which had so long been the glory and protection of that country." Although "Saxon ancestors held their land in absolute dominion," the Norman French conquest of 1066 unhappily imposed a feudal order "under which all lands were held in absolute right." Jefferson drew a parallel here with the growing tension between the Crown and the American colonies, in which he equated the policies of King George III with the Norman French usurpation of Saxon rights. Jefferson threatened to take action in the spirit of his Saxon ancestors: "For themselves they fought, for themselves they conquered, and for themselves alone they have a right to hold."[24]

John Adams wrote that Jefferson desired the Great Seal of the United States to display

> The Children of Israel in the Wilderness, led by a Cloud by day, and a Pillar of Fire by night, and on the other Side Hengist and Horsa, the Saxon Chiefs, from whom We claim the Honour of being descended and whose Political Principles and Form of Government We have assumed.[25]

The great seal committees decided against Jefferson's proposal; however, not only does his design demonstrate the influence of the Myth of the Wilderness in his thinking, it also speaks to his belief in the destined disappearance of Native Americans. Jefferson wrote in 1803:

> In truth, the ultimate point of rest & happiness for them is to let our settlements and theirs [the Indians'] meet and blend together, to intermix, and become one people. Incorporating themselves with us as citizens of the U.S., this is what the natural progress of things will of course bring on, and it will be better to promote than to retard it.[26]

He expressed an increasingly popular concept. Only by their absorption into the Anglo-Saxon world would Indians survive. Their world—their languages and ways of life—belonged to primitive and outmoded traditions destined to vanish. The only salvation for Indians rested in citizenship. The sooner they embraced the Anglo-Saxon customs based on the sanctity of private property, agricultural arts, and democracy, the better. Indeed, both the Israelites and the Angles and Saxons had absorbed (or

---

24. Thomas Jefferson, "A Summary View of the Rights of British America," https://www.history. org/almanack/life/politics/sumview.cfm (accessed June 4, 2016).

25. John Adams, "Letter from John Adams to Abigail Adams, 14 August 1776," http://www.masshist.org/digitaladams/archive/doc?id=L17760814ja (accessed June 4, 2016).

26. Thomas Jefferson, "Letter to Benjamin Hawkins, February 18, 1803," http://www.let.rug.nl/usa/presidents/thomas-jefferson/letters-of-thomas-jefferson/jefl150.php (accessed June 5, 2016).

killed off) the Indigenous Peoples whom they conquered—or so men, educated as Jefferson had been, believed.

Jefferson and his intellectual colleagues stood at a transitional point in the ongoing interest in the Anglo-Saxon past. Rooted in an Enlightenment worldview, they emphasized a rational and scientifically based study of human affairs; therefore, they focused their energies primarily on scholarly interpretations of Anglo-Saxon political institutions. But the late eighteenth-century emergence of Romanticism took Anglo-Saxonism into new territory. Romantics tended to stress the unique characteristics of individuals and peoples. German Romantics developed the notion of *Volksgeist* (the spirit of a people), a distinctive spirit collectively possessed by each nation, or "folk." Since both German- and English-speaking peoples shared an idealization of Anglo-Saxon ancestry, *Volksgeist* proved mutually influential. The *Volk* originated as a distinctly individual tribal community that eventually developed into a nation; thus, *Volksgeist* emphasized the uniqueness both of political institutions and of a wider common cultural identity shared by a given people, an identity that primarily depended on the distinctive language that bound its people as a nation.[27] These ideas existed in one form or another long before the time of the Romantics, but the shifting political climate, in no small part due to the American Revolution, lent them a new focus. Scottish antiquarian John Pinkerton expressed this Romantic worldview:

> It is a self-evident proposition, that the author of nature, as he formed great varieties in the same species of plants, and of animals, so he also gave various races of men as inhabitants of several countries. A Tartar, a Negro, an American [Indian] differ as much from a German, as a bull-dog or lap-dog, or shepherd's cur, from a pointer. The differences are radical; and such as no climate or chance could produce: and it may be expected that as science advances, able writers will give us a complete system of the many different races of men.[28]

The Pseudoscience of Race and the Myth of the Vanishing Indian

Now roundly discredited as having no basis in scientific fact, "race science" lent authority to assertions of Anglo-Saxon superiority in world affairs. It attempted to demonstrate inherent racial differences through skeletal evidence and through the claims of phrenology, a particularly popular branch of pseudoscience. According to mainstream phrenologists, cranial measurements indicated differing intellectual

---

27. See Horsman, *Race and Manifest Destiny*, 32–36.

28. John Pinkerton, *A Dissertation on the Origin and Progress of the Scythians or Goths: Being an Introduction to the Ancient and Modern History of Europe* (London: John Nichols, 1787), 33–34, https://archive.org/details/bub_gb_0CoPAAAAYAAJ (accessed June 5, 2016).

capacities between races. For Native Americans, the "discoveries" made by race science proved significant.

American physician and phrenologist Dr. Charles Caudwell (1772–1853) claimed that Indians faced certain extinction because their skulls proved inferior to those of White men:

> The average size of the head of the Indian is less than the head of a white man. . . . The chief deficiency in the Indian head lies in the superiour [sic] and lateral parts of the forehead, where are situated the organs of Comparison, Causality, Wit, Ideality, and Benevolence. . . . In the organs of Combativeness, Destructiveness, Secretiveness, Caution, and Firmness, the functions of which constitute the dominant element of the Indian character, the development is bold. This analysis . . . enables us . . . to understand the cause of the peculiar ineptitude of that race of men for civil life. [The] Indian is retreating before civilization, and disappearing with the buffalo and elk, the panther, and grisly [sic] bear.[29]

In plain English, the Indian race lacked the intellectual capacity for civilization, which Caudwell and his readers understood as the sole province of the White race. Phrenology "proved" that the Indian character excelled primarily in warfare and destruction. Like similarly doomed animal species, the Indian race withered, "retreating before civilization."

Phrenology absolved Whites of any acts of violence that they committed against Indians; nature determined that inferior races fell before the advance of superior races. Monumental works like Samuel George Morton's *Crania Americana; or, A Comparative View of the Skulls of Various Aboriginal Nations of North and South America* (1839) included nearly one hundred pictures of Native American skulls that Morton gathered in the course of his research. Among his methods for determining the intellectual capacity of various Indian nations, Morton poured millet seed into each cranial cavity in his collection. Seed volume—in conjunction with his elaborate caliper measurements—invariably led to the conclusion that Indians belonged to an inferior race.

Collecting Indian crania from gravesites could be a lucrative enterprise. Anthropologist Franz Boas, celebrated as the "father of American anthropology," asked a museum "whether they would consider buying skulls . . . for $600; if they will, I shall collect assiduously. Without having such a connection I would not do it."[30]

---

29. Charles Caudwell, quoted in R. W. Haskins, *History and Progress of Phrenology* (Buffalo, NY: Steele and Peck, 1839), 110–11.

30. Franz Boas, *The Ethnography of Franz Boas: Letters and Diaries of Franz Boas Written on the Northwest Coast from 1886–1931*, ed. Ronald P. Rohner (Chicago: University of Chicago Press, 1969), 88. The Native America Graves Protection and Repatriation Act (NAGPRA), enacted in 1990, provides a legal tool, however cumbersome, for returning the unlawfully obtained human remains and cultural objects of Native Americans. See "National NAGPRA: Resources for Tribes,

Phrenology helped to perpetuate the Myth of the Vanishing Indian by lending an aura of supposed scientific proof to stereotypes regarding the racial deficiency of Indians. It explained the resistance of Native Americans to White civilization; they could not adapt to it because they lacked the intelligence to understand its superior state, and this inability sealed their doom. As Morton explained, "Their proximity for more than two centuries to European communities has scarcely effected an appreciable change in the manner of life; and as to their social condition, they are probably in most respects the same as the primitive epoch of their existence."[31] He declared that God in His "wise purposes" provided the White race with "a decided and unquestionable superiority over all of the nations of the earth." Otherwise, the "soil which now rejoices the hearts of millions of freemen would be . . . overrun by lawless tribes of contending Barbarians. Thus it is that the White race has been able to plant and to sustain its colonies in every region of the habitable earth."[32] Against such a superior race, made so by God's "wise purposes," the Indian faced certain demise. Morton's "scientific" argument slides seamlessly between theologically based suppositions and unsupported historical assumptions.

George Morton's protégé Josiah C. Nott (1804–31) admitted that Whites mistreated Indians; however, wealth and power naturally gravitated to the White race, so nature could only take its course. The inability of Indians to survive stemmed from their racially determined lot as "lazy, intemperate, improvident savages."[33] Historian Francis Parkman (1823–93) observed that a "savage lethargy of mind" seriously handicapped any hope of "improvement" for the Indian race.[34] Archeologist Ephraim George Squier (1821–88) claimed that Indians, however degenerate in the nineteenth century, had probably destroyed the superior Mound Builders civilization in the distant past.[35] In brief, leading nineteenth-century scientists, historians, and archeologists left little doubt that the racial inferiority of Native Americans doomed them to certain extinction. The evidence presented by scholars percolated throughout the popular press. For many White Americans the inevitable disappearance of the Indian came as a forgone, "proven" conclusion.

Native Alaskan Villages and Corporations, and Native Hawaiian Organizations," https://www.nps.gov/nagpra/TRIBES/INDEX.HTM (accessed June 3, 2017).

31. Samuel Morton, *An Inquiry into the Distinctive Characteristics of the Aboriginal Race of America* (Boston: Tuttle and Dennett, 1842), 13–14.

32. Samuel Morton, *Brief Remarks on the Diversity of the Human Species and on Some Kindred Subjects* (Philadelphia, PA: Merrihew and Thompson, 1842), 21–22.

33. Josiah C. Nott, *Two Lectures on the Connection Between the Biblical and Physical History of Man* (New York: Bartlett and Welford, 1849), 34.

34. Francis Parkman, *France and England in North America*, Vol. 1 (New York: Library of America, 1983), 401.

35. Ephraim George Squier and Edwin H. Davis, *Ancient Monuments of the Mississippi Valley* (Washington, D.C.: Smithsonian Books, 1988), 44.

Some scholars who studied the Mound Builders published studies whose conjectures underscored stereotypes of Native American racial ineptitude. Built of earth, wood, and thatch, hundreds of mounds in the Ohio and Mississippi River Valleys and throughout the Southeastern region of the United States had long fascinated European and Euro-American explorers. Scholars now understand the mounds as evidence of several politically complex, hierarchically structured societies that enjoyed two eras of special efflorescence, the Adena-Hopewell Period (c. 500 BCE to c. 400 CE) and the Mississippian Period (c. 900 to c. 1300). During both eras, but especially for the Mississippians, a vast trade and communications network linked cities and villages over an area that, at its fullest extent, stretched from the Great Lakes to the Gulf of Mexico and from present-day Oklahoma to western New York. However, by the late thirteenth century, the highly centralized Mississippian world began to break down and transform into regional polities and more localized cultural identities. Although only partly understood, the shift probably arose from a combination of political factionalism, migration of new peoples, and deforestation, which led to soil erosion and the depletion of food sources. Inter-village warfare escalated. By the mid-thirteenth century, peoples of the eastern plains and the Mississippian heartland engaged in a state of war that decimated populations, destroyed villages, and severely crippled transregional trade. By the end of the thirteenth century, ongoing warfare probably contributed to the general depopulation of the people who inhabited the Ohio-Mississippi confluence, a region identified by nineteenth-century scholars as the Vacant Quarter.[36] Possibly introduced by Hernando De Soto's expedition through the present-day Southeastern region of the United States (1539–42), smallpox devastated sixteenth-century Mound Builder populations in the Mississippi and Ohio River Valleys.

The work of some nineteenth-century scholars remains useful to the current understanding of changes in the Mississippian world, an understanding far from complete. However, assumptions based on racial distinctions cloud the work of these academics. Many thought it inconceivable that the Indians they saw could have any relationship to the Mound Builders. As already noted, according to this line of thinking, the Mound Builders belonged to a superior and long-vanished race. Ephraim George Squier claimed that skulls unearthed from an Ohio River Valley site appeared similar to those described by Samuel George Morton as Toltec, a category that at the time referred to ancient Indians of Central and South America, whose civilization, although considered "primitive" by these researchers, ranked much higher than what North American Indians achieved.[37] Thus phrenological evidence led Squier to

---

36. Timothy R. Pauketat, *Ancient Cahokia and the Mississippians* (Cambridge, UK: Cambridge University Press, 2010), 145–62.

37. Historical identity of the Toltec as a people distinct from the Aztec remains contested, although some scholars periodize them between the tenth and twelfth centuries. For Morton, Toltec referred to a group of "civilized nations of Mexico, Peru and Bogata. . . . In reference to their cranial

theorize that the Mound Builders probably originated in a Toltec region. He bolstered his claim by identifying architectural similarities between the mounds and the Mesoamerican pyramids and by determining a resemblance between artifacts excavated in both regions. Although current archeological evidence indicates a probable north-south trade axis that moved some degree of goods and ideas between the Mississippian region, whose inhabitants had constructed an essentially Indigenous culture, and Mesoamerica, Squier's theory stood firmly on a racial foundation.[38]

The Myth of the Vanishing Indian stems in part from the skewed endeavors of individuals who used highly problematic methods to support predetermined conclusions. They firmly believed in the racial inferiority of Indians and then invented evidence to support their racist assumptions. Their methods actually make a mockery of science. Indeed, the steps involved today in professionally accepted scientific research systematically attempt to eliminate bias and proceed through rigorous testing to arrive at factually based conclusions. Unfortunately, the now scientifically rejected idea of a biologically determined hierarchy of races has yet to be fully scrubbed from contemporary worldviews. Stereotypes persist, regardless of the modern understanding of racial distinctions as socially—not biologically—constructed. The Vanishing Indian Myth straddles the myths of Noble and Ignoble Indians; it reinforces the notion that Indians somehow continue to vanish because of their unsustainable cultural purity or because indolent ways condemn them to disastrous ends.

U.S. Indian Policy and the Myth of the Vanishing Indian

Perhaps the most politically consequential myth of Native American history, the Myth of the Vanishing Indian underscores the multiple shifts in Indian policy administered by the federal government. Many elements of federal Indian policy stand on two sections of the U.S. Constitution. Article I, Section 3 declares that "Indians not taxed" remain excluded from the census for purposes of apportioning state representatives and taxes. This section politically disenfranchised Indians. Article I, Section 8 (the Commerce Clause) stipulated that Congress possesses the power "to regulate commerce with foreign nations, and among the several States, and with the Indian tribes." Article I, Section 8 served as the constitutional foundation for a series of Trade and Intercourse Acts passed between 1790 and 1834. Some of these acts attempted to regulate commerce between Whites and Indians through a licensing requirement

---

remains . . . we discover the great difference between the Toltecan and American families. In the arts and sciences of the former we see the evidences of an advanced civilisation." See Samuel George Morton, *Crania Americana; or, A Comparative View of the Skulls of Various Aboriginal Nations of North and South America* (Philadelphia, PA: J. Dobson, 1839), 83–84.

38. Early White settlers thought that the ancient Puebloan ruins outside Farmington and Mesa Verde, Arizona were Aztec, and the names "Aztec Ruins" and "Montezuma's Castle" remain fixed on them today.

for traders. Other acts attempted to control the sale of liquor in Indian Country and to preserve peace by declaring Indian Country off-limits to White settlement. The acts also aimed to promote Christianity and education among Indians and to instill in them a value system based on the sanctity of private property. The Trade and Intercourse Acts attempted contradictory goals of segregation and assimilation. The methods for achieving both goals assumed the incompatibility of Indians with the White world. But most policy makers as well as most White Americans believed that Indians stood little chance of survival against the forces of modernity. Across the nineteenth century, and into the twentieth century as well, policy decisions increasingly displayed the tension between a professed moral obligation to "save" the Indian and the work of race science that appeared to prove the Indian's inevitable extinction. Many alterations in Indian policy subsequent to the Trade and Intercourse Acts attempted in part to *ease* the Indian into extinction.[39]

The Civilization Fund Act of 1819 addressed increasing concern with the education of Indians. It encouraged benevolent societies to establish schools with money provided through a "civilization fund" appropriated annually by Congress. The act stood premised on the Myth of the Vanishing Indian:

> Be it enacted [that] for the purpose of providing against the further decline and final extinction of the Indian tribes, adjoining the frontier of the United States, and for introducing among them the habits and arts of civilization, the President of the United States shall be authorized . . . to employ capable persons of good moral character, to instruct [Indians] in . . . agriculture . . . and for teaching their children in reading, writing, and arithmetic.[40]

One early supporter of the act, Jedidiah Morse of New York's Northern Missionary Society, warned that Indians faced the grim prospect of wasting away in a few generations "to become extinct forever! This is no fancied picture. In a few years it will be sad reality unless we change our policy towards them; unless effectual measures be taken to bring them over this awful gulf, to the solid and safe ground of civilization."[41]

Many well-meaning policy makers, missionaries, and teachers saw before them a humanitarian emergency. They reasoned that Indians must be saved from themselves. Left to their own devices, Indians could only wither away into extinction. These assumptions did not take into account the fact that Indians knew full well

---

39. Brian W. Dippie, *The Vanishing American: White Attitudes and U.S. Indian Policy* (Lawrence: University Press of Kansas, 1982), 50–51.

40. "An act making provision for the civilization of the Indian tribes adjoining the frontier settlements, 516–17 U.S. Statutes at Large 3 (1819)," https://memory.loc.gov/cgi-bin/ampage?collId=llsl&fileName=003/llsl003.db&recNum=2 (accessed July 13, 2016).

41. Jedidiah Morse, *A Report to the Secretary of War of the United States, on Indian Affairs* (Washington, D.C.: Davis and Force, 1822), 66.

how to adapt to change. For thousands of years North America's Indigenous Peoples adjusted and transformed their societies to create new political and social orders, to shape their environment to better suit their needs, and to creatively confront periods of crisis. Nineteenth-century savants could be excused for their ignorance of more historically distant changes in Indian life, such as long-distance migrations and adaptations to new environments. However, one set of contemporary changes should have been obvious to them, namely Indians' ongoing adoption of new technology as it became available through trade within the networks of their own nations and through their trade with Whites. In many ways, the Myth of the Vanishing Indian assumed that Indians lived in a state of perpetual childhood. Often with the best of intentions, reformers attempted to erase Native American cultures, hastily replace them with the values of the White world, and thus turn Indians into functioning adults. To remain in a "childhood" state meant certain doom for Indians.

In part, the Trade and Intercourse Acts strove to slow the supposed extinction of Native Americans by protecting them from unscrupulous White traders. On their part, American fur companies regarded many of the acts as hindrances to their trade with Indians. In particular, companies argued that Congress' ban on the sale of liquor to Indians permitted an unfair advantage to less scrupulous traders and to British and French rivals operating on U.S. soil.[42] The 1796 act[43] that established government-controlled trading posts—the factory system whereby an authorized "factor," or merchant, maintained each post—further angered the fur companies. In part, the factory system stemmed from benevolent designs to ensure that Indians could purchase quality goods at reasonable prices. Long-range national security interests also operated through the factory system. Good trade relations could help build military alliances in the event of future conflict with the Canadian English. At the same time, Jefferson saw the factory system as a beneficial means for drawing Indians into debt with the U.S. government. To pay off the debt, Indians would be forced to cede their land.[44]

---

42. One stipulation of Jay's Treaty (1795) required English surrender of several pre-revolutionary forts on the Great Lakes to the United States; however, British and French traders could remain at the forts and operate on American soil.

43. "An Act for Establishing Trading Houses with the Indian Tribes 452–53, U.S. Statutes at Large 1 (1796)," https://memory.loc.gov/cgi-bin/ampage?collId=llsl&fileName=001/llsl001.db&recNum=2 (accessed July 13, 2016).

44. In 1803, President Jefferson wrote to the governor of Indiana Territory, William Henry Harrison: "We shall push our trading houses, and be glad to see the good and influential individuals among [the Indians living near the Great Lakes] run in debt, because we observe that when these debts get beyond what the individuals can pay, they become willing to lop them off by a cession of lands." See "President Jefferson to William Henry Harrison, February 27, 1803," in *Documents of United States Indian Policy*, ed. Francis Paul Prucha (Lincoln: University of Nebraska Press, 2000), 22.

But American fur companies claimed that the factory system threatened free enterprise by selling goods to Indians at rates cheaper than the companies wanted to—or could—offer. Moreover, following the War of 1812, the North American geopolitical map shifted. The British threat to the United States diminished, but the United States remained uneasy about the potential for tribal alliances with the British, fears that would soon inform removal policy. Meanwhile, pressure from private trading companies, and grave institutional mismanagement of the government's twenty-eight trading posts, led to Congress' termination of the factory system in 1822.

The government's Indian removal policy stood as another federal action that attempted to "benevolently" slow the presumed extinction of Indians. The policy germinated during Thomas Jefferson's presidency (1801–9), advanced significantly in James Monroe's administration (1817–25), and matured under President Andrew Jackson (1829–37). In 1825, President Monroe sent a Special Message to Congress regarding Indian removal. His argument concerned only the removal of the Cherokee Nation in Georgia, but the document exemplifies many aspects of pro-removal reasoning for decades to come:

> The removal of the [Cherokee] tribes from the territory which they now inhabit [in] Georgia, under a well-digested plan for their government and civilization . . . would not only shield them from impending ruin, but promote their welfare and happiness. . . . It is impossible to incorporate them . . . in any form whatever, into our system. . . . Without a timely . . . provision against the dangers to which they are exposed . . . their degradation and extermination will be inevitable. . . . By the establishment of . . . a government over these tribes with their consent [the United States becomes] in reality their benefactors. . . . Conflicting interests . . . between them and our frontier settlements will cease. There will be no more wars between them and the United States. Adopting such a government, their movement will be in harmony with us, and its good effect be felt throughout the whole extent of our territory to the Pacific. It may fairly be presumed that, through the agency of such a government, the condition of all the tribes inhabiting that vast region may be essentially improved; that permanent peace may be preserved with them, and our commerce be much extended.[45]

Framing Indian removal as an act of benevolence echoed Jefferson's reasoning and stood as an article of faith for many well-intentioned individuals. Just as often it provided mere political cover. Powerful voices promoting the interests of White settlers demanded removal, so they adopted the necessary rhetorical stances that served their purposes. Accordingly, removal benefited Indians because it saved them from certain extinction, but only if they took advantage of federal programs that provided them with the tools

---

45. James Monroe, "Special Message to the Senate and House of Representatives of the United States, January 27, 1825," http://www.presidency.ucsb.edu/ws/?pid=66430 (accessed June 14, 2016).

for becoming civilized. First they must be removed from their eastern homelands and relocated west of the Mississippi, far from White settlements of the time.

President Andrew Jackson's 1829 State of the Nation report to Congress introduced the current state of Indian affairs on a note of feigned sadness: "Their present condition, contrasted with what they once were, makes a most powerful appeal to our sympathies." Forced always farther westward, "some of the tribes have become extinct and others have left but remnants to preserve for a while their once terrible names." The Whites "by destroying the resources of the savage doom him to weakness and decay." Jackson declared, "Humanity and national honor demand that every effort should be made to avert so great a calamity." He wondered rhetorically what could be done "to preserve this much-injured race." Focusing then on the Choctaw, the Cherokee, and the Creek, he hoped for their voluntary removal from their lands in the southeast to resettlement in an "ample district west of the Mississippi, . . . to be guaranteed to the Indian tribes as long as they shall occupy it" with only marginal intercession by the U.S. government "as may be necessary to preserve peace on the frontier and between the several tribes." To assist the Indians in their new lands, the "benevolent may endeavor to teach them the arts of civilization, [promote] union and harmony among them, [and] raise up [a] commonwealth, destined to perpetuate the race and to attest the humanity and justice of this Government."[46]

Jackson's report follows the contours of Monroe's written report to Congress four years earlier. Both relied on the Myth of the Vanishing Indian to justify removal, and both ostensibly considered removal an act of benevolence that reflected well on the magnanimity of the federal government. Also in 1829, Superintendent of Indian Affairs Thomas McKenny saw Indians as culpable in their own supposed demise and warned, "If the Indians do not emigrate, and fly the causes, which are fixed in themselves, and have proved so destructive in the past, *they must perish!*"[47] A number of prominent voices opposed removal but also based their reasoning on the Myth of the Vanishing Indian. In 1830 Senator Peleg Sprague declared that "the doom of Providence" likely meant that Indians "must perish." Therefore, let them "live out all of their days, and die in peace; not bring down their gray hairs in blood, to a foreign grave."[48] President Jackson signed the Indian Removal Act in May 1830.[49]

---

46. Andrew Jackson, "State of the Nation, 1829," http://www.let.rug.nl/usa/presidents/andrew-jackson/state-of-the-nation-1829.php (accessed July 16, 2016).

47. Thomas McKenny, *"Address" Documents and Proceedings Relating to the Formation and Progress of a Board in the City of New York, for the Emigration, Preservation, and Improvement, of the Aborigines of America* (New York: Vanderpool and Cole, 1829), 37–38.

48. Peleg Sprague, "Speech of the Honorable Peleg Sprague, Senator from Maine, Delivered in the Senate of the United States, April 16, 1830" in *Speeches on the Passage of the Bill for the Removal of all Indians, Delivered in the Congress of the United States, April and May, 1830* (Boston: Perkins and Marvin, 1830), 66.

49. "An Act to provide for an exchange of lands with the Indians residing in any of the states or territories, and for their removal west of the river Mississippi," 411–422, U.S. Statutes at Large 4 (1830),

Forced removal befell most of the Choctaw, Creek, and Cherokee over the course of the 1830s. Prior to the Trail of Tears, discussed in the previous chapter, Elias Boudinot, editor of the *Cherokee Phoenix*, the first Native American newspaper in the United States, supported the voluntary migration of Native Americans to lands beyond the Mississippi. This placed him at odds with anti-removal forces within his own nation. But at the same time he recognized the fallacy in the Myth of the Vanishing Indian and also saw its lethal consequences:

> It is frequently said that the Indians are given up to destruction, and that it is the will of Heaven, that they should become extinct and give way to the white man. . . . The causes which have operated to exterminate the Indian tribes, that are produced as instances of the certain doom of the whole aboriginal family appear plain to us. These causes did not exist in the Indians themselves, nor in the will of Heaven, nor simply in the intercourse of Indians with civilized man; but they are precisely such causes as are now attempted by the state of Georgia.[50]

The bureaucratic complexity that grew apace with removal led Congress to pass a bill in 1834 aimed at streamlining the existing system of superintendents and agents in the Bureau of Indian Affairs.[51] This elaborately detailed piece of legislation further entangled the role of the government in the lives of Native Americans.

Policy decisions made in Congress often relied on reports filed by commissioners who oversaw the Bureau of Indian Affairs. These reports embodied the race-based assumptions of the time. In 1838, Indian Commissioner T. Hartley Crawford cautioned against a too-hasty program for lifting Indians "out of the mire of folly and vice in which they are sunk." Their education must advance by degrees: "To teach a savage man to read, while he continues a savage in all else, is to throw seed on a rock." Crawford advocated a system of manual labor schools and a system for the allotment of land to individual Indians, otherwise "you will look in vain for any general casting off of savagism. Common property and civilization cannot co-exist."[52]

Ten years later, Commissioner of Indian Affairs William Medill framed White acts of violence against Indians as "a contest of civilization with barbarism. [Always] the weaker party must suffer, [so the Indian] soon sinks . . . and perishes." Medill

https://memory.loc.gov/cgi-bin/ampage?collId=llsl&fileName=004/llsl004.db&recNum=458 (accessed June 16, 2016).

50. Elias Boudinot, "Editorial, July 28, 1829," in *Cherokee Editor: The Writings of Elias Boudinot*, ed. Theda Perdue (Athens: University of Georgia Press, 1996), 103–5.

51. "An Act to provide for the organization of the department of Indian affairs 735–39, U.S. Statutes at Large 4, (1834)," https://memory.loc.gov/cgi-bin/ampage?collId=llsl&fileName=004/llsl004.db&recNum=782 (accessed July 17, 2016).

52. Report of the Commissioner of Indian Affairs, 25th Cong., 3rd. sess., 1838, H. Doc. 1, serial 338, 450–56.

concluded that "natural and unavoidable causes [not] willful neglect, or . . . deliberate oppression and wrong" generally account for the "rapid decline and disappearance of our Indian population." The commissioner brightens, however, and recognizes that thanks to "a wise and beneficent system of policy . . . to colonize our Indian tribes" beyond the reach of White population, Indians stand a chance for survival. Confined within small districts, Indians first hunt game animals until they become so scarce that to survive they will be forced to adopt agriculture and to learn trades taught in a system of manual labor schools.[53]

Medill's plan for "civilizing" Indians continued Crawford's plan, one also taken up by Commissioner of Indian Affairs Luke Lea, who declared in 1851, "The civilization of Indians within the territory of the United States is a cherished object of the government."[54] The federal government's reservation policy further solidified during Lea's tenure. In 1850 he formulated a design in which "There should be assigned to each tribe, for a permanent home, a country adapted to agriculture, of limited extent, and well-defined boundaries." His plan focused primarily on the Dakota and Ojibwe nations, but "within our widely extended borders . . . the great work of regenerating the Indian race" required the extensive and increasingly ambitious involvement of the federal government to supply Indians with "stock, agricultural implements, and useful materials for clothing; encourage and assist them in the erection of comfortable dwellings, and secure to them the means and facilities of education, intellectual, moral and religious."[55]

As commissioner of Indian Affairs, Lea also bore responsibility for the Wisconsin Death March. The march began with the attempted removal of the Wisconsin Ojibwe to the newly created Minnesota Territory, a move favored by influential territorial politicians and by local traders who saw opportunities for profit, since the removal would mean transferring the location of annuity payments. The new location, Sandy Lake, proved only to serve as a gravesite for the Wisconsin Ojibwe. Having traveled by canoe and by foot across hundreds of miles in late 1850, they arrived at Sandy Lake to find that the payments needed for their supplies had been delayed. As the weeks passed and still no payments arrived, illness, hunger, and exposure caused the deaths of 170 Ojibwe at Sandy Lake and another 230 deaths on the journey back to Wisconsin, according to Wisconsin Ojibwe leaders. Although debate continues regarding the total number of deaths, historians generally recognize that about 12 percent of the Wisconsin Ojibwe population perished.[56] Attempting to deflect any

---

53. Report of the Commissioner of Indian Affairs, 30th Cong., 2d sess., 1846, H. Doc. 1, serial 537, 385–86.

54. Report of the Commissioner of Indian Affairs, 32d Cong., 1st sess., 1851, H. Doc., serial 636, 273.

55. Report of the Commissioner of Indian Affairs, 31st Cong., 2d sess., 1850, S. Doc. 1, serial 587, 35.

56. James A. Clifton, "Wisconsin Death March: Explaining the Extremes in Old Northwest Indian Removal," *Transactions of the Wisconsin Academy of Sciences, Arts, and Letters* 75 (1987): 25.

government responsibility for the Sandy Lake travesty, Minnesota Territory Governor Alexander Ramsey wrote Indian Commissioner Lea, claiming, "Far from famine or starvation ensuing from any negligence on the part of the Government officers, the [Indians] received all that the Government was under treaty obligations to furnish to them."[57] What happened at Sandy Lake further strengthened the resolve of Wisconsin's Ojibwe bands to resist any further attempted removals.[58]

But removing Indians to reservations remained the primary policy objective of the U.S. government. Policy makers couched their rationale in benevolent terms, but removal always served the interests of settler colonialism. In 1856, Indian Commissioner George W. Manypenny called for increasing government involvement in Indian affairs because "the existing laws of the protection of the persons and property of the Indian wards of the government[59] are sadly defective." He pressed for federal aid to preserve "the remnants of the Indian tribes now left to [the government's] oversight and guardianship."[60] In 1862, Indian Commissioner William P. Dole enthusiastically endorsed the reservation system, but he thought that Indians "are capable of attaining a high degree of civilization," so the time might come when they could earn "their ultimate admission to all the rights of citizenship."[61] The 1867 report by the Doolittle Committee exhibited the race-based rationale that regarded Indians as genetically inferior to Whites. This congressional committee chaired by Wisconsin senator James Doolittle concluded that most Indian tribes "are rapidly decreasing in numbers . . . by the irrepressible conflict between a superior and an inferior race."[62]

Treaties between Indian nations and European colonial authorities and, later, the federal government, served primarily as a means for effecting Indian removals. But in 1871, Congress formally ended the treaty-making era in a rider on an appropriations bill. According to the rider, Indian nations would no longer be considered independent political entities; thus, they no longer possessed the legal right to enter into treaties. Yet the rider also declared that all treaties formerly signed between the

57. Alexander Ramsey, *Annual Report of Commissioner of Indian Affairs* (Washington, D.C., 1850), 162.

58. Historian Erik M. Redix sees the Sandy Lake tragedy as an act of ethnic cleansing: "Few accounts of Minnesota history even mention the deaths at Sandy Lake. The events at Sandy Lake in 1850 constituted a deliberate act of ethnic cleansing worthy of inclusion in narratives of Minnesota history and American history." Erik M. Redix, *The Murder of Joe White: Ojibwe Leadership and Colonialism in Wisconsin* (East Lansing: Michigan State University Press, 2014), 55.

59. The infantilization of Indians as "wards of the government" originated in Chief Justice John Marshall's 1831 decision on *Cherokee Nation v. Georgia*. See Chapter 3, p. 62.

60. Report of the Commissioner of Indian Affairs, 34th Cong., 3d sess., 1856, S. Doc. 5, serial 875, 571.

61. Report of the Commissioner of Indian Affairs, 37th Cong., 3d sess., 1862, H. Doc. 1, serial 1157, 169.

62. Report of the Joint Special Committee: Condition of the Indian Tribes, 39th Cong., 2d sess., 1867, S. Rept. 156, serial 1279, 3.

United States and Indian nations would be respected as legally binding in full accord with the Constitution. Effectively, the bill perpetuated the central ambiguity in U.S. policy regarding the sovereignty of Indigenous nations. Senators expressed a variety of positions as they argued the question: Are Indigenous groups foreign—and therefore sovereign—or not? Kentucky senator Garret Davis opposed the rider and supported continued federal recognition of Indigenous sovereignty,[63] a position that prompted Iowa senator James Harlan to remark, "Nations of Indians that might have been so recognized years ago may now be well regarded as having deteriorated to such an extent as to justify the adoption of this declaration [the rider] on the part of the Congress."[64] Harlan relies here on the Vanishing Indian Myth, thus revealing the function of the myth in the rider itself. Accordingly, perhaps soon, complete Indian extinction would make all treaties moot.

Debate in the House of Representatives underscored the national project of vigorous expansion made possible by continually upholding the interests of White settlers. In the colonialist-settler worldview, Indigenous tribes occupied *American* land. Therefore, an end to treaty making meant, in the words of Ohio representative William Lawrence, that "hereafter, the land policy of Congress cannot be broken up and destroyed by Indian treaties. Henceforth the homestead policy has become the fixed policy of Congress."[65] The 1862 Homestead Act granted White settlers and freed slaves the right to claim 160 acres of federally held Western land, former homelands of Indigenous nations.

The right of Indigenous nations to maintain their historically sovereign status has undergone continual challenges by federal and state institutions. Another serious challenge came with the 1887 General Allotment Act.[66] The act attempted to break up reservation land held in common by tribes and divide it into privately held parcels. These ranged from 40 to 160 acres for males based on age and marital status. So-called Friends of the Indians saw the allotments as a means for "elevating" Indians by eliminating their tribal identities and replacing them with new identities as both private property holders and American citizens. Allotment represented an attempt to erase Indian identity through assimilation into mainstream American culture, effectively making the Indian vanish.

But at the same time, the government only grudgingly granted citizenship to Indians with allotments. The Dawes Act required that each allotment be held by the government in a trusteeship for twenty-five years, and only then could the allottee apply for a fee simple title to the land, and only then would citizenship

---

63. Kevin Bruyneel, *The Third Space of Sovereignty: The Postcolonial Politics of U.S.-Indigenous Relations* (Minneapolis: University of Minnesota Press, 2007), 72–74.

64. James Harlan, quoted in Bruyneel, *Third Space of Sovereignty*, 74.

65. William Lawrence, quoted in Bruyneel, *Third Space of Sovereignty*, 76.

66. Also known as the Dawes Severalty Act, named after its principal author, Massachusetts senator Henry Laurens Dawes.

follow. Moreover, the Dawes Act allotted reservation land with or without the consent of the Indians themselves. Some saw allotment as their best chance for making a living, while others resisted. Moreover, the act required that each tribe sell its unallotted land to the U.S. government, which then opened the so-called surplus land for White settlement. But the tribes did not receive the proceeds from the sales directly. Rather, the government held the money in yet another trust account that financed supplies for Indians. The act effectively perpetuated the subjection of Indians as wards of the state, however much it promised the eventual "reward" of citizenship.

Communally held tribal land had provided a home for all tribal members, but allotment nearly destroyed those communities and left only deepening Indian poverty in its wake. Tribes owned nearly 150 million acres in 1887. After the repeal of the General Allotment Act in 1934, less than 50 million acres remained in tribal hands.[67] In 1890, Commissioner of Indian Affairs Thomas J. Morgan declared:

> It has become the settled policy of the government to break up reservations, destroy tribal relations, settle Indians upon their own homesteads, incorporate them into national life, and deal with them not as nations or tribes or bands, but as individual citizens."[68]

In summary, allotment functioned as an assimilation project through which the government unambiguously attempted to make Native Americans disappear, to deliberately attempt to fulfill the Myth of the Vanishing Indian. The legal machinery of the General Allotment Act was aimed at grinding down tribal identities and making Indians conform to mainstream White values. But poor soil made many allotments unsuitable for farming. Even with good soil, allotees lacked money for equipment and seeds. Many who survived the twenty-five-year waiting period and gained title to their land could not afford its real estate taxes, so they either lost their land to foreclosure or sold it to White settlers.

Finally, after decades of mounting evidence, the government recognized allotment as a failed policy, and in 1934, the Indian Reorganization Act (IRA) was an attempt to reset policy by recognizing the sovereign status of Indian nations and by supporting reservation economies. The IRA mandated restoration of Indian land, and since its enactment, it has resulted in the restoration of several million acres to tribes, and by reason of the act, the government currently holds approximately 56 million acres in

---

67. Stephen L. Peaver, *The Rights of Indians and Tribes* (New York: Oxford University Press, 2012), 9.

68. Thomas J. Morgan, *Message from the President of the United States to the Two Houses of Congress at the Beginning of the Second Session of the Fifty-First Congress, with the Reports of the Heads of Departments and Selections from Accompanying Documents* (Washington, D.C.: Government Printing Office, 1891), 690.

trust for them.[69] Although the Bureau of Indian Affairs recognizes tribes as sovereign governments on these lands, the continuing ambiguous nature of tribal sovereignty itself fuels ongoing legal disputes.

In 1928, Commissioner of Indian Affairs John Collier recognized the historical damage done by the Myth of the Vanishing Indian and called it out for its false assumptions and for the policy consequences that stemmed from them:

> For nearly 300 years white Americans, in our zeal to carve out a nation made to order, have dealt with the Indians on the erroneous, yet tragic, assumption that the Indians were a dying race—to be liquidated. We took away their best lands; broke treaties, promises; tossed them the most nearly worthless scraps of a continent that had once been wholly theirs. But we did not liquidate their spirit. The vital spark which kept them alive was hardy. So hardy, indeed, that we now face an astounding, heartening fact. Actually, the Indians, on the evidence of federal census rolls of the past eight years, are increasing at almost twice the rate of the population as a whole. . . . Dead is the centuries-old notion that the sooner we eliminated this doomed race, preferably humanly, the better.[70]

But Collier's speech could not magically eliminate the myth. It persists today as a common misconception. Non-Native Americans have internalized the myth often because they simply do not encounter Indians in their daily lives, especially in cities or in regions of the country that do not have high Indian populations. Therefore, they assume that the Indian must, indeed, be vanishing. The negative stereotype of Indians as drunks helps to fortify the notion that all Indians must not be long for the world. The stereotyped idea that Indians are—or already have—vanished also stems from the false perception that Indians lived only in the Wild West (itself a mythical land), and since those days are gone, Indians must have gone with it. Ignorance, both willful and innocent, continues to drive the Myth of the Vanishing Indian.

Canadian Indian Policy and the Myth of the Vanishing Indian

Significant Indian policy differences between the United States and Canada reflect divergences in the historical paths of the two nations. However, similarities persist, and federal policy decisions made by both governments often stand premised on the Myth of the Vanishing Indian. Canada's assimilation policy dates at least to the 1876

---

69. Bureau of Indian Affairs, https://www.bia.gov/WhoWeAre/BIA/OTS/FTT/index.htm (accessed June 5, 2017).

70. *Annual Report of the Secretary of the Interior for the Fiscal Year Ended June 30, 1938* (Washington, D.C.: Government Printing Office, 1938), 209, https://archive.org/details/annualreportof-se8231unit (accessed June 21, 2016).

Indian Act, which remains in effect today. Although attempting to "erase" Indigenous cultures, the act's complexities resist simple characterization, as indicated by its continued support by many prominent First Nation voices.

In 1967, Canada celebrated its confederation centennial. The world's fair in Montreal, Expo 67, served as the centennial's highlight. Although lavishing attention on Canada's White founders, the fair also included an Indians of Canada Pavilion. But confrontations between Expo 67 authorities and First Nation artists commissioned to design the pavilion demonstrated an official desire to control the Indigenous narrative. Artist Alex Janvier, of Dene Suline and Saulteaux descent, remarked: "How come our people are dying in the jails and rotting in the mental hospitals and here we're going to tell the world we're doing great? Let's tell it as it is"[71]

Thus the pavilion departed significantly from museum representations of Aboriginal culture common since the late nineteenth century in which displays of "pure" and "authentic" Indians trapped in a distant past often implied that assimilation alone provided their only means of survival. The pavilion stressed Indigenous grievances and featured negative images of contact with Whites. Although its message also embraced the past, the displays followed the principle that "the Past should not dominate the Present and the Future; the Present is the crucial part which should be projected."[72] The political statement made by the pavilion came as a shock to many fairgoers. It challenged stereotypes and faulted White Canadians for historical acts of aggression against Indians.

The pavilion's politics belonged within a growing national awareness of the marginalized position of First Nations in Canadian society. Indeed, in 1963 the federal government appointed anthropologist Harry B. Hawthorn to investigate the social, educational, and economic conditions of Canada's Indigenous Peoples. His report alarmed many of its readers: poverty, political disenfranchisement, and poor educational opportunities characterized the common lot for most Indigenous Peoples throughout Canada.[73]

Partly as a result of the Hawthorn Report came the 1969 white paper. Minister of Indian Affairs and Northern Development[74] Jean Chrétien (later prime minister of Canada) directed the new government policy that, in the words of the white paper, would enable Indians "to be free—free to develop Indian cultures in an environment of legal, social and economic equality with other Canadians."[75] In its zeal for the

---

71. Alex Janvier, quoted in Ruth B. Phillips, *Museum Pieces: Toward the Indigenization of Canadian Museums* (Montreal, Canada: McGill-Queen's University Press, 2011), 37.

72. Quoted in Phillips, *Museum Pieces*, 39.

73. Olive Patricia Dickason and William Newbiggig, *A Concise History of Canada's First Nations* (Toronto: Oxford University Press, 2010), 250.

74. Since November 2015, the designation is minister of Indigenous and Northern Affairs.

75. "Statement of the Government of Canada on Indian Policy (the White Paper)," https://www.aadnc-aandc.gc.ca/eng/1100100010189/1100100010191 (accessed July 11, 2016).

supposed benefits of complete assimilation into mainstream Canadian society, the white paper did not recognize Aboriginal rights; moreover, it called for the cancellation of all treaties.

Widespread criticism came swiftly, and it packed lethal consequences for the white paper. Dave Courchene, president of the Manitoba Indian Brotherhood, proclaimed:

> I feel like a man who has been told he must die and am now consulted on the method of implementing this decision. . . . A hundred or more years of acceptance on the part of the Indians, of policies and programs fostered by political experts who at the same time considered themselves amateur sociologists has led us once again up the garden path of false hopes, broken promises, colossal disrespect and monumental bad faith.[76]

Harold Cardinal, leader of the Indian Association of Alberta, called the white paper "a thinly disguised programme of extermination through assimilation."[77] In 1970 the association rejected the white paper in its document *Citizens Plus*, which became popularly known as the "red paper." It declared, "There is nothing more important than our treaties, our lands and the well-being of our future generations," and it served as a rallying point for Aboriginal associations throughout Canada.[78] The white paper survived less than two years. Prime Minister Pierre Elliott Trudeau conceded, "The government was very naïve . . . too theoretical . . . too abstract . . . not pragmatic enough or understanding enough,"[79] and the white paper's formal retraction came in March 1971.

The discredited white paper had proposed to abolish the 1876 Indian Act and to dismantle the Department of Indian Affairs and Northern Development. Regardless of the problems with both the act and the department, the white paper's wide-sweeping assimilation program would have meant the erasure of legal distinctions, rights, and land long possessed by Canada's Indigenous Peoples. Legally, the white paper made the Indians vanish.

The 1876 act built on the foundation of two previous Indian policy acts.[80] The Gradual Civilization Act (1857), which failed miserably in its goal to assimilate Indigenous Peoples into White society, and the Gradual Enfranchisement Act

---

76. Dave Courchene, quoted in Arthur J. Ray, *Illustrated History of Canada's Native People: I Have Lived Here since the World Began* (Montreal, Canada: McGill-Queen's University Press, 2011), 334.

77. Harold Cardinal, *The Unjust Society: The Tragedy of Canada's Indians* (Edmonton, Canada: M. G. Hurtig, 1969), 1.

78. *Citizens Plus*, *Aboriginal Policy Studies* 1, no. 2 (2011): 188–281, http://www.sabar.ca/glossary-term/citizens-plus/ (accessed July 11, 2016).

79. Pierre Elliott Trudeau, quoted in Frédéric Bastien, *The Battle of London: Trudeau, Thatcher, and the Fight for Canada's Constitution* (Toronto, Canada: Dundurn, 2014), 48.

80. The Indian Act's ancestry ultimately dates to the Royal Proclamation of 1763, which recognized Indians as a distinct political unit within the colonial system and constructed the constitutional framework for treaty negotiations between England and Canada's Indian nations.

(1869), which proved far more successful than its predecessor, primarily because it granted unprecedented control to the superintendent general of Indian Affairs and simultaneously restricted the power of band councils to oversee their own affairs. (Enfranchisement refers to the legal process for terminating an individual's Indian status and replacing it with Canadian citizenship.) With confederation in 1867, the newly empowered federal government sought to write a single code of laws to govern all Aboriginal groups. The diversity of political structures within and between groups of Indigenous Peoples fell under a single system of control, the Indian Act of 1867, which effectively defined Indians as wards of the state.

Among the many amendments attached to the Indian Act over time—and up to the present day—one of the most controversial came in 1884. Popularly known as the Potlatch Law, it banned perhaps the most important ceremony for Indians living in the Pacific Northwest, the potlatch ceremony, a gift-giving feast essential to the social fabric of these nations. The potlatch marked important occasions and served a crucial role in the distribution of wealth within First Nation communities. Canadian colonists and missionaries saw the ceremony as excessive and wasteful. Moreover, they thought that the communal nature of the ceremony interfered with assimilation tactics. Wealth redistribution must give way to the sanctity of private property.

Resistance to the law was sharp and persistent.[81] Namgis chief Dan Cranmer hosted an underground potlatch in British Columbia's Alert Bay to celebrate a wedding. The ceremony stretched over six days in late December 1921, until authorities arrested about fifty guests, confiscated hundreds of potlatch items—masks, regalia, and food—and later sentenced twenty-two guests to jail for two months.[82] Judge Alfred Scow, the first Aboriginal judge appointed to the Provincial Court of British Columbia, described the Potlatch Law:

> This provision of the Indian Act was in place for close to 75 years and what that did was it prevented the passing down of our oral history. It prevented the passing down of our values. It meant an interruption of the respected forms of government that we used to have, and we did have forms of government be they oral and not in writing before any of the Europeans came to this country. We had a system that worked for us. We respected each other. We had ways of dealing with disputes.[83]

Alarmed by the increasing political activity of Aboriginal groups in the 1920s, particularly in their pursuit of land claims, the federal government amended the Indian Act to outlaw the hiring of lawyers and legal counsel by Indians. This effectively

---

81. Douglas Cole and Ira Chaikin, *An Iron Hand upon the People: The Law against the Potlatch on the Northwest Coast* (Seattle: University of Washington Press, 1994), 1–24.

82. Ibid., 119–20.

83. Alfred Scow, *Royal Commission on Aboriginal People*, 344–45, http://scaa.sk.ca/ourlegacy/solr? query=ID%3A30466&start=0&rows=10&mode=view&pos=0&page=4 (accessed July 18, 2016).

barred Indigenous Peoples from access to Canadian courts. Indeed, further amendments strictly prohibited Indians from any type of gathering, forcing Aboriginal political organizations to disband or to go underground.

But changes made to the Indian Act in 1951 reflected the government's growing recognition that the injustice and poverty experienced by many Aboriginal people required legal and economic remedies. In part, Canada's commitment to the United Nations Universal Declaration of Human Rights led to the deletion of the more onerous laws that restricted freedom of movement and denied the practice of traditional tribal ceremonies. The changes included a striking down of the Potlatch Law, a lifting of the prohibition that required Indians to receive official permission to leave their reserves in ceremonial dress, and eliminating the ban against gambling by First Nations people. Laws against the consumption of alcohol by Indians, however, remained. Changes made to the act also allowed Indians to organize politically and hire legal counsel, and Indian women could once again vote in band councils.

Gender discrimination, however, appeared in several sections of the Indian Act. According to Section 12, an Indian woman's marriage to a White man automatically terminated her legal identity as an Indian, so she lost treaty benefits, health benefits, the right to live on her reserve, inherit her family property, and be buried with her ancestors.

Lengthy court battles culminated in a 1982 ruling by the United Nations Human Rights Committee that identified Section 12 as a human rights abuse. Three years later, in an amendment to the Indian Act, lawmakers attempted to reinstate the rights of Aboriginal women; however, weaknesses in the amendment continue to contradict Canada's Charter of Rights and Freedoms, which constitutionally guarantees gender equality. Marginalization of Aboriginal women in Canada remains an ongoing issue today.

The Assembly of First Nations describes the Indian Act as a form of apartheid. However, the act acknowledges and affirms the historical and constitutional relationship between First Nations and the Canadian government; therefore, efforts to abolish the Indian Act continue to meet with widespread resistance. Harold Cardinal explained in 1969:

> We do not want the Indian Act retained because it is a good piece of legislation. It isn't. It is discriminatory from start to finish. [But] we would rather continue to live in bondage under the inequitable Indian Act than surrender our sacred rights. Any time the government wants to honour its obligations to us we are more than happy to help devise new Indian legislation.[84]

First Nations peoples have refused to "vanish" in accord with federal laws that sought to legally terminate their identities. Paradoxes inherent in the Indian Act and its many amendments made over that past 140 years underscore the complex historical relationship between First Nations and the Canadian government.

---

84. Cardinal, *Unjust Society*, 140.

Indian Education Systems: Curricula for the Vanishing Indian

Social Darwinism (popularly known as "survival of the fittest," a phrase coined by Herbert Spencer in 1864 based on his understanding of Charles Darwin's theory of evolution) provided some of the philosophical underpinnings for the establishment of Indian education programs in the United States and Canada in the nineteenth century. Proponents of these programs argued that education would quicken the process for Indian children to rise from "savagery" to the highest stage of social evolution, that of Western civilization.[85]

In 1877, Congress began appropriating money for Indian education. Three types of schools would soon be established—the reservation day school, the reservation boarding school, and the off-reservation boarding school. Two years later, following a study of Indian education in the United States, Canada launched its own system, which included day schools and on- and off-reservation residential schools.

Both systems suffered from chronic underfunding, perennially unqualified teachers, and, in the boarding and residential schools, a toxic physical environment that contributed to persistent smallpox and tuberculosis epidemics.[86] In 1907, Canadian government medical inspector P. H. Bryce reported that 24 percent of previously healthy Aboriginal children across Canada died while attending school. But schools frequently sent critically ill students home. Bryce reported that 47 to 75 percent of these discharged students died shortly thereafter.[87] Underfunding meant that students often spent most of the day growing food, cooking, baking, mending and washing clothes, and performing janitorial work. The schools operated with zero tolerance for students who spoke in a language other than English. Penalties included corporal punishment and solitary confinement. Indeed, the prime directive called for eradication of all traces of Indian culture. The students must be remade as productive American or Canadian citizens. Ultimately, they would not need reservations, so their land would be sold. In short, the Indian would be eliminated. A mission of ethnic cleansing informed nearly every aspect of the schools.

Now recognized as a shameful chapter in Canadian history, the residential school era from 1879 to 1986 displayed the consequences of rigorous social engineering designed to erase Indian identities. During treaty negotiations, First Nation representatives requested schools on their reserves, and in Treaty One (1871) the government promised to "maintain a school on each reserve . . . whenever the Indians of

---

85. For example, Commissioner of Indian Affairs Thomas J. Morgan intoned: "Time as an element in human progress is relative, not absolute. A good school may thus bridge over for [the Indians] the dreary chasm of a thousand years of tedious evolution." Qtd. in David Wallace Adams, *Education for Extinction: American Indians and the Boarding School Experience, 1875–1928* (Lawrence: University Press of Kansas, 1995), 19.

86. Ibid., 131–35; John S. Milloy, *A National Crime: The Canadian Government and the Residential School System, 1879–1986* (Winnipeg, Canada: University of Manitoba Press, 2006), 77–78.

87. Milloy, *National Crime*, 91.

111

the reserve should desire it."[88] Subsequent treaties continued to include language that promised reserve schools. However, instead of the desired system of day schools in which children continued to live at home, the federal government developed a system of residential schools. Often removed forcefully from their homes, Aboriginal children spent months and even years away from their families to attend these schools. As instruments of assimilation, residential schools operated primarily to indoctrinate children into Euro-Canadian society. Residential schoolchildren would then become the last generation of Indians, and the Indigenous Peoples of Canada would vanish from the earth.

The system owes much to a study of industrial schools for Indian children in the United States that Prime Minister Sir John A. Macdonald learned about from the journalist and politician Nicholas Flood Davin. Davin recommended that Canada follow the "aggressive civilization" model that he found in the United States: "If anything is to be done with the Indian, we must catch him very young. The children must be kept constantly within the circle of civilized conditions."[89] Laws for the compulsory attendance of Indian children in residential schools escalated over the decades, and in 1920, amendments made to the Indian Act required mandatory attendance at residential schools for all Indian children and outlawed their attendance at any other educational institution.[90]

In 1996, the Royal Commission on Aboriginal Peoples interviewed Indigenous People across Canada about their residential school experiences. Based on the commission's recommendations, the Canadian government publicly apologized to former students for the physical and sexual abuse they suffered in the residential schools, and it established a $350 million plan to aid communities affected by the residential schools. In 2005, the Assembly of First Nations won a class action lawsuit against the Canadian government for the long-lasting harm inflicted by the residential school system. In 2008, the House of Commons gathered in a nationally televised ceremony to again publicly apologize for the government's involvement in the residential school system. The apology met a range of responses. Some thought it marked a new, positive era in relations between the federal government and First Nations; others considered it superficial and doubted that relations would change much.[91]

The boarding school system in the United States solidified under Grant's Peace Policy of 1869–70, which, in an effort to institute a humane policy free of corruption, turned over the administration of Indian reservations to Christian denominations that would establish both day and boarding schools on reservation lands. These

---

88. Articles of a Treaty, *Sessional Papers of the Dominion of Canada* 5 (1872): 20.

89. Nicholas Flood Davin, "Report on Industrial Schools for Indians and Half-Breeds," https://archive.org/stream/cihm_03651#page/n5/mode/2up (accessed July 13, 2016).

90. J. R. Miller, *Shingwauk's Vision: A History of Native Residential Schools* (Toronto, Canada: University of Toronto Press, 2012), 169.

91. Hanson, "Indian Act," 140.

Christian groups used this authority to evangelize and to attempt to stamp out Indigenous religious beliefs—often by force. Then in 1879, Richard Pratt founded Carlisle Indian Industrial School as the first off-reservation boarding school. He argued that schools situated on reservations defeated efforts to assimilate the children into American society. They must be removed entirely from the influence of their families. He proposed a system whereby children would be taken far from their homes at an early age and not returned until adulthood.

Pratt proposed to "kill the Indian in him and save the Man."[92] Carlisle served as a template for Indian boarding schools throughout the United States. Generally, the schools prepared Indian boys for lives of manual labor and Indian girls for domestic work, effectively replacing their former Native American identities with the gender roles common to White American culture. Rather than returning them to their homes for the summer, the schools often leased children out to White homes as menial laborers.

By 1900, twenty-five off-reservation schools enrolled a total of 7,430, and eighty-one boarding schools on reservations enrolled 9,600 students.[93] Situations in boarding schools varied widely across the system. Some graduates spoke well of their education and reported generally positive experiences at their schools. Moreover, some scholars argue that the off-reservation boarding school experience fostered a politically beneficial pan-Indianism. Although formerly separated by language and culture, students from areas throughout the country lived and worked together, developed friendships, and often married former classmates. Many found work in the Indian Service, and others returned to their reservations to seek active roles in tribal politics.[94] Sometimes local Indigenous People managed to exercise considerable control over the direction taken by school authorities, as, for example, in the Albuquerque and Santa Fe Indian Schools. Largely because a number of Pueblo communities surrounded both schools, parents could influence curriculum decisions and could allay assimilation measures that otherwise sought to erase their children's Indian identities.[95]

However, boarding school students often spent their school years as common laborers, field hands, custodians, servants, and laundresses, and they received negligible educations. By the late 1920s, and throughout the following decades, increasing

---

92. Richard Pratt, "The Advantages of Mingling Indians with Whites," in *Americanizing the American Indians: Writings by the "Friends of the Indian" 1880–1900*, ed. Francis Paul Prucha (Cambridge, MA: Harvard University Press, 1973), 260.

93. Francis Paul Prucha, *The Great Father: The United States Government and the American Indians*, abridged ed. (Lincoln: University of Nebraska Press, 1986), 280.

94. Brenda Child, "Boarding Schools," *Encyclopedia of North American Indians*, ed. Frederick E. Hoxie (Boston: Houghton Mifflin, 1996), 80.

95. For case studies of these schools, see John R. Gram, *Education at the Edge of Empire: Negotiating Pueblo Identity in New Mexico's Indian Boarding Schools* (Seattle: University of Washington Press, 2015).

public and federal scrutiny revealed the dire conditions in which many students lived and the substandard educations they received. By midcentury most schools had closed their doors, and by the 1970s, community-based schools and tribal colleges managed by Indian nations began to be established on reservations throughout the country. Today, thirty-two tribal colleges and universities enroll approximately thirty thousand full- and part-time students.[96]

The residential Indian school system in the United States left a disgraceful record. In the year 2000, the Bureau of Indian Affairs (BIA) marked its 175th anniversary. During an anniversary ceremony, Assistant Secretary of Indian Affairs Kevin Gover acknowledged the error of the BIA's efforts to eliminate Native American languages and cultures through the boarding school system:

> This agency forbade the speaking of Indian languages, prohibited the conduct of traditional religious activities, outlawed traditional government, and made Indian people ashamed of who they were. [The BIA] committed these acts against the children entrusted to its boarding schools, brutalizing them emotionally, psychologically, physically, and spiritually. . . . The trauma of shame, fear and anger has passed from one generation to the next, and manifests itself in the rampant alcoholism, drug abuse, and domestic violence that plague Indian country. . . . And so today I stand before you as the leader of an institution that in the past has committed acts so terrible that they infect, diminish, and destroy the lives of Indian people decades later, generations later.[97]

Today, there are 567 federally recognized Indian nations in the United States. According to the 2010 census, 5.2 million people identify as Native American or Alaska Native, including those of more than one race. The U.S. Census Bureau projects that the population of Native Americans and Alaska Natives, including those of more than one race, will increase to 8.6 million by 2050.[98] In light of these statistics, the Myth of the Vanishing Indian must be put to rest once and for all.

---

96. Department of Education: Tribal Colleges and Universities, https://sites.ed.gov/whiaiane/tribes-tcus/tribal-colleges-and-universities/ (accessed June 5, 2017).

97. Kevin Gover, "Ceremony Acknowledging the 175th Anniversary of the Establishment of the Bureau of Indian Affairs, September 8, 2000," http://www.twofrog.com/gover.html (accessed July 14, 2016).

98. U.S. Census Bureau, https://www.census.gov/newsroom/releases/archives/facts_for_features_special_editions/cb11-ff22.html (accessed July 7, 2017).

5. No Feather, No Indian: The Myth of the Authentic Indian

Our warriors kicked full speed into their mounts and went racing after [the buffalo], whooping wildly to strike terror in the herd and make them break in confusion. "Therump, therump, therump"—the ground fairly shook under the beat of our horses' pelting hoofs. . . . Most of [the warriors] were using their bows and arrows first, and they would not pull a string until they were racing along right over the left shoulder of the buffalo. Then, "fluck!"—and a long, steel-tipped arrow would bury itself deep in the shaggy withers of the beast, and it would take a few steps and pitch forward, pierced through the heart. But the buffalo died hard—they rolled and mooed and struggled valiantly for a second or two before shivering and stiffening out under the final thrust of death. One of our boys, Shakes-the-Other-Fellow . . . went crashing right into the pile of rolling buffalo. [He] became so excited . . . that he shoved his hands deep into the wool of one of their backs and took a mighty hold on it. . . . The buffalo [raced] away wildly with the boy sitting upon its back with his hand sunk into its wool. Some of the warriors saw this and they galloped after it [for] nearly a half-mile. They shot it four times before it hit the ground . . . and sent young Shakes-the-Other-Fellow sprawling to the turf. [Next] we travelled northeastward [to] the big Sun Dance camp . . . where for ages past the Blackfeet had sent their young men through the terrible tortures of "brave-making." The massive camp . . . was about two miles long. The hundreds of beautifully painted teepees were thrown in a huge circle [and] in the center of the campus we could see the skeleton of the Sun Dance lodge.[1]

As told by Chief Buffalo Child Long Lance in his 1928 autobiography, these and other childhood adventures charmed many readers, and his book produced highly favorable reviews in both the United States and Canada. However, for some readers, the book did not seem quite plausible. By the time of Long Lance's childhood days in the 1890s, bison no longer roamed the plains; indeed, by then they faced extinction. Moreover, by then nations of the Blackfoot Confederacy to which he claimed membership lived generally impoverished lives on American reservations and Canadian reserves. Warriors

---

1. Chief Buffalo Child Long Lance, *Long Lance* (New York: Cosmopolitan Books, 1928), 116–22.

no longer raced across the plains in pursuit of thundering herds of bison. At best, Long Lance described a way of life that belonged to decades long gone by the 1890s. Long Lance did not write an autobiography. He wrote a book of fiction. In fact, he lived a life of fiction. Finally, his masquerade fell apart. Exposure proved fatal. He committed suicide in 1932.

Although both his mother and father, Joe and Sallie Long, claimed Indian ancestry, they also descended from African American slaves and from White slaveowners. Because the "one drop [of Negro blood]" rule automatically classified them as Black, the Longs could not hope for opportunities and privileges freely open to Whites, especially in the Jim Crow days of the American South.[2] The child who became Long Lance grew up as Sylvester Clark Long in a segregated Winston, North Carolina neighborhood. His parents and the local Black preachers promised rewards in the next world if he, and all other African Americans, humbly accepted their lot. But he chaffed against enforced subservience to Whites, ever-present racial taunts, and even the threat of lynching by White mobs. After elementary school, he started Slater Normal School in Winston, thinking that he might train as a teacher, a lawyer, or a journalist, but he could never hope to work outside of African American neighborhoods; facing an insufferably race-restricted future, he dropped out. Only by reinventing himself could he hope to escape.[3]

Claiming a half-blood Cherokee ancestry, he gained admission to the Carlisle Indian Residential School in Carlisle, Pennsylvania. His classmates came from Indian nations across the country, including the Cherokee, and most students eyed him suspiciously. Sylvester had, however, picked up a few words of Cherokee during his brief stints as a circus worker, enough to convince Carlisle authorities of his authenticity. Moreover, his light complexion and his straight black hair helped him "pass" as an Indian, but questions about his true identity continued for the rest of his life.[4]

After graduating from Carlisle, his masquerade grew increasingly complex. Three years at St. John's Military Academy led to an appointment from the War Department for the West Point entrance exams, which earned him a *Washington Post* story that described him as a full-blooded Cherokee destined to bring honor to his race.[5] He failed the entrance exams, but with the newspaper clipping in his scrapbook

---

2. According to the "one drop" rule, an individual with any demonstrable African ancestry became socially and legally classified as Black. See F. James Davis, *Who Is Black: One Nation's Definition* (University Park: Penn State University Press, 2001). In North Carolina, where Sylvester grew up, in order to be classified "White," a person had to be less than one-eighth "African"; in other words, the single African ancestor had to be more distant than a great grandparent.

3. Donald B. Smith, *Chief Buffalo Child Long Lance: The Glorious Imposter* (Red Deer, Canada: Red Deer Press, 2000), 22–32.

4. Sylvester's father claimed one-quarter Eastern Cherokee ancestry, and his mother claimed one-quarter Croatan ancestry. See Smith, *Chief Buffalo Child Long Lance*, 33–34 and 41–42.

5. Ibid., 69.

augmenting his Indian identity from half-blood to full-blood Cherokee, he enlisted in the Canadian armed forces in August 1916, declaring West Point as his previous military experience. He served with distinction, took shrapnel in his legs, and after the war returned to Canada. A talented writer, he worked for a number of major Canadian papers under the byline, Long Lance.

Although transformed from African American to full-blood Cherokee, he did not stop there. While living in Calgary, he refashioned himself as a member of the Blood, one of the Blackfoot Confederacy nations. He managed to gain adoption into the tribe and to earn a new name, Buffalo Child. Nonetheless, the Blood considered him a mere honorary member of the nation, in part as a sign of appreciation for Long Lance's sympathetic newspaper stories regarding Canadian injustice against Indians, but they questioned whether he actually came from any Indian background whatsoever. His intention to profit commercially from his new identity soon became clear, much to the dismay of the Blood.[6]

But as a writer, and as a well-paid lecturer, he aimed exclusively at a White audience. There, Blood disapproval went unheard. He claimed descent from warriors, invented his Indian childhood wholesale, and even gave himself the title of chief. He staged widely published photographs in which he wore traditional tribal clothing that often ignored cultural and historical accuracy. For one photo he donned pants that probably came from the Crows in Montana, a tobacco pouch from the Blood, a Blackfoot vest, and a headdress used in the Blackfoot Chicken Dance, his short hair hidden under a wig with two long braids.[7] The mash-up appeared fully authentic to White eyes. Members of the Blood Nation knew otherwise.

His readers and listeners marveled at his adventure stories of exotic warriors and at his arrestingly detailed explanations of the ceremonies, dances, and daily lives of Plains Indians; moreover, he often placed himself squarely in the midst of the action. The more stories he told, the more authentic he became. Knowing what the White world thought it already knew about Indians, he displayed a genius for confirming the stereotype. Well-crafted fictions with the ring of authenticity, his tales beguiled American and Canadian audiences. This handsome, powerfully built, erudite, and impeccably dressed man further enhanced his credibility as an Indian by continually professing a deep admiration of the White world, of "civilization." Again, he knew how to gratify his audience. International fame, invitations to high-society ballrooms, and easy access to women infatuated by his exotic charm—all would have been denied him had his true identity been known.

His starring role in *The Silent Enemy* (1930) solidified his image as an Authentic Indian. As Baluk, a fictional Ojibwe hunter, he battles blizzards, wolves, and mountain lions in the Canadian north to save his people from starvation by tracking down

---

6. Ibid., 81–135.

7. Ibid., 148.

The Caption Reads: "Arrayed in full festive regalia of his tribe, Chief Buffalo Child Long Lance, author of 'When the Indians Owned Manitoba,' presents a picturesque and striking appearance. The Chief is in reality a full-blooded Indian chief. He is a graduate of Carlisle University in the United States. An all-around athlete, for several years he was a member of the famous Carlisle football team and played along with Jim Thorpe, of international fame." Chief Buffalo Child Long Lance, "When the Indians Owned Manitoba," *Winnipeg Tribune*, February 10, 1923.

a migrating herd of caribou. However, shortly before its release, the film's legal counsel received disturbing information regarding the star's true identity. When the day of reckoning finally came, one of his wealthy admirers, Irvin S. Cobb, who also wrote a glowing introduction to Long Lance's autobiography, profanely summarized the shock felt in the White world: "To think that we had him in our house. We're so ashamed! We entertained a nigger."[8]

Sylvester Long knew that Whites often felt guilty about their historical injustices against Indians. His masquerade provided a means by which they could assuage

---

8. Irvin S. Cobb, quoted in Smith, *Chief Buffalo Child Long Lance*, 273.

their guilt. Social circles from New York to Hollywood took pride in having an Authentic Indian at their parties. He manipulated White guilt, capitalized on it, and expanded his celebrity through it. The stress of the charade, however, began to take its toll on him long before his ultimate exposure. His story provides essential insight into the racial divides of his time, but his ability to pass himself off in the White world first as a Cherokee and then as a Blood speaks directly to the Myth of the Authentic Indian.

The Indian image created by Sylvester Long in his "autobiography" appeared authentic because it drew on popular stereotypes found in traveling Wild West shows, Hollywood Westerns, dime novels, and the advertising industry. The image, however, then and now restricts Native Americans to a narrow historical range and to a limited set of characteristics. Authentic Indians roam the Western plains where they hunt buffalo from horseback, live in tipis, wear feathered headdresses, and prefer peace but go to war with the slightest provocation. By the turn of the twentieth century, and due mostly to the power of the emerging film industry, the Authentic Indian solidified into a reliable type. Moreover, Cowboy and Indian movies tended to collapse the Myth of the Authentic Indian with the Myth of the Vanishing Indian. Since Authentic Indians belong to the past, films may eulogize their bygone days, but modernity holds no place for them except as a memory invoked on the silver screen.

The Myth of the Authentic Indian marks the beginning of a relatively recent phase in historical myths about Indians, one that includes the remaining two myths covered in this book, the Myths of the Ecological Indian and the Mystical Indian. Although all three rely on the Myths of the Noble Savage and the Ignoble Savage—which, as demonstrated in previous chapters, trace their roots to antiquity—these myths owe their emergence, in part, to twentieth-century changes in communications technology. Film, radio, television, and the internet have provided the means for a mass production of stereotypes. Instantly recognizable, often as the one wearing the feather, and likely speaking in halting English, the Western movie Indian and the broadcast Indian conformed to a single type. That type lived in the Wild West and could not survive outside of it. Manufactured for decades in films, radio programs, and television shows, the Authentic Indian thrived as a commoditized image. The brand sold well, and it still turns a good profit in certain corners of popular culture.

Wild West Shows: The Premiere of the Authentic Indian

In the grassland stretching across the North American midlands—the Great Plains—buckskin-clad William F. Cody guided wealthy tourists and honed his image as the mythic horse-mounted hunter and Indian fighter, Buffalo Bill. The tourists expected to see Indians as part of their Wild West experience, and once Cody hired several Pawnee to stage an attack against himself and a client, who tore off terrified, running for his life.[9] But such added levels of realism cost money, so he preferred to work alone as a guide and to rely primarily on his storytelling powers. Ever the gifted showman, Cody wove together fact and fiction in tales of the Indian wars, of the prowess of Indians as hunters, and of their once noble and free lives on the Great Plains.[10] His compelling yarns alone generally left his campfire audiences satisfied. In the Nebraska and Kansas regions, where he conducted most of his guide work, he crafted a romanticized illusion of Native American lives as the preferred substitute for nuanced historical reality.

He worked as a guide from 1868 through the mid-1870s, years that he also hired himself out to the army as a scout. This role with the military helped him earn his fame as an Indian fighter, and he gloried in his battlefield exploits, but in later years as a Wild West showman he also spoke with a sense of respect and even sentimentality regarding his Native American enemies. Moreover, throughout his life he adhered to the common wisdom that Indians would soon disappear altogether, in accord with the Myth of the Vanishing Indian.

As the dime novel hero in Ned Buntline's highly fictionalized *Buffalo Bill: The King of the Border Men* (1869), and in many other stories that commandeered Buffalo Bill in their titles, Cody embodied the American West for admirers across the country and across the Atlantic. So attempts to distinguish between William F. Cody and his persona, Buffalo Bill, stand akin to the work involved in untangling the historical West from the mythical West. After his stints as both guide and scout, and following several years as a Broadway star, Cody fully launched his Wild West show in 1883.[11] Under his direction, the Indians who performed in his arenas also blended history and myth, as he sought to both inform and entertain his audiences. From that mixture, and through the power of his celebrity, the image of the Authentic Indian emerged in the popular imagination. Cody's influence on the early years of the movie industry helped to transfer that image to film.

Buffalo Bill's Wild West show generally featured Plains Indians. But despite the many warriors whom he killed in battle with the Lakota, Cheyenne, Apache, Comanche, and Pawnee, he learned little about the rich varieties of Native American cultures and met few Indians in person.[12] On stage this did not matter. He merely invented a history of the American West and placed himself at the center of it. Decades of national and international touring helped to imprint the popular notion that all or most Native Americans acted according to their "authentic" portrayals in his elaborate productions. Spectators watched Plains Indians attack settlers and stagecoaches, burn settlements, track down bison, and go to war with the U.S. Cavalry.

---

9. Louis S. Warren, *Buffalo Bill's America: William Cody and the Wild West Show* (New York: Alfred A. Knopf, 2005), 146.

10. Ibid., 144.

11. Ibid., 211.

12. Ibid., 190.

William F. Cody created Buffalo Bill as a supreme authority on Indians and then presented the Wild West show as a historically accurate pageant. Audiences glimpsed the final days of a proud and exotic people who followed the migrating bison across the plains long before the advent of the White man. These romanticized aspects of Native American history also tended to leave the impression that nineteenth-century Plains Indians had been following the same way of life for untold years stretching far back into a timeless past.

But most nineteenth-century Plains Indian nations moved into the region only over the course of the previous century. The Comanche and Kiowa began venturing onto the plains of Texas and Kansas from their farther Western homelands in the early 1700s.[13] At about the same time the Shoshone expanded throughout the northern plains.[14] The migrations of the Lakota, Arapaho, and Cheyenne to the plains generally date from the early to the mid-1700s.[15] These migrations displaced older plains inhabitants, including the Arikara, Hidatsa, Mandan, and Pawnee. Hunting and warrior cultures remained important to all plains peoples, although horticulture also accounted for much of their diet, and existing intertribal rivalries for hunting grounds intensified with the mid-nineteenth-century arrival of White settlers. The end of the Civil War led to a jump in settlement, as thousands of former soldiers sought farmland and ranchland in the trans-Mississippi West. At the same time, the U.S. Army focused on protecting the interests of new settlers as well as the interests of the transcontinental railroad. Thus multiple competing forces fed the Indian Wars era during the 1860s and 1870s, a period that served as the central dramatic focus for Buffalo Bill's Wild West show.

The show glorified the Anglo-Saxon conquest of the American West as the final step in the march of Manifest Destiny across the continent. In essence, Buffalo Bill told a story that his White audiences wanted to hear, and he represented everything good that they wanted to believe about themselves. Simultaneously, they believed in the authenticity of the Indians who raced around the arena in feathered savagery. In short, if the story rang true, so did the Indians in it. The power of spectacle helped to imprint the notion that all Indians lived like the ones on the showground. Thus, in the popular imagination, all or most Native Americans tended to blur into a single composite based on the horse-mounted hunters and warriors presented by Buffalo Bill.

However, any assumption that Cody exploited or humiliated the Indians who worked for him runs contrary to the facts, and it shortchanges the business sense of those Indians. Hundreds of mostly Pawnee, Sioux, and Cheyenne actors found good-paying jobs with the show, and Cody scripted plots that generally blamed White

---

13. Pekka Hämäläinen, *The Comanche Empire* (New Haven, CT: Yale University Press, 2008), 18.

14. Ibid., 22.

15. Loretta Fowler, *Arapahoe Politics, 1851–1978* (Lincoln: University of Nebraska Press, 1986), 16.

aggression for the Indian Wars.[16] Indeed, in 1879 Cody claimed that he never killed an Indian without feeling sorry about it. "Although I have had many a tough fight with the red man my sympathy is with him entirely, because he has been ill-used and trampled on by those whose duty it was to protect him."[17] Such statements contradict other, mostly earlier, broad boasts of his Indian fighting—and Indian hating—days, but he learned to adjust to his public's changing tastes. He aimed to please the growing number of middle-class ticket buyers who recognized the need to kill Indians but who found it insensitive to hate them. Generally, the Indians who worked for Cody understood White perceptions and the expectations of the show's North American and European audiences. Most Indians who worked for Cody knew the marketplace and lived with its ambiguities.[18]

Robert Altman's film *Buffalo Bill and the Indians* (1976) depicts Indians as naïve victims exploited by Cody's chicanery. But the historical record does not support Altman's political agenda, one that too easily demonizes Whites and perpetuates the notion of Native Americans as one-dimensional primitives. More than a thousand Indians performed in the show during the course of its thirty-three-year run. In the arena they played noble and ignoble stereotypes; however, as individual employees they received the same high level of respect from Cody that he usually accorded all his actors and show hands.[19]

By the 1880s, most Plains Indians faced lives as impoverished wards of the state and severe restrictions on any off-reservation travel. But a job with the show meant a steady income and a chance to see the world. Thus, as noted, Indian actors willingly played fictionalized roles that fulfilled an audience's expectation of their authenticity. To mistake the actor for the act here discounts Indians as individuals navigating the complexities of an entertainment industry. They knew their own value to the show. Without them, Cody would have had no show.

Many Lakota actors took pride in their *oskate wicasa* (show man) status. Moreover, the show helped them preserve dances and ceremonies that federal authorities banned on reservations. Cody placed no restraints on Lakota religious practices. Also, assimilation policies that emphasized private property ownership and placed children in distant boarding schools tended to drive families apart and break up communities. But if they worked for Cody, families lived together in tipis near the show grounds and freely conducted their own community affairs. Indeed, Cody helped to keep families together because not only did he employ the Lakota men as actors, he paid

---

16. In a perhaps surprising note of praise, Vine Deloria, Jr., a harsh critic of White injustice against Indians, stated: "Buffalo Bill's relationship with the Indians, absent the aura of show business, seems above average in the positive human qualities of justice and play." Vine Deloria., Jr., in Warren, *Buffalo Bill's America*, 196.

17. William F. Cody, quoted in Warren, *Buffalo Bill's America*, 195–96.

18. Ibid., 190–97.

19. Ibid., 358–59.

the Lakota women as well to prepare food for the hundreds of workers, to keep the actors' clothing in repair, and to assist in other domestic chores on the show grounds. Tightly enforced travel restrictions on their reservations kept families apart, but Cody allowed the Lakota to go wherever they pleased.[20]

Turn-of-the-century reformers, so-called friends of the Indians, tended to regard Buffalo Bill's Wild West and other similar touring shows as havens of debauchery. Therefore, so the theory went, Indians who worked in "show business" (the term arose in the 1880s often to disparage traveling amusements) faced ruin as they fell victim to unscrupulous promoters who exploited them for cheap entertainment that possessed little if any socially redeeming value. Prejudice against actors, and especially against traveling shows, goes back centuries. But this anti-theatrical prejudice had a special twist. Regarding Indians, perceptions of their show business exploitation by Whites often assumed that Indians themselves lacked the capacity to control their own affairs, weigh their own options in life, and make their own decisions.

The Office of Indian Affairs (OIA) and Indian school officials militated against Indian employment in Wild West shows. The OIA regulated the employment of Indians in Wild West shows, ostensibly to protect Indians from exploitation. But it also believed that such employment defeated assimilation efforts to "civilize" Indians, and Indian school newsletters agreed.[21] OIA and Indian school officials were all White, and their paternalism effectively infantilized Indians. In other words, Indians lacked the sense of responsibility necessary to make their own employment decisions.

Cody's show, along with other, smaller Wild West shows, hired their performers through the OIA. Although the OIA signed contracts with the shows and provided them with Indian performers for decades, its stated policy appeared to contradict this long-standing practice. In 1890, OIA commissioner Thomas Jefferson Morgan informed all Indian agents that, "the influence of 'Wild West' and other similar shows has been harmful both to the Indians individually participating in the 'shows' and also to the Indians generally. [It is] the duty of this Office to use all its influence to prevent Indians from joining such exhibitions."[22] Yet OIA contracts with Wild West shows continued.

A certain irony accompanied the reform efforts that targeted Cody. Many Lakota *oskate wicasa* praised Cody for his financial generosity and legal protection and for protecting their right to perform music, dance, and other traditions, including ceremonies that involved the sweat lodge, all otherwise banned on reservations. Powwows performed today can trace their legacy back to the Wild West show. Indeed, in 2004 the Lakota dancer and singer Calvin Jumping Bull, a descendent of Sitting Bull and

---

20. Ibid., 362–63.

21. Linda Scarangella McNenly, *Native Performers in Wild West Shows* (Norman: University of Oklahoma Press, 2012), 39.

22. Thomas Jefferson Morgan, quoted in McNenly, *Native Performers*, 43.

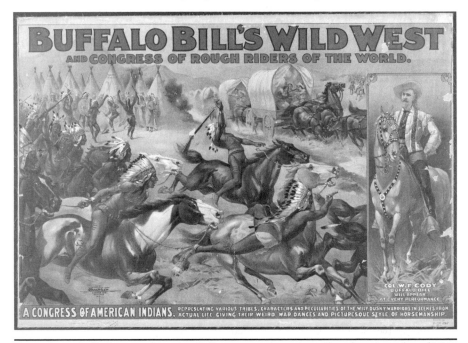

The caption reads: "A Congress of American Indians, representing various tribes, characters and peculiarities of the wily dusky warriors in scenes from actual life giving their weird war dances and picturesque style of horsemanship." Note the cavalry in the upper right coming to rescue the wagon train besieged by Indians. "Buffalo Bill's Wild West and Congress of Rough Riders of the World," 1899. Chromolithograph poster. Library of Congress, Prints and Photographs Division. Reproduced from http://www.loc.gov/pictures/resource/ppmsca.13514/.

Black Elk, both of whom Cody famously featured in his show, credited Buffalo Bill for preserving freedom of expression for the Lakota people.[23]

Considering the many thousands of Native American performers who worked in Wild West shows, the range of their experiences varied widely. Breaches of contract and complaints about working conditions generated paperwork. Good experiences did not leave much of a paper trail. This built-in documentary bias must be taken into account when attempting to assess the working lives of Indians in the shows.[24] But employment opportunities on reservations were few, so Wild West shows provided employment, generally good pay, and good working conditions. Guy Dull Knife, Jr., a Lakota Indian, recounted stories about his grandfather George Dull Knife, who worked for Cody and who explained that Native performers lived in a camp that

23. Warren, *Buffalo Bill's America*, 364.
24. McNenly, *Native Performers*, 46.

"began to resemble the camps they had always lived in on the Plains."[25] While the OIA denigrated traditional kinship-based Lakota society and promoted assimilation, Cody's Wild West Show provided Native American performers and their families a place to live together wherever the show took them.

William F. Cody stands as the sum of his contradictions. Each *oskate wicasa* certainly knew something of Cody's past as an Indian fighter and Indian hater, yet to simplify the Indians who worked for him as exploited Wild West dupes denies their own human complexity and historical agency. Moreover, as the best known public figure of his time, Buffalo Bill left his mark on popular culture, and in subtle and not so subtle ways his influence continues down to the present day.

Cody's focus on Plains Indians and on the Indian Wars era etched the Myth of the Authentic Indian into the popular imagination. Although his romanticized and melodramatic stage productions contained an element of historical accuracy, that history effectively ignored other Native American histories and other eras. As an entertainment spectacle, one repeated decade after decade to audiences throughout North America and Europe, the show created an Indian of the imagination on a mass scale. By the turn of the nineteenth century into the twentieth century, Cody's growing financial and personal difficulties in combination with the advent of the cinema marked the beginning of the end for Buffalo Bill's Wild West. But when transferred to cinema, and later to radio and television, the Authentic Indian, based on stereotypes of a handful of Plains Indian nations, reached an ever-widening audience.

The Authentic Indian on the Silver Screen

Cody's foray into film brought him only limited success. *The Indian Wars* (1914), now lost except for a few fragments, marked his only effort to broach the new medium. Always attempting to produce "authentic" portrayals of the Wild West, Cody secured permission from the secretary of war to use actual soldiers instead of actors. Thus, *The Indian Wars* featured the Twelfth Cavalry under the command of retired General Nelson A. Miles. Moreover, Cody promised the Department of the Interior, which exercised authority over all Native Americans at the time, that the historically reenacted battles would be followed by scenes of contemporary Lakota learning to assimilate into White American society. Thus, the film concluded with scenes of uniformed Indian children in their schools saluting the American flag and with clips of Indians diligently working away on their farms.[26] With the cavalry's role in "taming the West" in mind, the Army probably planned to use *The Indian Wars* as a recruitment tool; also, the Department of the Interior wanted the film to send an encouraging message

---

25. George Dull Knife, quoted in McNenly, *Native Performers*, 65. McNenly, *Native Performers*, 68; Warren, *Buffalo Bill's America*, 362.

26. Warren, *Buffalo Bill's America*, 537.

about the purportedly excellent quality of life experienced by contemporary Indians. The propaganda efforts of both the Army and the Department of the Interior seemingly achieved a level of success.[27] One reviewer deemed *The Indian Wars* a fine example of "the great leaders of our army [and] the great chiefs of our Indian tribes . . . in the open world that has been made sacred by the heroic blood of the nation's fighting heroes."[28]

The Indian Wars portrayed the Battles of Summit Springs (1869) and Warbonnet Creek (1876) and the Wounded Knee Massacre (1890). Cody hired Arnold Short Bull, a Wild West show veteran, No Neck, and Woman's Dress for lead roles and to act as interpreters for the several hundred Oglalas and Brules who performed for the film. By all accounts, the Native American actors understood the battles that Cody paid them to recreate, and some had fought in them.[29] However, a month after filming ceased, the New York *World* claimed that Cody duped the Indians into thinking they played roles in merely fictitious battles, and, indignant over Cody's deception, the actors intended to file a formal protest with the federal government. Rumors also circulated that the government refused to release the film because Cody presented the army unfavorably, especially in its action at Wounded Knee. Yet another rumor, circulated months before the film's release, claimed that Cody cast himself as a hero at Wounded Knee in which, historically, he did not participate. This rumor originated with Indian policy reformer Chauncy Yellow Robe, one of Cody's long-time critics. Historians sometimes repeat these various allegations, taking them at face value.[30] Yet extensive records indicate that the Oglala and Brule actors knew they played roles in historical, not fictitious battles. Cody did not appear in the Wounded Knee massacre scenes but did reenact both the "heroic" role of his purported scalping of the Cheyenne warrior Yellow Hand at the Battle of Warbonnet and his supposed killing of Tall Bull at the Battle of Summit Springs. Lastly, no government censorship occurred. Indeed, General Miles[31] joined Cody in the first screening of the film in January 1914, and a month later the National Press Club hosted another screening in conjunction with the Department of the Interior.[32]

The Indian Wars embodied one of the storylines destined for expansion and repetition in hundreds of Cowboy and Indian films over the following decades. Warbonneted and horse-mounted plains warriors would fall to their cinematic deaths left and right against the charging cavalry as the American Western grew into one of the most

---

27. Kilpatrick, *Celluloid Indians*, 20.

28. Quoted in Kilpatrick, *Celluloid Indians*, 20.

29. Reddin, *Wild West Shows*, 152.

30. L. G. Moses, *Wild West Shows and the Images of American Indians, 1883–1933* (Albuquerque: University of New Mexico Press, 1996), 231–44.

31. Miles, a Medal of Honor recipient and well-known Indian fighter, sternly criticized the Wounded Knee Massacre and tried, unsuccessfully, to secure compensation for the survivors of that massacre.

32. Moses, *Wild West Shows*, 231–44.

successful and influential genres in movie history. But Cody's film did not originate the genre. That honor can be traced to one of the first films in cinematic history, *Sioux Ghost Dance* (1894). Produced in Thomas Edison's West Orange, New Jersey studio, the film features eight Oglala and Brule Sioux touring the East at the time with Buffalo Bill's Wild West show. They performed a portion of the Ghost Dance for Edison's camera, a production that led to a story in the *New York Herald* headlined "Red Men Again Conquered":

> A party of Indians in full war paint invaded the Edison laboratory at West Orange yesterday and faced unflinchingly the unerring rapid fire of the kinetograph (camera). It was indeed a memorable engagement, no less so than the Battle of Wounded Knee, still fresh in the minds of the warriors. It was probably more effective in demonstrating to the red men the power and supremacy of the white man, for savagery and the most advanced science stood face to face, and there was an absolute triumph for one without the spilling of a single drop of blood.[33]

Sioux Ghost Dance does not tell a story—it does not edit scenes into a narrative sequence—it serves primarily as an ethnographic document, a purportedly authentic glimpse into "savagery."

The quest for ethnographic authenticity also drove Edward S. Curtis' *In the Land of the Head Hunters* (1914), which attempted to illustrate the lives of the Kwakwa̱ka'wakw (Kwakiutl) of the Northwest Coast before the White man came. With Curtis' fame as a photographer already well established through his multivolume portfolio, *The North American Indian*,[34] he turned to filmmaking to record an "Indian epic drama," in the phrase of one publicity poster.[35] Simultaneously, he presented audiences with "Genuine Indian pictures [that] will be far more valuable than regular dramatic subjects."[36] W. Stephen Bush reviewed the film for *Moving Picture World*:

> Mr. Curtis has extracted from his vast materials nothing but the choicest and nothing but that which will please the eyes and stir the thoughts of an intelligent white audience. All the actors are full-blooded Indians. The Indian mind is, I believe, constitutionally incapable of acting; it cannot even grasp the meaning of acting, as we understand it. Probably nobody understands this fact better than Mr. Curtis. The picture speaks volumes

33. "Red Men Again Conquered," *New York Herald*, September 25, 1894, 12.

34. See Chapter 4.

35. Quoted in Brad Evans and Aaron Glass, eds., *Return to the Land of the Head Hunters: Edward S. Curtis, the Kwakwa̱ka'wakw, and the Making of Modern Cinema* (Seattle: University of Washington Press, 2014), 21.

36. Edward S. Curtis, quoted in Alison Griffiths, "Science and Spectacle: Native American Representations in Early Cinema," in *Dressing in Feathers: The Construction of the Indian in American Popular Culture*, ed. S. Elizabeth Bird (Boulder, CO: Westview Press, 1996), 88.

of the producer's intimacy with the Indians and his great power over them. They are natural in every move: the grace, the weirdness and the humor of their dances have never been brought home to us like this before.[37]

Three years earlier, Bush identified "moving picture absurdities" about Indians, although in the process he substituted one set of stereotypes for another:

> We have [the Indian] in every variety but one. We have . . . "red" men, recruited from the Bowery and upper West End Avenue. . . . The only kind we lack are the real Indians. Tradition credits the Indian with uncommonly keen sight, which he seems to lose when transferred to celluloid, for on an average every Indian in the picture shades his eyes, as if it hurt him to look, on an average about eight times during a scene. . . . There is no medium of morality about him. He is either wholly good, seemingly transplanted from the skies or else a fiend and an expert scalper in constant practise [sic]. Those who know him best describe the Indian as stoic and unemotional, but what a change when the red brother poses before the moving picture camera. He is as busy and talkative as the "villain" in the first two acts of the old-fashioned melodrama.[38]

For Curtis, an Indian remained authentic as long as he or she remained uncontaminated by Whites. This often led him to suppress evidence of the contemporary lives of the Indians that he photographed, in effect freezing his Native American subjects in a timeless past. He claimed that his method served the interests of scientific accuracy, the same claim that he made for his 1914 film, a mythic melodrama largely of his own invention. *In the Land of the Head Hunters* freely manipulated and sensationalized aspects of Kwakwaka'wakw culture, especially practices eventually abandoned following contact with White traders and missionaries and generations before Curtis arrived with his camera. But two central elements in the film, headhunting and sorcery, authenticated the Kwakwaka'wakw for him. White culture disrupted the pristine timelessness of Indians, an illusion that Curtis mistook for reality.

Curtis intertwines a potlatch, a whale hunt, and various ceremonial dances within the plot line. He did strive and often succeeded in his attempts at historical accuracy due to his careful attention to the knowledge of Kwakwaka'wakw actors themselves. Indeed, collaboration between the Kwakwaka'wakw and Curtis made the film possible in the first place. But at the same time he invented a fantasy world, one borrowed in part from Longfellow's epic poem *Song of Hiawatha*, and threaded thematic and

---

37. Stephen W. Bush, "In the Land of the Head-Hunters," *Moving Picture World*, December 19, 1914, 1685.

38. Stephen W. Bush, "Moving Picture Absurdities," *Moving Picture World*, September 16, 1911, 773, http://www.curtisfilm.rutgers.edu/ (accessed September 8, 2016).

visual elements of the poem throughout the film.[39] The Myth of the Vanishing Indian in Longfellow's poem found its echo in Curtis. The Authentic Indian works in conjunction with the Vanishing Indian.

Curtis did not necessarily see a contradiction between his scientific aims and his mythologized storyline, as he hoped to both inform and entertain, all the while assuring his audiences of the authenticity of his Indians. However, authenticity relied on mythologized notions of noble and ignoble Indians, and the film's storyline depended less on Kwakwa̱ka̱'wakw culture and more on stories drawn not only from Longfellow but from European culture as well, as noted in W. Stephen Bush's film review:

> Mr. Curtis conceived this wonderful study in ethnology as an epic. It fully deserves the name. Indeed, it seemed to me that there was a most striking resemblance all through the films [sic] between the musical epics of Richard Wagner and the theme and treatment of this Indian epic. The fire-dance, the vigil journey with its command of silence and chastity, the whole character of the hero were most strangely reminiscent of Parsifal and the Ring of Nibelungs. I have indicated but a few general outlines, anyone can pursue the likeness in all its details to his heart's content.[40]

Bush's influential review assured readers that *In the Land of the Head Hunters* relies, in part, on Western dramatic models to legitimate its story, one purportedly dealing with Native American history. Of course, Wagner's operatic cycle takes place on a purely mythical Germanic plane, perhaps underscoring the myth that masquerades as history in Curtis' film. One playbill advertised the film as an "Indian Trojan War,"[41] a comparison that unwittingly refers less to any historical reality regarding the war and more to Homer's well-known ancient Greek mythical account of it in his epic poem *The Iliad*.

In 1915, one year after Curtis released his film, American poet Vachel Lindsay published one of the earliest works in the field of film study, *The Art of the Moving Picture*. He presented, in effect, a partial guideline for producing an Authentic Indian and in the process singled out Curtis' film:

> The photoplay of the American Indian should in most instances be planned as a bronze in action. The tribes should not move so rapidly that the panther-like elasticity is lost in the riding, running and scalping. On the other hand, the aborigines should be far from the temperateness of marble. . . . Mr. Edward S. Curtis, the super-photographer, has made an Ethnological collection of photographs of American

---

39. Mick Gidley, *Edward S. Curtis and the North American Indian, Incorporated* (Cambridge: Cambridge University Press, 2000), 232.

40. Bush, "Land of the Head-Hunters," 1685.

41. Evans and Glass, *Return*, 21.

Indians. This work of a lifetime, a supreme art achievement, shows the native as a figure in bronze. Mr. Curtis's photoplay, the Land of the Headhunters, . . . a romance of the Indians of the North-West, abounds in noble bronzes.[42]

In Redface

Throughout the silent era, Westerns continued to regularly employ Native Americans in lead roles and as extras. However, resistance from the Bureau of Indian Affairs, which claimed that the burgeoning industry only exploited the Indians who worked for it, along with changes in movie-making techniques, especially the 1927 advent of the sound stage, meant fewer jobs for Indians and increasing reliance on cheap and plentiful White actors hungry for work. In Hollywood Westerns, the White Indian became the new Authentic Indian.[43]

To create a *speaking* Indian, filmmakers relied on existing stereotypes, and attempts to represent authentic-sounding Indian languages led to innovative techniques. For the sound era serial *Scouts to the Rescue* (1939), White Indian actors first recorded their dialogues in English, and then technicians printed the recordings in reverse for the film, the gibberish passing for an authentic-*sounding* Indian language.[44] Many movie Indians also relied on stoical silences punctuated by grunts, and they usually spoke English in stilted article-free monotones, a style, as already noted, most famously associated with the Lone Ranger's sidekick, Tonto.[45]

Indians continued to find work in Westerns, usually as extras and stuntmen and often as members of nations other than their own. The Twentieth Century Fox picture *Buffalo Bill* (1944) employed Navajos from Tuba City, Arizona to play Cheyenne and Sioux in the Utah mountains. A 1944 article in Colliers describes some of the Navajos' reactions to their absurd situation:

> When it came time to have the war paint smeared on their faces by the makeup experts from Hollywood, the Navahos [sic] objected at first. They thought this was a bit thick, and that Hollywood was overdoing the thing. . . . They laughed and joked over their costumes. . . . When Chief Thundercloud [Cherokee actor and the film's historical advisor, Victor Daniels] explained a torture scene in the picture, wherein the Cheyenne

42. Vachel Lindsay, *The Art of the Moving Picture* (New York: Modern Library, 2000), 69.

43. Moses, *Wild West Shows*, 250–51.

44. John A. Price, "The Stereotyping of North American Indians in Motion Pictures" in *The Pretend Indians: Images of Native Americans in the Movies*," ed. Gretchen M. Bataille and Charles L. Silet (Ames: Iowa State University Press, 1981), 80.

45. See the Introduction, p. xxi.

proved his bravery by having his back cut, the Navahos laughed uproari-ously; they thought such action was downright nonsense. There is noth-ing stoic about the Navahos [sic]. They do not bear pain with fortitude nor do they practice self-torture as a sign of bravery.[46]

Buffalo Bill focuses on the Battle of Warbonnet. Joel McCrea played Buffalo Bill Cody and Mexican American actor Anthony Quinn portrayed the Cheyenne warrior Yellow Hand (Heova'ehe), who is killed by Cody. Quinn also played a Cheyenne Indian in *The Plainsman* (1936), the Oglala Lakota leader Crazy Horse in *They Died with Their Boots On* (1941), and Seminole leader Osceolo in *Seminole* (1953). Quinn's history of Native American roles typifies the careers of multiple non-Indian actors who played Indians in Hollywood westerns. Jeff Chandler portrayed the Apache leader Cochise in *Broken Arrow* (1950), although the film also features Canadian Mohawk actor Jay Silverheels (most famous as Tonto) in the role of Geronimo; Burt Lancaster played Massai in *Apache* (1954), and Henry Brandon played Scar in *The Searchers* (1956),[47] to name only a few.

White actors in redface remained acceptable in the movie industry for decades after it abandoned racist blackface performances. The first talkie, or picture with sound, *The Jazz Singer* (1927), featured White actor Al Jolson in blackface, and between 1927 and 1953 at least seventy films featured blackface performances.[48] From 1953 to 1963, studios produced nearly three times that number of films featuring redface per-formances, with scores of redface films continuing to fill the screens in the following decades.[49] Like blackface, redface predated the rise of the cinema. Both originated on the American stage. Edwin Forrest performed perhaps the most famous early redface role when he portrayed Metamora in John Augustus Stone's *Metamora; or the Last of the Wampanoags* (1829). Forrest played Metamora for over forty years, work that won him fortune, fame, and the title of "the American tragedian."[50] Stone's play made him a nineteenth-century superstar.

Metamora represents Metacom (1638–76), the sachem, or chief, of the Wampa-noags who lived in southern New England. Known also as King Philip, he led a war against English settlers in 1675, sparking the so-called King Philip's War (1675–78). Following his death in battle, Plymouth colonials cut off Metacom's head and stuck

---

46. James F. Denton, "The Red Man Plays Indian," *Colliers* 113 (March 18, 1944): 18–19, http://www.unz.org/Pub/Colliers-1944mar18-00018 (accessed August 17, 2016).

47. See Chapter 3, pp. 42–44.

48. Corin Willis, "Meaning and Value in *The Jazz Singer*" in *Style and Meaning: Studies in the Detailed Analysis of Film*, ed. John Gibbs and Douglas Pye (Manchester: Manchester University Press, 2005), 127.

49. Michael Hilger, *Native Americans in the Movies: Portrayals from Silent Films to the Present* (New York: Rowman and Littlefield, 2016), 416–24, passim.

50. Sally L. Jones, "The First but Not the Last of the 'Vanishing Indians': Edwin Forrest and the Mythic Re-creations of the Native Population," in Bird, *Dressing in Feathers*, 13.

it on a pike in the middle of town. Indeed, on August 17, 1676, the citizens of Plymouth celebrated his death in a day of thanksgiving.

Several days earlier, Captain Benjamin Church, a principal leader of colonial forces in the war, commanded his soldiers to drag Metacom's corpse from the swamp where he had been slain. Church declared that since the sachem "had caused many an Englishman's body to be unburied, and to rot above ground, not one of his bones should be buried."[51] Thus he had the body hacked into quarters, ordered his men to hang each limb on four neighboring trees, and then hauled the sachem's head to Plymouth. The Indian's severed head, hung high above the ground, provided the thanksgiving centerpiece.[52] Fifty-five years earlier, Massasoit, Metacom's father, attended the 1621 thanksgiving, the gathering now memorialized every November in the United States as the "Pilgrims' First Thanksgiving."[53]

By the time of Stone's 1829 play, Metacom transformed in the popular imagination from a "bloody and crafty wretch,"[54] as Puritan divine Increase Mather wrote in 1702, into a sentimentalized tragic hero. Felled by Church and his soldiers, Metamora (Metacom) utters a curse at the end the play:

> My curses on you, white men! May the Great Spirit curse you when he speaks in his war voice from the clouds! Murderers! The last of the Wampanoag's curse be on you! May your graves and the graves of your children be in the path the red man shall trace! And may the wolf and panther howl o'er your fleshless bones, fit banquet for the destroyers! Spirits of the grave, I come! But the curse of Metamora stays with the white man![55]

Here, and throughout the play, Stone establishes a relatively sympathetic understanding of Metacom. However overwrought dramatically, the sachem at least possesses a voice, a conscience, and a sense of righteous indignation over the wrongs committed against him and his people. Most previous histories denied him these human qualities and did not miss opportunities to venomously condemn him, although the level of sadistic violence committed by both Whites and Indians during King Philip's War made it difficult to discern which side committed the greater evils.

---

51. Benjamin Church, quoted in Jill Lepore, *The Name of the War: King Philip's War and the Origins of American Identity* (New York: Alfred A. Knopf, 1999), 173.

52. Ibid., 174.

53. Regarding Massasoit, see Chapter 1, p. 7.

54. Increase Mather, *Magnalia Christi Americana: Or the Ecclesiatical History of New England*, Vol. 1 (London: Thomas Parkhurst, 1702), 54.

55. John Augustus Stone, *Metamora; or the Last of the Wampanoags* (Brookline, ME: Feedback Theatrebooks, 2009), 38–39.

Approvingly or not, critics noted Stone's transformation of Metacom from demon to tragic hero. However, they tended to focus less on the historical figure of Metacom and more on the actor Edwin Forrest, identified in the play's epilogue as "a native actor"[56] not because he possessed a Native American heritage, but because he stood on the stage as a native-born *American*. Forrest, who commissioned the play from Stone, saw his performance as a statement of American artistic independence from British culture. Indeed, one critic noted in 1848: "He has created a school of art, strictly American, and he stands forth as the very embodiment, as it were, of the masses of the American character."[57] Forrest appropriated a historical Indian figure and retooled him for the nation's ongoing quest for an identity separate from old Mother England and from Europe in general.

Stylistically, Forrest relied on an expansive and forceful stage presence, while English actors of the time tended to deliver their lines in a reserved and somewhat cerebral fashion. But aesthetic differences in stage presence also embodied potent political statements in the often bitter antipathy between England and the United States that continued to simmer long after the revolution. Indeed, rivalry between Forrest and his equally famous British counterpart, Charles Macready, came to a head on the night of May 10, 1849. That night Macready starred in Shakespeare's *Macbeth* at the Astor Opera House in New York. An estimated 10,000 people filled the streets outside the theater, all fueled to one degree or another with nationalist disdain for the British, and Macready provided a ready focus for their energies. The mob laid siege to the theater, pelting its windows with rocks, attempting to burn it to the ground, and terrifying the audience trapped inside. Macready managed to finish his performance. Meanwhile, the Astor Place Riot left at least 22 people dead and 150 wounded.[58]

A redface performance stood at the heart of the combat, as did the issue of the purported "authenticity" of that performance. According to one of his biographers, "When [Forrest] came to impersonate Metamora . . . it was the genuine Indian who was brought up on the stage. . . . The counterfeit was so cunningly copied that it might have deceived nature herself."[59] Other critics joined in the chorus over the decades to sing the praises of Forrest's "authentic portrayal" of the Wampanoag sachem. Thus at the center of a nationalist effort to identify the United States as a country uniquely separate and even superior to hoary old England stood not a living Indian but a White Indian. That White Indian, Forrest's Metamora, focused his mighty curse on England itself. Put another way, the Indian made Forrest authentically American.

---

56. Ibid., 39.

57. Lepore, *Name of the War*, 199.

58. Ibid.

59. William Rounseville Alger, *Life of Edwin Forrest, The American Tragedian*, Vol. 1 (Philadelphia, PA: Lippincott, 1877), 240.

No Feather, No Indian

The Myth of the Authentic Indian persists today. To many, the Indian somehow remains incompatible with modernity. Perhaps the myth provides a subtle—or not so subtle—means for continuing to control Indians by conceptually limiting their ability to participate fully in the twenty-first-century world. The myth locks Indians away into a set of stereotyped roles. As mere relics from a bygone era, their presence in modern career paths or professions appears anomalous. Moreover, those who adhere to the myth effectively question Indian identity itself, as noted by Duane Champagne, citizen of the Turtle Mountain Band of Chippewa in North Dakota:

> The cultural complexities of contemporary Indian communities tend to confuse non-Indians who are expecting and often demand traditional cultural expression and personas from contemporary Indian people. If a person does not look and act like an Indian—usually a stereotypical image of a Plains Sioux Indian—then many non-Indians doubt the Indian authenticity of tribal member. . . . Unfortunately, much contemporary discussion about Indian authenticity focuses more on U.S. definitions of authenticity than tribal understandings, which are less well known and understood by the U.S. public and many ethnic Indians.[60]

Authenticity is imposed upon Indians by cultural forces that have historically looked into Indian Country from the outside and then passed judgments, in manners alien to Indians themselves, on who *is* and who is *not* an Indian. But the multitude of individual tribal histories, and the individual tribal identities intertwined with those histories, militate against simplistic generalizations that perpetuate the misperception of Indian authenticity. Moreover, tribal membership tends to be defined today according to either blood quantum (the amount of one's Indian blood) or lineal descent. In other words, Indian tribes themselves determine their own identities according to their own rules, and not to rules imposed upon them from outside. But rules governing both blood quantum and lineal descent are far from simple. Indeed, contentious debate regarding their rationale remains ongoing within Indian communities.

The historic roots of blood quantum for Native Americans reach back to the early eighteenth century in colonial Virginia. Officials used it as a means for legally discriminating against anyone with 50 percent or more of Native blood. With some irony, the term took on its current application due to the Indian Reorganization Act

---

60. Duane Champagne, "Authenticity: Ethnic Indians, Non-Indians, and Reservation Indians," *Indian Country Today*, January 6, 2014, https://indiancountrymedianetwork.com/education/native-education/authenticity-ethnic-indians-non-indians-and-reservation-indians/ (accessed July 7, 2017).

of 1934, according to which Indians could be defined as "persons of one-half or more of Indian blood,"[61] and the act identifies benefits attached to tribal enrollment.

Today, tribal enrollment requirements based on blood quantum vary from tribe to tribe. Typically, membership is defined as "quarter-blood," "half-blood," "one-eighth," or "one-sixteenth."[62] For example, White Mountain Apache Tribe members must be half-blood, and the Eastern Band of Cherokee in North Carolina requires one-thirty-second Indian blood for enrollment.[63] Blood quantum requirements for a given tribe deny enrollment for those who self-identify with that tribe but lack its blood percentage.

Tribes that base their enrollment on lineal descent cast a wider net than those that rely on blood-quantum-based enrollment. However, some argue that lineal descendancy may be overly inclusive. Others argue for dispensing with genetic determinants for enrollment and for adopting a cultural approach based on language acquisition and participation in the tribal community. Some fear that, barring more inclusive measures, plummeting enrollments may threaten the future viability of some Indian nations. But membership rules remain a tribal prerogative, and the complex issues of Native American identity stands beyond the purview of anyone other than Native Americans themselves.

---

61. "Wheeler-Howard Act (Indian Reorganization Act), June 18, 1934" in Francis Paul Prucha, editor *Documents of United States Indian Policy* (Lincoln: University of Nebraska Press, 2000), 225.

62. Matthew L. M. Fletcher, "Tribal Membership and Indian Nationhood," *American Indian Law Review* 37 (2012–13): 4.

63. Eric Beckenhauer, "Redefining Race: Can Genetic Testing Provide Biological Proof of Indian Ethnicity?" *Stanford Law Review* 56 (2003): 167.

6. A Life in Balance: The Myth of the Ecological Indian

The old Indian was not wasteful of his resources. He picked no more berries than he needed to stay the cravings of his hunger, and scrupulously avoided injuring trees and bushes which bore anything edible. He killed no more game than he needed for himself and his camp, and ate every part of what he did kill. When he built a fire, he used only the fuel that was necessary, and before quitting the spot extinguished the flame with care. Along came the White man, the finished product of centuries of civilization, and reversed nearly everything the Indian was doing. . . . He professed to be the follower of a Prince of Peace, yet his distinguishing insignia were weapons for destroying life. . . . He was always decrying waste, yet threw away enough to subsist a fellow man. If he hunted, his trail was strewn with untasted meats. If he built a fire for a night's camp, it must be big enough to illuminate a whole canyon.[1]

As appraised by Indian Commissioner Francis E. Leupp (1849–1918), the White man compares poorly with the Indian. Frugal and thoughtful, the Indian lives in balance with nature, whereas the profligate White man knows only how to squander and lay waste to his world. Rooted in nineteenth-century Romanticism, although traceable to even earlier centuries, this popular dichotomy proved especially useful to critics of an increasingly industrialized world. They saw the growing extraction of natural resources that fueled the factories, which in turn seemed only to blacken the skies over the ever-expanding cityscapes, as wanton destruction of the environment. Many writers, artists, and intellectuals sought solutions to the problems of modernity through their idealization of Native Americans, whose reputed reverence for the natural world precluded the exploitation of its resources. And herein resides yet another Indian stereotype.

The Myth of the Ecological Indian takes many cues from the Myth of the Noble Savage. Primitive yet virtuous dwellers of forest and plain, Indians always lived in harmony with the earth. Charles Eastman (Ohiyesa) (1858–1939), a Santee Dakota who graduated from Boston University Medical School, also wrote several popular books that ennobled Indians through romantic tales of lives long lost. He often contrasted

---

1. Francis E. Leupp, *In Red Man's Land: A Study of the American Indian* (New York: Fleming H. Revell Company, 1914) 66–68.

an idyllic Indian past with the complexities of the modern industrial world. *The Soul of an Indian* (1911), perhaps his most famous book, opens with a stanza from English Romantic poet Samuel Taylor Coleridge that extolls the virtues of nature and attributes them to the utterances of God. Thus situating himself squarely within the Romantic tradition, Eastman nostalgically recalls an altruistic childhood, paints it with reverent flourishes, and then condemns his present role as an educated professional:

> Long before I ever heard of Christ, or saw a white man, I had learned from an untutored woman the essence of morality. With the help of dear Nature herself, she taught me things simple but of mighty import. I knew God. I perceived what goodness is. I saw and loved what is really beautiful. Civilization has not taught me anything better! As a child, I understood how to give; I have forgotten that grace since I became civilized. I lived the natural life, whereas I now live the artificial. Any pretty pebble was valuable to me then; every growing tree an object of reverence. Now I worship with the white man before a painted landscape whose value is estimated in dollars![2]

Heavily influenced by Eastman, as well as by the novels of James Fenimore Cooper,[3] naturalist Ernest Thompson Seton (1860–1946) thought Whites could learn much from Indians. In his book *The Gospel of the Red Man: An Indian Bible* (1936), he explains the path he took to achieve his "vision of the perfect man," the one who stands:

> Athletic, fearless, kind, picturesque, wise in the ways of the woods, and without reproach of life. And by a long, long, trail, with ample knowledge of histories and of persons, I was led, as many before have been, to choose the ideal Red man. By all the evidence at hand, his was a better system, a better thought, because it produced far nobler, better men. He, more than any type I know, is the stuff that fires our highest dreams of manhood, realized complete. Him therefore, I proclaim as the model for an outdoor life, our travel guide on the fourfold way that leads to perfect manhood.[4]

Seton's "fourfold way" integrated body, mind, spirit, and service, and it stood at the core of Woodcraft, an organization that he built to teach boys the virtues of the outdoor life. In Woodcraft he idealized: "The Red man [as] the apostle of outdoor life,

---

2. Charles Eastman, *The Soul of an Indian* (Mineoloa: Dover Publications, 2003), 23.

3. Regarding Cooper, see Chapter 1.

4. Ernest Thompson Seton, *The Gospel of the Red Man: An Indian Bible* (San Diego: The Book Tree, 2006), 113.

his example and precept are what young America needs today above any other ethical teaching of which I have knowledge."[5]

Born in England, raised in Canada, and trained as an artist in several European schools, he eventually gained greatest fame for his scientific articles as a naturalist and as a popular author of animal tales. Having married into a wealthy family, he enjoyed a luxurious New York City apartment and a country estate in New Jersey called Wyndygoul, which he landscaped to simulate an idealized Indian camp with miles of walkways and thick woods. (All were protected by a ten-foot-high fence topped with barbed wire.)[6] In 1902 he took the name Black Wolf and enthralled neighborhood boys with tales of Indians and of life on the plains. He wrote, "Gauging my stories in a steady crescendo till I had renewed the Fenimore Cooper glamour of romance, and heightened it to a blaze of glory, [he could] feel the thrill of intense interest [and] their regret that the noble red men were gone before their day."[7]

He gave himself the title of Medicine Man and conducted an election among the forty-two boys for the head chief; a wampum chief, or treasurer; the chief of the painted robe, or secretary; and the chief of the council fire, who made the fire and policed the grounds. Along with other elected officials, these officers constituted the Council of Twelve. The head chief called meetings to order with a two-fingered "buffalo horn" salute. Seton instructed the boys to "think Indian" and developed "Woodlore" activities that included archery, tracking, and handicrafts. Those who excelled in Woodlore work received a feather. The boys adorned their blankets and made headdresses with their accumulated feather awards. Campers took Indian names, dressed in moccasins, erected Siouan tipis, and built fires not with matches but by rubbing sticks together or using bow drills. Primarily, Seton imparted his notions of the close spiritual connection that Indians maintained with the natural world. His stories thrilled the young campers, who easily idolized Black Wolf as they embraced the opportunity to play Indian in the woods. Following a series of articles that Seton published in *Ladies' Home Journal* about his camp activities with local boys, Woodcraft chapters proliferated throughout New Jersey.[8]

Woodcraft served as a template for the Boy Scouts; however, the latter's emphasis on patriotism seemed to Seton a betrayal of Woodcraft's foundation in Indian ways. The Boy Scout concept originated in England. Its founder, Sir Robert S. S. Baden-Powell, based the organization on two army manuals that he published in 1884 and 1899.[9] Although he originally worked with Seton, Baden-Powell envisioned Boy

---

5. Ibid., 1–2.

6. H. Allen Anderson, *The Chief: Ernest Thompson Seton and the Changing West* (College Station: Texas A&M University Press, 1986), 108–9.

7. Ernest Thompson Seton, quoted in ibid., 139.

8. Ibid., 139–41.

9. Ibid., 152.

Scouts not as an organization devoted to playing Indian but as a means for creating a loyal and disciplined citizenry. Soon after the formation of Boy Scouts of America in 1910, Seton abandoned Woodcraft altogether, petulantly disgusted with Baden-Powell's de-emphasis of Indian lore and suggesting that the Scout motto, "Be Prepared" meant "Be prepared (for war)."[10]

The experience only sharpened Seton's belief in the superiority of Indian culture over White culture. However, he took heart in the establishment of Camp Fire Girls, which adopted many of the principles from his Woodcraft manual, *Birch Bark Roll*. The first Camp Fire Girls meeting in 1910 established the organization's motto, "Wo-He-Lo," an Indian-sounding word that combined the first two letters of "Work, Health, and Love."[11] The girls took part in outdoor recreation and learned about natural science. They originally wore fringed ceremonial gowns and headbands, adopted Indian names, and received strings of shells and colored beads (not feathers, as with Woodcraft braves) for their achievements.[12]

Woodcraft, Boy Scouts, and Camp Fire Girls all enshrined many honorable and worthy ideas. However, an unintended consequence arose from their idealizations of Indian culture, namely, the perpetuation of Indian stereotypes. Sentimentalized notions of Indian history dehumanize Native Americans as much as the belief that they possess an inherent savagery.

A simplistic idealization of the relationship between Indians and their environment must give way to a nuanced, complex, and often contradictory historical record. As noted above, the Myth of the Ecological Indian arose initially as a critique of European and Euro-American culture. As such, the myth obscures any accurate portrayal of Native American environmental history itself. Moreover, the Myth of the Ecological Indian relies on the popular, although scientifically challenged, myth of the balance of nature. The notion that North American Indians historically achieved an ongoing mystical balance with their environment rests on the assumption that a balance of nature exists in the first place.

The Balancing Act

Godfrey Reggio's film *Koyaanisqatsi: Life Out of Balance* (1983) takes its title from the Hopi word defined at the end of the film as: "1. Crazy life. Life in turmoil. 2. Life out of balance. 3. Life disintegrating. 4. A state of life that calls for another way of living."[13] Reggio contrasts images of pristine landscapes with those of polluted, crowded, and mechanized cityscapes. Time-lapse sequences instill a sense of

---

10. Seton, quoted in ibid., 155.

11. Ibid., 166.

12. Ibid.

13. *Koyaanisqatsi: Life Out of Balance*, directed by Godfrey Reggio, 1983 (IRE Productions).

frantic mindlessness to the urban environments. Slow-motion panoramic sweeps characterize the serene balance supposedly present in the "natural" world. Reggio also employs time-lapse sequences of rolling clouds and the shadows they cast across the land, sunrises, and sunsets. But the message here appears to suggest harmony and stability, as the land itself remains unchanged, until powerlines, mining operations, and thermonuclear detonations enter the picture. Reggio's eighty-minute montage imbeds a harsh critique of industrialized modernity and idealizes Native American wisdom about the danger of disrupting the balance of nature. Reggio supplies the translation of a Hopi chant strung throughout the film: "If we dig precious things from the land we will invite disaster. Near the Day of Purification, there will be cobwebs spun back and forth in the sky. A container of ashes might one day be thrown from the sky, which could burn the land or boil the oceans."[14] But neither the word *koyaanisqatsi* nor the chant shed light on the actual environmental history of the Hopi. Moreover, Reggio likely implies that these extracts from Hopi philosophy represent an ecological wisdom inherent to all Native Americans.

Beliefs themselves inform, but they do not comprise the actual environmental history of Indians anywhere in North America. Too often the popular imagination substitutes a system of beliefs for history itself. The Myth of the Ecological Indian paints a noble portrait. The *historical* picture, however, represents the engagement of North America's Indigenous Peoples with multiple environments across the continent that exist not in steady balanced states but in dynamic states of flux that often bring unpredictable and dramatic change. Moreover, Indigenous Peoples altered their landscapes through irrigation works, building projects, fires, and deforestation. Not stereotypes or myths, but human beings make history, and like human beings anywhere, Native Americans historically possessed neither more nor less than their share of judgment about their world. They lived with both the intended and unintended consequences of their actions.

In the West, the notion of a balance of nature arose in Greek antiquity, if not earlier. Aristotle (384–322 BCE) believed in an eternally balanced cosmos. Events in nature occurred in a repetitive and orderly fashion, all guided by a divine plan. Nearly two thousand years later, this worldview remained about the same, as the prevalent notion of a "clockwork universe" permeated late medieval and Enlightenment science. Here the universe ran according to predictable and unchanging laws put into motion by God at Creation.[15]

---

14. Ibid.

15. Regarding the "clockwork universe," see: Stephen D. Snobelen, "The Myth of the Clockwork Universe: Newton, Newtonianism, and the Enlightenment," in *The Persistence of the Sacred in Modern Thought*, ed. Chris L. Firestone and Nathan Jacobs (Notre Dame: University of Notre Dame Press, 2012), 149–84.

The idea of a law-abiding and orderly state of nature more or less endured among scientists until the nineteenth century, when evolutionary biology arose to challenge it.[16] Based on fossil evidence, scientists began to understand that biological species undergo adaptations and extinctions; thus, the natural world undergoes continual changes, however imperceptible these might be to human perception. In tandem with these biological findings, mounting environmental evidence indicated that shifts in climate entailed profound historical consequences for human populations. Extreme droughts or floods have decimated once well-populated areas. Ecological ground rules continually change.

Yet the notion of an intrinsically balanced natural world continues, partly due to deep cultural beliefs in a divinely created universe as a perfectly conceived—and therefore perfectly balanced—work. Moreover, many ecologists maintain that ecosystems eventually attain a state of equilibrium, which in turn ensures the balance of nature wherein competition among species becomes minimal or even nonexistent. In this view, vegetation and animal species reach a state of balance in so-called climax communities that remains more or less unchanged in perpetuity. Thus many conservationists argue that ecosystems disrupted by industrial development should be allowed to return to their original state of self-regulating balance.[17]

To the contrary, many scientists now no longer rely entirely on models of a balanced state of nature; rather, they employ the term "stochastic" (randomly determined) to describe the element of random unpredictability within ecosystems.[18] Theoretical formulations that incorporate stochastic models might help to better characterize the changing historical relationships between people and their environment. But the antiquity of the idea of the balance of nature remains of central relevance to the Myth of the Ecological Indian, itself a Western construction bolstered by similar Native American concepts. As popularly employed, the myth primarily serves political and cultural agendas. These erase nuance and contradiction from the historical record and substitute simplistic notions of an inherently beneficent Native American relationship with the environment and an inherently destructive Euro-American relationship with that same environment.

As much as that dualistic model might be erroneous in its naïve simplicity, there is one fact that cannot be denied. Today, as will be explored in a section below, numerous programs developed by Native American organizations focus on sustainable agricultural practices and on the development of green energy. These programs have proven beneficial ecologically and economically.

---

16. John Kricher, *The Balance of Nature: Ecology's Enduring Myth* (Princeton: Princeton University Press, 2009), 36–38.

17. Ibid., 86–87.

18. Ibid., 128.

Adapt or Perish

Archeologists and climatologists continue to piece together the story surrounding the extinction of thirty-five large North American animal species at the end of the Pleistocene era, approximately 11,000 years ago. One theory, now generally dismissed, claimed that Indigenous Peoples hunted the animals into extinction during a 350-year "blitzkrieg." According to this scenario, the wooly mammoth, giant sloth, and others all fell victim to an unstoppable wave of overzealous and wasteful hunters engaged in a rapid and lethal trek across the continent. However, current evidence suggests that climate change played a greater part in the extinctions than did the efforts of North America's thinly scattered human populations.[19] Regardless, stereotyped images of early hunters bringing down wooly mammoths with volleys of spears remain common. But on a regular basis, most hunters probably went after much smaller game, and people survived not only by hunting; they also harvested and processed a wide range of edible plants. Survival depended on adaptation. This included the need to establish new cultural practices and to invent new technologies, sometimes in response to climate change but also due to crises caused by Native Americans themselves, including resource depletion and environmental degradation. Those who adapted survived; those who did not perished.

The Ancestral Puebloans

By about 1000 CE, in the Four Corners region of the American Southwest, the Ancestral Puebloans[20] had established nearly one hundred multistory urban centers, or "great houses." Sophisticated roadways connected the great houses and communicated with up to twenty thousand smaller towns and tens of thousands of farmsteads. Among the trade items that moved across these roads, workers hauled an estimated 215,000 ponderosa trees cut down with stone axes in forests twenty to thirty miles away from the major building sites. These logs, up to thirty feet long, served primarily as great house roof beams.[21] Construction projects led people to travel long distances

---

19. In 1967 archeologist Paul Martin (1928–2010) advanced his influential "Pleistocene overkill" theory and defended it throughout his career, continually dismissing climate change as a significant factor in the extinctions. See Paul Jentz, "Quantitative Analysis of Megafaunal Extinctions and the Tenacity of Pleistocene Overkill: Archeology and the World Historian," *World History Bulletin*, 29 (2013): 12–14.

20. The term *Ancestral Puebloans* replaces *Anasazi*, a term formerly used by scholars but which contemporary Puebloans find offensive, as the word derives from Navajo and means "ancestors of our enemies." See Linda S. Cordell and Maxine E. McBrinn, *Archeology of the Southwest* (New York: Routledge, 2016), 36–37. However, the term *Anasazi* remains in use, as for example in the name of the Anasazi Heritage Center at the Canyons of the Ancients National Monument in Delores, Colorado.

21. David E. Stuart, *Anasazi America* (Albuquerque: University of New Mexico Press, 2004), 78.

for materials, especially because ongoing local needs for firewood resulted in expanding rates of deforestation. Indeed, when deforestation coincided with drought, populations often declined and people commonly abandoned their communities.[22]

Most great houses clustered in Chaco Canyon, located about one hundred miles northeast of present-day Gallup, New Mexico. All roads led here. By 1050, a three-level cultural and economic hierarchy emerged in the Ancestral Pueblo world, with farmsteads occupying the lowest rung, followed by district great houses, with the greatest concentration of power in the Chaco Canyon great houses.[23] But the high-point of cultural, technological, and architectural accomplishments, the so-called Chaco Phenomenon, lasted only from approximately 1020 to about 1130. And then within about forty years, extended periods of drought led to starvation, increased warfare, and the relatively rapid fragmentation of society.

The Ancestral Puebloans had experienced any number of extended droughts throughout the thousands of years that they lived in the Southwest.[24] During times of famine their numbers decreased. Poor nutrition led to fewer births, as undernourished women ovulate less frequently than healthy women. Moreover, the Ancestral Puebloans probably practiced infanticide to maintain low populations, therefore helping to ensure their survival as a people during periods of famine.[25] They took advantage of periods of regular rainfall when they cleared land on an ever-increasing scale for crops. The Chaco Phenomenon, for all its grandeur, rested on a fragile ecological foundation. The massive population base, and the thriving trade networks made possible by it, relied on a period of dependable precipitation to enrich the tens of thousands of farmsteads scattered throughout the 40,000-square-mile Four Corners region. But then the rains stopped.[26]

The drought in 1090 devastated the world of the Ancestral Puebloans. Levels of warfare rose due to the increasingly desperate search for food. However, after a few years the rains returned, until 1130, when an extended period of drought returned. Climate refugees of their time, communities that had not already left after the previous drought abandoned their farmsteads, towns, and cities and migrated into often distant regions that promised better prospects of survival.

---

22. Timothy A. Kohler, "Prehistoric Human Impact on the Environment in the Upland American Southwest," *Population and Environment*, 13 (1992): 258–60. Also see Margaret C. Nelson and Gregson Schachner, "Understanding Abandonment in the North American Southwest," *Journal of Archeological Research*, Volume 10, no.2, 2002: 167–206.

23. Stuart, *Anasazi America*, 108.

24. Archeological evidence indicates sporadic occupation of the Four Corners region by at least 7000 BCE. See Stephen Plog, *Ancient Peoples of the American Southwest* (London: Thames and Hudson, 2009), 93.

25. Stuart, *Anasazi America*, 20.

26. Ibid., 120.

By the mid-fourteenth century, the once densely populated Puebloan homeland lost one-half to three-quarters of its people due to starvation, war, and the continued unreliability of rainfall. One scholar correlated this dramatic population loss with the number of deaths predicted for modern America if it suffered a nuclear war.[27] As their previously diverse geographical region became agriculturally untenable, the shrunken world of the Ancestral Puebloans clung to the rivers and consolidated along their narrow corridors. Village life there replaced the previously centralized political and economic system of the Chacoan era in which power emanated from great house elites. Villages now emphasized self-containment, although former trade networks remained relatively intact.

For many of these self-contained villages, arroyo farming proved relatively more successful than dry farming techniques common to the uplands.[28] Relying on a well-watered arroyo (a gully cut out by running water), farmers implanted fields of maize, beans, and squash and hunted a plentiful range of wild game. One such village, Acoma Pueblo, with origins dating to approximately 1150 CE, remains inhabited today, making it the oldest continually inhabited community in North America. But in the face of general upheaval and depopulation, the many pueblos followed no single pattern, as the histories of Arroyo Hondo and Pecos Pueblo bear witness.

Founded in about 1310, Arroyo Hondo, five miles south of present-day Santa Fe, expanded within a single generation to encompass blocks of mostly two-story buildings containing one thousand rooms for an estimated one thousand people. The buildings surrounded several plazas, where cooking, pottery making, corn drying, weaving, and other daily activities took place. Agricultural prosperity fueled trade, and Arroyo Hondo's long-distance trade connections brought Pacific coast abalone and olivella shell to the region for use by jewelry makers.[29]

And then the rains stopped again. By 1345, Arroyo Hondo stood virtually abandoned. Briefly reinvigorated around 1370 when the rains returned, another drought in 1410 again emptied the town. By 1425, Arroyo Hondo effectively ceased as a viable community. People did not return to the arroyo until the Spaniards settled Santa Fe in 1610. But even at the arroyo's agriculturally most productive level, high infant mortality rates and ongoing malnutrition remained common. Arroyo Hondo's history exemplifies the fate of numerous other villages throughout the Four Corners region.[30]

---

27. Ibid., 154.

28. Charles L. Redman, *Human Impact on Ancient Environments* (Tucson: University of Arizona Press, 1999), 118–19.

29. Stuart, *Anasazi America*, 155. Earlier, by about 900 CE, with the emergence of Chaco Canyon as a political-cultural-economic center on the rise, a lucrative trade in turquoise gemstones began along the so-called "Turquoise Trail," which connected Ancestral Puebloans with customers and merchants in the central Valley of Mexico. Eric A Powell, "The Turquoise Trail," *Archeology* 58 (2005): 24–29.

30. Stuart, *Anasazi America*, 157–58.

Pecos Pueblo fared better than Arroyo Hondo. Founded in the early fourteenth century near the Arroyo del Pueblo about eighteen miles southeast of Santa Fe, this mesa top village survived until the early nineteenth century. By the early fifteenth century, villagers raised walls around the entire mesa, and this easily defended stronghold benefited from the geographical diversity of the land beneath it. Farmers constructed irrigation works to nourish miles of grid formation gardens and fields. They raised several varieties of maize, beans, and squash, and they harvested *piñon* nuts, yucca fruits, and wild berries. Hunters pursued buffalo, antelope, deer, and rabbit. Similarly, other pueblos along the Rio Grande and Charma rivers housed thousands of people by the late fifteenth century. Just north of present-day Albuquerque, New Mexico stood Kuaua. Visited by the Coronado expedition in 1540, Kuana contained over 1,200 ground-floor rooms. About one hundred miles away, Sapawe, perhaps the largest pueblo ever built, contained an estimated 2,524 rooms on the ground floor, with second-story rooms bringing the total closer to 4,000. By the early sixteenth century, as many as two hundred pueblos of various sizes dotted the Southwest. Generally, the life spans in these Puebloan people averaged slightly above those of Arroyo Hondo, and diseases caused by malnutrition, especially osteoporosis, developed at rates slightly below Arroyo Hondo's levels.[31]

By the fourteenth century, the most resilient Puebloan communities had developed new crop varieties, field locations, and planting techniques. Farmers in some villages cultivated multiple strains of maize adapted to different altitudes and to numerous temperature and precipitation ranges. Different varieties resisted cold or tolerated drought. Farmers developed strains based on root depths, speeds of maturation, and color. Blue, yellow, white, and mixed kernels all possessed specific qualities designed for a range of grinding and cooking methods.[32] This increasingly diversified agricultural economy relied in part on a complex irrigation infrastructure. Some communities invested heavily in the labor needed for the development and ongoing expansion of canal networks. Workers regularly dredged channels, regulated check dams, and monitored water catchments.[33]

Some romanticized notions of the Puebloan past stand on the assumption that sixteenth-century Spanish colonials encountered native communities that had remained relatively unchanged for hundreds, if not thousands, of years. Yet only by continually adapting to a changing environment did certain groups survive. Regardless of any "balance of nature" ideology, innovation in the face of dire circumstances—droughts, floods, and warfare—meant the difference between life and death.

---

31. Ibid., 159–62.
32. Ibid., 164.
33. Cordell, *Archeology of the Southwest*, 168.

The Hohokam

The confluence of the Salt and Gila rivers in southern Arizona's Sonoran Desert served as the Hohokam people's core region for approximately 1,500 years. Then in the mid-fifteenth century, a combination of overpopulation, environmental degradation, resource depletion, ineffective leadership, and social fragmentation led the Hohokam to finally abandon their homeland.[34] They dispersed throughout the American Southwest and into adjacent northwestern Mexico. Some oral histories of today's Akimel O'odham (River People) and Tohono O'odham (Desert People) nations of the Sonoran Desert claim descent from the Hohokam.[35] The term "Hohokam" derives from the O'odham word *huhugam*, which means "something that is all gone."[36]

The sprawl of the present-day city of Phoenix, Arizona stands on much of the Hohokam's original homeland. Modern urbanization compromises archeological research required to understand Hohokam history.[37] But the city itself also serves as a testament to Hohokam technical skills, as some routes followed by current irrigation projects run along courses laid down by Hohokam engineers centuries ago.[38]

Primarily tapping the lower Salt River and the middle Gila River, the Hohokam drew water into fourteen irrigation networks with an aggregate length of approximately three hundred miles. The product of ongoing expansion and contraction over the centuries, the system at times irrigated four hundred square miles of Hohokam cropland.[39] The expanse of the network, and the need to coordinate labor required for construction and maintenance, if only on a seasonal basis, suggests some degree of centralized administration in Hohokam communities. Differences in river levels due

---

34. David R. Abbott, Cory Dale Breternitz, and Christine K. Robinson, "Challenging Conventional Conceptions," in *Centuries of Decline during the Hohokam Classic Period at Pueblo Grande* (Tucson: University of Arizona Press, 2003), 4–5.

35. Donald M. Bahr, "O'odham Traditions about the Hohokam," 123–29, in *The Hohokam Millennium*, edited by Suzanne K. Fish and Paul R. Fish (Santa Fe: School for Advanced Research Press, 2007). For an examination of the role played by the international boundary between the United States and Mexico and the distinctions between the Pimas and the Tohono O'odham that arose from it see: Andrae M. Marak and Laura Tuennerman, *At the Borders of Empires: The Tohono O'odham, Gender, and Assimilation, 1880–1934* (Tucson: University of Arizona Press, 2013).

36. Daniel Lopez, "Huhugam," in *The Hohokam Millennium*, 118.

37. William H. Doelle, "Laws, Dollars, and Scholars: The Business of Hohokam Archeology," in *The Hohokam Millennium*, 109–15.

38. Kim Whitley and Jeri Ledbetter, *Hohokam Canal System*, Arizona State University. http://www.azheritagewaters.nau.edu/loc_hohokam.html (accessed September 30, 2016).

39. David E. Doyle, "Irrigation, Production, and Power in Phoenix Basin Hohokam Society," in *The Hohokam Millennium*, 83; Cordell, *Archeology of the Southwest*, 164–70.

to floods, droughts, and salinization required both the periodic abandonment of canal alignments and the construction of new lines.[40]

Between 1286 and 1316, increased frequencies of floods and droughts in the Pueblo Grande region—present-day Phoenix—proved catastrophic, primarily because of the region's growing dependence on maize. Destroyed crops meant famine. And while maize became increasingly central to the Pueblo Grandean diet, the availability of other food resources apparently also declined, for reasons not yet clear. The climate crisis began at a point of high population growth due to both natural increase and the immigration of people perhaps fleeing adverse climate conditions elsewhere. With irrigation systems failing due to the fluctuations in rainfall, Pueblo Grande-ans probably tried a number of tactics for confronting food shortages. Perhaps they changed methods for growing and processing maize, or they attempted to broaden their trade routes or restructure their population distribution. The Pueblo Grandeans likely exceeded the carrying capacity of their land for wild foods, including saguaro fruits and mesquite beans, and the demand for mesquite wood as fuel endangered the availability of the beans. The situation resulted in a major reduction in population, a process likely accompanied by structural changes in Pueblo Grandean society.[41]

The Eastern Woodland Indians

Eastern Woodland Indians[42] domesticated their forestlands for millennia. They burned and cleared trees and underbrush for fields and for creating grasslands on which to hunt grazing wildlife. They cultivated trees, bushes, and plants from which they harvested a variety of foods and medicines.[43] European colonies often settled on sites already cleared by Indians. These burned-over areas usually covered about 100 to 150 acres, and some represented the sites of former Indian villages, locations of which changed approximately every ten to twenty years. Reasons for moving included soil

---

40. Jerry B. Howard, "System Reconstruction: The Evolution of an Irrigation System," 162–94. Jerry B. Howard and Gary Huckleberry, *The Operation and Evolution of an Irrigation System: The East Papago Canal Study* (Phoenix: Soil Systems Publications in Archeology, Number 18, 1991). Scott M. Kwiatkowski, "Evidence for Subsistence Problems," in *Centuries of Decline*, 63–67.

41. Kwiatkowski, "Evidence for Subsistence Problems," in *Centuries of Decline*, 48–69.

42. Eastern Woodland Indians include groups who lived east of the Mississippi in five geographical zones, thus scholars often refer to the Northeast, Southeast, Great Lakes, Prairie Woodland, and Mississippian peoples. The Woodland Period stretched from approximately 1000 BCE to the time of European contact.

43. In his highly popular travelogue, Timothy Dwight (1752–1817), the president of Yale College, wrote: "The aborigines of New England customarily fired the forests that they might pursue their hunting with advantage. [. . .] Such to a great extend were the lands [that] they were probably burned over for more than one thousand years." Timothy Dwight, *Travels in New England and New York*, Barbara Miller Solomon, ed., 4 vols. (Cambridge: Harvard University Press, 1969), 1:72. Originally published posthumously, 1821–22.

exhaustion, depletion of local game, and the need for strategic military positioning for protection from regional enemies.[44]

Scholars, writers, and artists have generally romanticized eastern forests as virgin expanses, dense and unbroken by human hands, until the Europeans arrived. These perceptions persist today.[45] In a 1950 book—reissued in 1989—one scholar imagined "great forests that swept across the United States, unbroken from the Atlantic coast to the Great Plains, [until the advent of] the destructive white man."[46] This re-inscribes the erroneous notion that Native Americans had always lived in a passive relationship with their environment, somehow surviving on the land without leaving a mark on it, whereas the active—although demonized—White man alone can effect change in the landscape.

Among Woodland Indians, one of the most extensive alterations in the landscape belongs to the Mississippian Mound Builders. Indeed, deforestation around some of their larger urban centers led in some cases to extensive erosion and long-term soil depletion.

Mound construction history in the lower Mississippi region dates to about 3400 BCE, when people living in present-day Louisiana created some of the first monumental structures in the Americas. Watson Brake site in Ouachita Parish contains mound architecture surrounding a central plaza and shows evidence of intermittent habitation and expansion over the course of five hundred years.[47] The earliest signs of habitation at Poverty Point, a World Heritage Site situated in Louisiana's far northeast, date between 1740 and 1530 BCE.[48]

Because of the intermittent habitation of urban centers that featured mound architecture, the transmission of identifiable traditions of social organization across the millennia (and across an extensive geographical region occupied by mounds) remains an open question.[49] But evidence of a relatively cohesive cultural network solidified by at least 900 CE.[50] By then, Mississippians had constructed earthen, wood, and thatch monumental structures and built extensive housing in cities both within and beyond

---

44. Stephen J. Pyne, *Fire in America: A Cultural History of Wildland and Rural Fire* (Seattle: University of Washington Press, 1997), 46–47. Also see Gordon M. Day, "The Indian as an Ecological Factor in the Northeastern Forest," *Ecology* 34 (1953): 329–46.

45. See Chapter 4.

46. John Bakeless, *The Eyes of Discovery: America as Seen by the First Explorers* (New York: Dover, 1989), 407–8.

47. Timothy R. Pauketat, *Ancient Cahokia and the Mississippians* (Cambridge: Cambridge University Press, 2010), 7.

48. Jenny Elerbe and Diana M. Greenlee, *Poverty Point: Revealing the Forgotten City* (New Orleans: Louisiana State University Press, 2015), 28.

49. Pauketat, *Ancient Cahokia*, 48. Pauketat also notes that the stereotype of Native Americans as "traditional" peoples implies that they do not change, that their ways remain relatively static regardless of migration and resettlement, and that by nature they resist innovation.

50. Ibid., 55, 60.

Serpent Mound. This effigy mound in Adams County, Ohio, originated around 300 BCE, with subsequent construction periods dating to approximately 1070 CE. Photo by Eric Ewing (CC BY-SA 3.0).

the Mississippi's watershed. Home to hundreds of thousands of people, these political centers provided focal points for trade and communication that linked people of the Great Plains with those of the Gulf Coastal regions and the northeastern woodlands. The different types of mounds and their associated structures provide insight into Mississippian modes of government, social order, and religious beliefs. The Coles Creek mounds in Louisiana, Mississippi, and Arkansas probably functioned as sacred spaces for the performance of religious rites witnessed by the crowds below. About 1000 CE, these flat-topped mounds became the foundations for buildings that rose yet farther above the surrounding plaza. These buildings likely served as political and religious centers of power, local authority probably operating along the lines of small-scale chiefdoms. But in Illinois, Wisconsin, Ohio, and Iowa, mound construction took on distinctly different characteristics from those of Coles Creek. These so-called effigy mounds resembled birds, bears, snakes, and an array of other creatures of localized cultural significance. Burials also took place on effigy mounds. Those interred likely came from the ranks of the local leadership.[51]

Mississippians mined the Ozark region for salt, lead, iron, red claystone, and chert (flint). Lead and iron ores provided essential ingredients for mineral-based paints. The easily carved red claystone became statues in the hands of Mississippian craftworkers. Chert proved especially suitable for the manufacture of axes and other woodworking tools. These distinctive statues and tools served as popular trade items and have turned up in archeological sites as far away as Wisconsin, Oklahoma, and Tennessee, and catlinite carvings at Mississippian sites show that they were tied into trade emanating from present-day Pipestone, Minnesota. Furthermore, ancient Ozark miners

---

51. Pauketat, *Ancient Cahokia*, 8–9, 49, 53.

not only extracted valuable resources from the soil, they also left petroglyphs depicting animal, human, and geometric shapes throughout the region's rocks and caves. Indeed, petroglyphs associated with the Mississippians extend into Kentucky, Tennessee, and southern Illinois.[52]

Around 1050 CE came the establishment of Cahokia, a city near the confluence of the Mississippi, Missouri, and Illinois Rivers in present-day East Saint Louis, Illinois, that at times became home to upward of twenty thousand people. Because of Cahokia's size and strategic riverine location, the city's elites likely exerted significant political and economic power across the region. They probably conscripted labor for building projects, coordinated supply chains for securing and storing the city's food resources from the surrounding fields, and managed trade networks, many of which possibly found their most lucrative markets in the populous urban environment.[53]

Cahokians manufactured distinguishing types of pottery, arrowheads, beads, and stone axes that found their way as popular items along trade routes from Lake Superior to the Gulf Coast. Long-distance trade also placed conch and whelk shells from the Gulf of Mexico into the hands of Cahokian artisans, and from the north they acquired Lake Superior copper. Routes along which these items moved would eventually be used by European colonists, and some evolved into today's paved roadways.[54]

Continual competition probably arose between Mississippian communities for agricultural land, particularly the highly desirable Mississippi floodplains—the bottomlands. But the desire to escape the region's land rivalries might also have resulted in the establishment of new cultural, political, and economic centers. Increasingly complex interregional relationships probably maintained some cohesion, as expanded kinship networks likely grew apace with continued emigrations.[55]

A combination of factors led to Cahokia's fourteenth-century population dispersal and economic decline. Climate change probably shortened growing seasons, thus curtailing food production. Deforestation, due to the many centuries of land clearing required for agricultural expansion and the ongoing use of wood for fuel and building material likely resulted in increasing levels of soil erosion. The degraded environment probably led to recurrent social unrest due to spreading food shortages. One of the city's most ambitious building projects began around 1150 CE, when political turmoil required the extensive defensive measure of constructing a wooden wall around the city. This fifty-year-long project used up about twenty thousand logs. Thus, the trifecta of climate

---

52. Ibid., 32–35. For a focused examination of Mississippian rock art, see Carol Diaz-Grandos and James R. Duncan, *The Petroglyphs and Pictographs of Missouri* (Tuscaloosa: University of Alabama Press, 2000).

53. Ibid., 103–10, 145–50.

54. Ibid., 33–35.

55. Ibid., 41–42

change, deforestation, and political unrest meant that by the time European colonials first set eyes on the region in the sixteenth century, a much diminished city stood before them.[56]

Upon examining the ruins of Cahokia and other mound complexes found throughout the southeast, many nineteenth-century observers theorized that Native Americans could not have constructed such sophisticated structures. It seemed more plausible that the builders originated in ancient Israel, or perhaps they came from Atlantis. Pointing to the fancied resemblance between the mounds and Aztec pyramids, some scholars thought that only Aztec engineers possessed skills enough to build them. As we saw in Chapter 4, one generally accepted theory for the mound builders' downfall was a supposed savage onslaught by jealous Indians—ancestors of those living in the vicinity of abandoned mounds. But by the end of the century researchers from the Smithsonian's Bureau of American Ethnology officially laid these myths to rest, although they persist in popular histories.[57]

Considering the complex historical relationship between the Mississippians and their environment, the Myth of the Ecological Indian must be put to rest. Like the Ancestral Puebloans and the Hohokam, the Mississippians learned how to coax a living from the land. They possessed a keen working knowledge of their environment. Their very existence depended on this knowledge. But the Myth of the Ecological Indian would have them living only in noble harmony with the earth, carefully preserving and balancing its resources across the millennia. The myth does not leave room for errors in judgment, long-term soil degradation, or changes in climate that sometimes benefited and sometimes devastated societies. In part, the myth uses stereotyped notions of Native American spirituality as evidence for an idealized, steady-state Indian past, a fantasy history. But food shortages, overpopulation, disease, and the conflicts that arose from competition for resources all ensured that cultures regularly grappled with changes that forced them to reinvent themselves. Sometimes this meant the adoption of new methods for governing, planting crops, acquiring a new range of food sources, or migrating into more promising regions. The myth glosses over the dynamic history of Native Americans and the transformations their cultures underwent when confronted with environmental changes. Moreover, the myth does not leave room for understanding the structural shifts that their societies underwent because of these changes.

The Ancestral Puebloans, the Hohokam, and the Eastern Woodland Indians can only in the most general sense serve as representative examples of the variety of North American Indigenous environmental histories. But throughout these histories, land use does not stand opposed to ecological thinking; however, economic

---

56. Ibid.

57. Robert Silverberg, *Moundbuilders of Ancient America: The Archeology of a Myth* (Greenwich: New York Graphic Society, 1968), 59–96. A Meso-American connection, at least a minor one, consisting of intermittent trade and communication between Mississippians and Meso-American peoples remains a probability. See Pauketat, *Ancient Cahokia*, 72–73.

pressures have at times led to compromising ecological principles, and environmental changes required adaptations and the development of new technologies and infrastructures.

Industrialization in the Four Corners

In 1968, the United Nuclear Corporation (UNC) opened its underground uranium mining operations in Church Rock, New Mexico. By 1978, the Church Rock Mill produced over two million pounds of uranium oxide annually. This supplied the yearly fuel requirements for about five nuclear power plants. The mill stored its radioactive waste—wet sand and mill liquids—in three lagoons surrounded by a fifty- to seventy-five-foot earthen dam. On July 16, 1979, the dam burst, spilling 1,100 tons of radioactive waste into the Rio Puerco. This remains the single largest accidental release of radioactive material in U.S. history.[58]

The Rio Puerco runs through Navajoland (Diné Bikéyah), which borders the mill.[59] The river provides many Navajo (Diné) people with water for irrigation, livestock, and recreation. Moreover, at the time of the accident, the mill employed about two hundred Navajo workers. Within weeks of the accident, Navajo authorities requested disaster assistance from New Mexico's governor, Bruce King, who denied the request. The UNC made an effort to remove some of the radioactive material but managed to clean up only about 1 percent of the contaminated riverbed. Moreover, UNC refused to accept responsibility for Diné livestock that died from drinking the water. Claiming depressed market conditions, the UNC closed Church Rock Mill in 1982.[60]

The next year the Environmental Protection Agency (EPA) declared the mill a superfund site. Over the next ten years, the EPA expanded the range of its study to include all uranium mines located in Diné Bikéyah. Escalated rates of cancer and other diseases associated with radiation exposure continue to plague the reservation. Some of these illness probably stem from exposure to the contaminated river, from drinking contaminated well water, or from working in the uranium mines. Cleanup of the Church Rock Site, and of Diné Bikéyah's contaminated water and soil, remains an ongoing effort.[61] In 2014, The General Accounting Office reported that the Navajo

---

58. Doug Brugge, Jamie L. deLemos, and Cat Bui, "The Sequoyah Corporation Fuels Release and the Church Rock Spill: Unpublicized Nuclear Releases in American Indian Communities," *American Journal of Public Health* 97 (2007): 1595–1600.

59. Diné Bikéyah extends over 27,000 square miles of land in Utah, Arizona, and New Mexico.

60. Brugge, et al., "The Sequoyah Corporation." 1600.

61. Valerie Rangel, "Church Rock Tailing's Spill: July 16, 1979," *New Mexico Office of the State Historian*, http://dev.newmexicohistory.org/filedetails.php?fileID=24161 (accessed October 10, 2016).

people continue to live with radiation-related illnesses from over five hundred abandoned uranium mines located on their reservation.[62]

Many of these mines originated in 1941 with the Manhattan Project, which refined uranium into plutonium for the world's first atomic bombs. Diné Bikéyah's uranium helped to build the U.S. Cold War stockpile of thermonuclear weapons and to fuel reactors for the atomic energy industry. Thus, not only have the Diné grappled with changes brought by industrialization, but they also faced—and continue to face—the consequences of radioactive pollution, one of the most lethal costs of industrialization. Uranium mining has employed over three thousand Diné miners, and radioactive tailings—rocks and soil separated from the uranium ore during processing—litter the reservation landscape. By the mid-1980s, a downturn in the uranium market led to the closure of most mines; however, in 2005, the market improved, and many mines reopened. Also in 2005, the Navajo Nation resisted the resurgence of uranium mining by passing the Diné Natural Resources Protection Act. This placed a moratorium on new mines on the nation's land.[63]

The relationship between the Navajo Nation and the uranium industry had always been uneasy. During the 1940s and 1950s, the Diné generally found mine work preferable to other options, most of which required travel far from their homes, including railroad work or California farm labor.[64] But by the late 1960s, over two hundred Diné uranium workers had died of radiation-related diseases.[65] Death from radiation-related diseases plagued uranium workers throughout the Southwest.[66] The health risks of mine work, downplayed by both the federal government and the uranium industry for decades, became increasingly clear.

By the mid-1960s, the Navajo Tribe financed most of the site development, construction, and worker training for seventeen different industrial plants located both in and near its reservation land in New Mexico. However, when tribal subsidies expired, most companies shuttered their operations. Despite these efforts made by the Navajo

---

62. Trip Jennings, "Native American Project: Remembering the Largest Radioactive Spill in U.S. History," *New Mexico in Depth*, http://nmindepth.com/2014/07/07/remembering-the-largest-radioactive-spill-in-u-s-history/ (accessed October 10, 2016).

63. Traci Brynne Voyles, *Wastelanding: Legacies of Mining in Navajo Country* (Minneapolis: University of Minnesota Press, 2015), 3. Thousands of uranium mines lay scattered across the American West. For several decades, the uranium industry meant jobs, and plenty of them. In some areas, this led to the rise of company towns, so-called "Yellowcake Towns." (The name refers to semi-refined uranium, a yellow powdery substance called "yellowcake.") For an examination of these towns see Michael A. Amundson, *Yellowcake Towns: Uranium Mining Communities in the American West* (Boulder: University Press of Colorado, 2004).

64. Voyles, *Wastelanding*, 13.

65. Ibid., 21.

66. Three out of four uranium miners during the 1950s and 1960s lived in non-Indian yellowcake towns. See Amundson, *Yellowcake Towns*, 13.

Nation to broaden and diversify its economic base, most development on the reservation remained in uranium, oil, gas, and coal extraction. Indeed, also by the mid-1960s, the Four Corners region yielded enough mineral wealth to make New Mexico the leading uranium-producing state in the union and to make it the seventh leading state in total mineral yield.[67]

In 1961, the Navajo Tribal Council signed a contract with the Four Corners Power Plant, and in 1964 the council entered into a contract with the Peabody Coal Black Mesa strip mine. Yet the council recognized that neither contract provided satisfactory control of Navajo resources.[68] Continued attempts to gain control of resources on Navajo land, and on the land of other Southwestern Indian nations, led Peter McDonald, chairman of the Navajo Nation, to organize the Council of Energy Resource Tribes (CERT) in 1975.

Currently CERT comprises fifty-four tribes in the United States and four First Nation Treaty Tribes in Canada. Its recently approved Thunderbird project involves the long-term development agreement for up to $3 billion in biofuel and bioenergy projects. Plans include the creation of a worldwide renewable jet fuel business and projects for environmental toxin remediation on tribal lands. The Thunderbird agreement calls for the construction of ten refineries that will produce a combined annual output of up to 250 million gallons of jet fuel and diesel fuel. The project also includes the development of five waste to energy plants for converting waste biomass into molasses for food production, and into ethanol, and other biochemicals. In the United States, CERT currently holds "absolute control" over 30 percent of the coal west of the Mississippi River, 40 percent of known uranium reserves, and 9 percent of known oil and gas reserves.[69]

CERT's focus on renewable energy, and its attention to reclamation projects for polluted land, express the organization's sense of environmental responsibility. But the Myth of the Ecological Indian would only simplify and distort the complexities involved in developing an economically feasible approach to industrial development that also minimizes the environmental impact of those industries. In 2013, Diné Citizens Against Ruining our Environment (Diné CARE) protested against the tribe's purchase of the Navajo Mine in Fruitland, New Mexico. The seller, BHP Billiton, had operated the coal mine profitably since 1984 and pumped about $41 million annually into the Navajo Nation's economy. Advocates of the sale declared that 10 percent of the mine's profits would help finance research into renewable energy. However, Diné CARE criticized the sale, arguing that ownership of the mine burdens the tribe with

---

67. Voyles, *Wastelanding*, 125.

68. Ibid., 126.

69. "Council of Energy Resource Tribes Enters $3 Billion Biofuels and Bioenergy Agreement," *Indian Country Today Media Network*, September 25, 2012. http://indiancountrytodaymedianet-work.com/2012/09/25/council-energy-resource-tribes-enters-3-billion-biofuels-and-bioenergy-agreement-135584 (accessed October 13, 2016).

continued economic dependence on an energy industry notorious for its damage to the region's air and water.[70] Currently, the Navajo Mine employs about 375 workers, 80 percent of whom are Navajo. The mine supplies coal to its sole customer, Arizona Public Service Company's Four Corners Power Plant (FCCP), one of the largest coal-fired plants in the United States. Constructed on Navajo land between 1963 and 1970, FCCP operates under a lease from the Navajo Nation.[71] In April 2016, Diné CARE and other environmental groups filed a lawsuit challenging the U.S. Department of the Interior's twenty-five-year extension of operations at FCCP and the Navajo Mine.[72] But Steve Gundersen, chairman of the company created by the Navajo to help acquire and manage the mine, stated:

> The most immediate purpose for buying the mine was to preserve the stability of the Navajo Nation's economy. If the mine and power plant were removed from the Navajo economy, the results, within a year, would have been devastating. We needed to preserve the business and income.[73]

Thus, within the Navajo Nation, tensions between economic interests and environmental concerns remain ongoing, regardless of what the Myth of the Ecological Indian says. According to the myth, any development that endangers the environment belongs solely to the White world, while the Indian retains an instinctive reverence for the natural world. Attractive as this simplified construction might be to some people, it operates only through denial of the complex political, economic, social, and environmental issues historically navigated by Native Americans.

Sustainable Agriculture

Five current Native American sustainable agriculture organizations are Traditional Native American Farmer's Association (TNAFA),[74] White Earth Land Recovery

70. Anne Minard, "Diné CARE Opposing 'Bad Business Decision' That Is the Navajo Mine, *Indian Country Today Media Network*, December 23, 2013, http://indiancountrytodaymedianetwork. com/2013/12/23/dine-care-opposing-bad-business-decision-navajo-mine-152842 (accessed October 13, 2016.)

71. James Fenton, "Navajo Mine Owners Ready to Take Over From BHB," *Farmington Daily Times*, June 25, 2016, http://www.daily-times.com/story/money/industries/coal/2016/06/25/navajo-mine-owners-ready-take-over-bhp/85856610/ (accessed October 13, 2016).

72. James Fenton, "Feds sued Over Fruitland Power Plant, Mines," Farmington Daily Times, April 22, 2016, http://www.daily-times.com/story/money/industries/oil-gas/2016/04/20/feds-sued-over-fruitland-power-plant-mine/83288808/ (accessed October 13, 2016).

73. Steve Gundersen, quoted in Rebecca Fairfax Clay, "Tribe at a Crossroads: The Navajo Nation Purchases a Coal Mine, "*Environmental Health Perspectives*, Volume 122, Number 4, April, 2014. http://ehp.niehs.nih.gov/122-a104/ (accessed October 14, 2016).

74. Traditional Native American Farmer's Association, http://www.tnafa.org (accessed July 7, 2017).

Project,[75] San Ildefonso Pueblo Community Farm Program,[76] Tohono O'odham Community Action,[77] and Mvskoke Food Sovereignty Initiative.[78] The TNAFA provides one definition of sustainable agriculture as "the harmonious integration of landscape and people, providing food, energy, shelter, and other needs . . . for all species."

Formed in 1992 in Gallup, New Mexico, the TNAFA currently represents seventy-two farming families from seventeen Native communities in New Mexico and Arizona. Through the TNAFA, Native farmers and elders address multiple issues surrounding genetic seed loss. Their programs preserve and conserve traditional seeds in the interests of biological and cultural diversity. Also, the TNAFA is devoted to regenerating and stabilizing the culture, health, and economy of Native communities by focusing not on agribusiness models but on community-based organic farming. The TNAFA sees the loss of traditional diets as the primary cause for the high rates of obesity, heart disease, and diabetes in its communities, and it works to reverse the health crisis by growing crops from traditional seeds and by adhering to traditional food processing and consumption.

The White Earth Land Recovery Project see its mission as "the recovery of the original land base of the White Earth Indian Reservation [in Minnesota] while preserving and restoring traditional practices of sound land stewardship, language fluency, community development, and strengthening our spiritual and cultural heritage." It markets traditional food under the label Native Harvest; operates Niiji Radio, KKWB, with programs in both Anishinaabemowin (Ojibwe) and English; and installs solar heaters in homes on the White Earth Reservation.

Since 2010, the San Ildefonso Pueblo Community Farm Program has been using traditional dry farming techniques to raise ancestral crop varieties. Based near Tucson, Arizona, the Tohono O'odham Community Action organized in 1996. It trains community members to cultivate traditional and nontraditional crops. It publishes the magazine *Native Foodways*, operates the Desert Rain Café, and works with Tohono O'odham schools to serve traditional foods in their cafeterias. In Okmulgee, Oklahoma, the Mvskoke Food Sovereignty Initiative works to provide the Mvskoke people with food produced through sustainable agriculture techniques and offers courses in farming and ranching.

Food sovereignty stands as a goal for Indigenous programs that promote sustainable agriculture. Tohono O'odham Community Action, for example, endorses the 2007 Declaration of Nyéléni in Sélingué, Mali, an event that drew five hundred representatives from over eighty countries. The declaration defines food sovereignty as

75. White Earth Land Recovery Project, https://welrp.org (accessed July 7, 2017).

76. San Ildefonso Pueblo Community Farm Program, http://www.sanipueblo.org/farm-program.aspx (accessed July 7, 2017).

77. Tohono O'odham Community Action, http://www.tocaonline.org (accessed July 7, 2017).

78. Mvskoke Food Sovereignty Initiative, http://www.mvskokefood.org (accessed July 7, 2017).

"the right of peoples to healthy and culturally appropriate food produced through ecologically sound and sustainable methods, and their right to define their own food and agricultural systems."[79]

Indigenous agricultural sustainability, then, stands as a political issue on a global scale.

Dispense with the Myth

Dispensing with the Myth of the Ecological Indian makes room for Native American environmental history to speak for itself. That history of experimentation and technological innovation that yielded new crop varieties and expanded arable land bases also includes a record of resource depletion caused by either human activity or environmental change, or by a combination of the two; thus, Indigenous societies needed to continually reinvent themselves to survive. The Myth of the Ecological Indian freezes that history. In effect, the myth creates yet another Indian caricature.

The myth arose in part as a means for criticizing the environmental degradation—the air and water pollution—caused by industrialization; thus, as we have seen, the myth started to gain traction especially by the late nineteenth century. One telling modern use of the myth came in 1971, when the nonprofit organization Keep America Beautiful launched a public service announcement (PSA) that introduced the "crying Indian." The PSA featured Iron Eyes Cody, an Italian American actor (born Espera Oscar de Corti) who portrayed Native American characters in over two hundred Hollywood films. With the PSA, he serves a multipurpose role by combining the Myths of the Noble, Authentic, and Ecological Indian.[80]

In the PSA, Cody canoes through a polluted urban landscape. When he steps ashore, someone tosses a bag of garbage from a speeding car. The bag lands at his feet. The camera cuts to his face, revealing a single tear rolling down his cheek. Meanwhile, the voice-over tells us: "Some people have a deep abiding respect for the natural beauty that was once this country, and some people don't." In another PSA, Cody rides a horse through a pristine forest and then comes upon a trash-strewn landscape, as the voice-over intones: "The first American people loved the land. They held it in simple reverence. And in some Americans today that spirit is reborn. . . . But all around us are reminders of how far we still have to go." Cue the tear.

The good intentions behind these PSAs are not in question. At issue stands the simplistic binary that places, on one side, a stereotyped Indian used as a symbol of

---

79. Declaration of Nyéléni, https://nyeleni.org/spip.php?article290 (accessed June 7, 2017).

80. To his credit, he supported Native American causes throughout his life. See: http://css.khwebs.com/ (accessed June 23, 2017).

ancient ecological wisdom and, on the other side, a world destroyed by industrialization and ignorance. Locked in the past, the Indian has no place in modernity; he merely rides through it and laments its many follies. This good versus evil melodrama serves only a social agenda and cannot substitute for the complexities of history. The repetition of Indian stereotypes merely re-inscribes unexamined perceptions of both past and present actions and issues regarding Native Americans.

7. Shopping at the Indian Myth Boutique: The Myth of the Mystical Indian

The Rainbow bridge to a renewed Earth was first shown to me in a vision given me by White Buffalo Calf Pipe Woman, the mysterious holy woman who came many generations ago to a small group of Lakota people, bringing the Sacred Pipe that represents the Oneness and holiness of the Circle of Life. She . . . has been an inner guide and teacher to me and to many others of this generation. [She took me to the edge of a chasm.] On the other side was a radiantly golden world. . . . Two-leggeds went about peacefully and joyfully . . . nibbling for their sweet taste the fruits and plants that grew about them in profusion. It was a glorious place—a golden dream for us and all Our Relations. . . . Then I turned back to look behind me. . . . There was smog on the horizon and acridness in the air. . . . There was arguing and fighting and warring, repression and prejudice. . . . The scream of chain saws bespoke cutting the precious trees on the hills. [Then] White Buffalo Woman [sent] a rainbow of light that jumped across the chasm to rest on the other side. [She said,] "To make a rainbow, all colors of light must be included. None can be left out, or there will be no bridge. [The rainbow] reminds you that you will find joy and happiness by creating them through singing, dancing and celebrating together in gratefulness for the beauty the Creator has given. . . . Rather than working for it, you must dance *your lives as the old ones did*. Nurturing ceremony and joyful celebration will be not only the hallmarks but also the means into this wonderful future."[1]

Brooke Medicine Eagle (Daughter of the Rainbow of the Morning Star Clan Whose Helpers Are the Sun and the Moon and Whose Medicine Is the Eagle) here relates her mystical initiation into shamanism. Throughout her book *The Last Ghost Dance: A Guide for Earth Mages* (2000), and elsewhere, she signals her right to speak with authority on Native American spiritual beliefs by claiming White Buffalo Woman as "an inner guide and teacher." She claims Crow, Nez Perce, Lakota, Cree, Piegan, and Cherokee ancestry.[2] Indeed, her website once featured her Crow nation enrollment

---

1. Brooke Medicine Eagle, *The Last Ghost Dance: A Guide for Earth Mages* (New York: Ballantine, 2000), xv–xvii. Italics in original.

2. "About Brook Medicine Eagle," http://www.medicineeagle.com/meet-brooke/ (accessed October 24, 2016.)

card, until Crow officials revealed the card as a forgery. After deleting the card,[3] she bestowed upon herself the status of "a non-traditional member of the Crow tribe in Montana,"[4] probably attempting, as one blogger noted, "to come up with a reason why she would not be able to present an enrollment card. . . . 'Traditionality' however defined, is not a prerequisite to gain enrollment."[5] Currently, her website asserts, "She has always identified with the richness of all humanity, rather than any one tribe or people."[6] This tactic conveniently sidesteps enrollment issues. No tribe in either the United States or Canada recognizes her as a valid member. In 1984, the American Indian Movement identified Brook Medicine Eagle as a White charlatan who profits from her charade as a Native American spiritual leader.[7] By proclaiming, "My baseline spirituality is Native American,"[8] she blurs historical and cultural distinctions between dissimilar Indigenous Peoples. Moreover, she imports Christianity and astrology into her "baseline spirituality":

> The seed of truth . . . will grow in its own time. [We] are standing on Earthly ground as the seed unfolds into the light again after being set by Dawn Star 2000 years ago. We are the heirs of the Ghost Dancers from the 1600s to the 1800s. That seed's sprouting into the light was the Harmonic Convergence which occurred on August 17, 1987.[9]

---

3. Although removed from Brooke Medicine Eagle's website, the card remains available here: http://web.archive.org/web/20050410203451/http://www.medicine-eagle.com/tribal_certificate.htm (accessed October 24, 2016).

4. "About Brook Medicine Eagle."

5. "Brooke 'Medicine Eagle' Edwards—Plastic Shaman with 40 years of Experience in Fleecing," https://blog.psiram.com/2015/04/brooke-medicine-eagle-edwards-plastic-shaman-with-some-40-years-of-experience-in-fleecing/ (accessed October 24, 2016).

6. "About Brook Medicine Eagle."

7. Graham H. Harvey and Robert J. Wallis, *Historical Dictionary of Shamanism* (Lanham, MD: Rowman and Littlefield, 2016), 21.

8. "Private Time with Brooke," http://www.medicineeagle.com/private-work-with-brooke/ (accessed October 24, 2016).

9. Brooke Medicine Eagle, *Last Ghost Dance*, 57. Note her conflation of the 1680 Pueblo Rebellion led by Popé with the late nineteenth-century Ghost Dance, an amalgam of Native American and Christian religious beliefs largely associated with the Paiute leader Wovoka. The astrological term "harmonic convergence" refers to a planetary alignment considered by New Age adherents as mystically propitious. For the Pueblo Rebellion, see Andrew L. Knaut, *The Pueblo Revolt of 1680: Conquest and Resistance in Seventeenth-Century New Mexico* (Norman: University of Oklahoma Press, 1995). For the Ghost Dance, see Michael Hittman, *Wovoka and the Ghost Dance* (Lincoln: University of Nebraska Press, 1997) and Gregory E. Smoak, *Ghost Dances and Identity: Prophetic Religion and American Indian Ethnogenesis in the Nineteenth Century* (Berkeley: University of California Press, 2008). For the harmonic convergence, see Philip Jenkins, *Dream Catchers: How Mainstream America Discovered Native Spirituality* (New York: Oxford University Press, 2004), 194–95.

Through her shamanic supervision, her followers (those who purchase her books and merchandise available through her online Rainbow Trading Post or perhaps pay $2,000.00 for her seven-day FlowerSong Retreat[10]) can be assured of receiving authentic spiritual guidance, thanks to her mystical connection with White Buffalo Calf Pipe Woman.

To the contrary, many Lakota believe that Ptehincala Ska Win, usually translated as White Buffalo Calf Woman, taught sacred ceremonies and gave the *canupa*, the pipe, only to them and to no one else. Accordingly, by appropriating Lakota religious beliefs, and by profiting from them, Brooke Medicine Eagle effectively commits sacrilege.[11] Likewise, some Christians might find her reference to Christ as Dawn Star offensive. However, here she taps into the popular notion that some traditional Native American beliefs appear to stem from an ancient North American visit by Christ. Accordingly, the Indian Great Spirit stands analogous to the Christian God. But Brooke Medicine Eagle also turns elements of Hinduism, ancient Celtic beliefs, paranormal activity, and magic spells into expressions of Native American spirituality. According to her, Indians possesses a naturally mystical aptitude for insight into religious ideas throughout the world. Accordingly, Native American shamans—like herself—train to bring these spiritual and psychic connections to light.

The Myth of the Mystical Indian drives the profits of a lucrative publishing, merchandising, and lecture circuit industry. Brooke Medicine Eagle's work typifies the methods taken by a multitude of mostly Euro-American writers and artists who capitalize on promoting the myth. Moreover, banking on equations between Native American spiritual beliefs and reverence for the earth, the Myth of the Mystical Indian turns the Myth of the Ecological Indian into a for-profit enterprise.

From Heathen Snares to Tourist Traps

The Myth of the Mystical Indian builds on several centuries' worth of misconceptions about Native American religious beliefs. European colonists sometimes viewed these beliefs sympathetically; however, perceptions of Indians as savage heathens dominated early records. Later Euro-American commentators generally followed suit. But by the end of the nineteenth century—after Indians no longer posed a threat to White settlement—romanticized notions of Native American spiritual values took hold of the popular imagination. These notions accelerated across the twentieth century. Two world wars, the Cold War, and especially the cultural fracturing that came with the Vietnam War, all in their turn led growing numbers of White Americans to question

---

10. "Private Time with Brooke."

11. Nick Estes, "Protect He Sapa, Stop Cultural Exploitation," July 14, 2015, *Indian Country Today*, http://indiancountrytodaymedianetwork.com/2015/07/14/protect-he-sapa-stop-cultural-exploitation (accessed October 25, 2016).

the mainstream values of their society. Some saw Christianity as a tool for hypocrites who prayed on Sunday and went to war on Monday. Answers seemed to lie in the direction of Native American religions. Enter the Mystical Indian.

The Myth of the Mystical Indian initially gathered momentum in the nineteenth century. It arose partly as a reaction to long-standing prejudiced distortions of Native American religious beliefs. As seen in Chapter 2, the distortions first developed when North American colonials attempted to frame these beliefs within European world-views. The result enhanced existing White animosity against Indians. A compatriot of Virginia's Jamestown colony Henry Spelman (1595–1623) wrote, "For the most part they worship the divell, which the conjurers who are ther preests, can make apeare unto them at ther pleasure, yet never the less in every country they have a severall Image whom they call ther god."[12] William Strachey, (1572–1621), another Virginia commentator, corroborated and expanded Spellman's view:

> The Inhabitants have not a Religion. . . . Their chief god they worship is no other indeed than the devil. . . . Indeed their Priests being ministers of Satahn (who is very likely visibly conversant amongst them) feare and tremble lest the knowledge of god and of our Saviour Jesus Christ should be taught in those parts.[13]

Even Roger Williams (1603–83), a trusted friend of New England's Narragansetts, believed that Indians practiced witchcraft; moreover, he wrote, "After being in their houses and beholding what their worship was, I durst never bee an eye-witness, spectator, or looker on, lest I should have been a partaker of Satan's inventions and worships."[14]

In a similar vein, the Jesuit Joseph de Jouvancy (1643–1719) wrote of his experience with the Indians whom he encountered in New France:

> There is among them no system of religion, or care for it. They honor a Deity who has no definite character or regular code of worship. They perceive, however, through the twilight, as it were, that some deity does

---

12. Henry Spelman, "An English Boy among the Indians: 1609–11," in *Captain John Smith: Writings with Other Narratives of Roanoke, Jamestown, and the First English Settlement of America*, ed. James Horn (New York: The Library of America, 2007), 969.

13. William Strachey, "The Indians of Virginia: 1612," in Horn, *Captain John Smith*, 1070–71.

14. Roger Williams, quoted in *Witches of the Atlantic World: An Historical Reader and Primary Sourcebook*, ed. Elaine G. Breslaw (New York: New York University Press, 2000), 197. Alfred Cave's analysis of Williams' statement deserves attention. He argues that, on balance, Williams understood that unlike common English perceptions of witches as primarily maleficent, Native American shamans manipulated purportedly evil spirits and warded them off in order to heal the sick. See Alfred Cave, "Indian Shamans and English Witches," in *Witches of the Atlantic World: An Historical Reader and Primary Sourcebook*, ed. Elaine G. Breslaw (New York: New York University Press, 2000), 196–203.

exist. . . . They call some divinity, who is the author of evil, "Manitou," and fear him exceedingly. Beyond doubt, it is the enemy of the human race, who extorts from some people divine honors and sacrifices.[15]

Protestant luminary Cotton Mather (1663–1728) identified connections between New England's Indians and Satan:

Though we know not *when* or *how* these Indians first became inhabitants of this mighty continent, yet we may guess that probably the Devil decoyed these miserable salvages hither in hopes that the gospel of the Lord Jesus Christ would never come here to destroy or disturb his *absolute empire* over them.[16]

Notions of Indians as "Red Devils" persisted, but by the eighteenth century, if not earlier, some commentators discerned more charitable comparisons between Native American beliefs and Christianity. Naturalist William Bartram's (1739–1823) observations on Southeastern Indians concentrated on the common ground that he perceived between their beliefs and a Christian worldview. He took solace in their recognition of an all-powerful deity who rewarded the departed faithful with a spiritual paradise of eternal bliss:

These Indians . . . adore the Great Spirit, the giver and taker away of the breath of life. . . . They believe in a future state where the spirit exists, which they call the world of the spirits, where they enjoy . . . a serene, unclouded, and peaceful sky . . . where there is fullness of pleasure uninterrupted.[17]

His willingness to at least meet Indians halfway on the metaphysical plain contrasts markedly from ideas of Indians as agents of Satan.

Along with the perceived Great Spirit/Christian God equation, writers also searched Native American beliefs for evidence of a messiah, a Christ figure. Both approaches exhibit an early Euro-American appropriation of Indian culture. Writers construed certain Indian stories into proofs that a proto-Christian worldview permeated the forests and plains. There dwelled God's red children. Such views validated Native American religious beliefs, not in their own right but because they appeared to resemble basic Christian tenets. The Indians imagined by Henry Wadsworth Longfellow conformed to Western models and adhered to religious beliefs familiar to his

---

15. Joseph de Jouvancy, *Concerning the Country and Manners of the Canadians, or the Savages of New France* (Rome: Printing House of Giorgio Placko, 1710), 287.

16. Cotton Mather, quoted in *The Puritans: A Sourcebook of Their Writings*, Vol. 2, edited by Perry Miller and Thomas Johnson (New York: Harper, 1963), 503.

17. William Bartram, *Travels and Other Writings* (New York: The Library of America, 1996), 489–96.

Christian audience. In his *Song of Hiawatha*, the godhead Gitche Manito speaks to the assembled tribes:

> On the great Red Pipe-stone Quarry,
> Gitche Manito, the mighty,
> He the Master of Life, descending
> On the red crags of the quarry
> Stood erect, and called the nations,
> Called the tribes of men together.
>
> . . .
>
> I will send a Prophet to you,
> A Deliverer of the nations,
> Who shall guide you and shall teach you,
> Who shall toil and suffer with you.[18]

When President Grant launched his Peace Policy, which partnered Protestant churches with the federal government in order to bring "civilization" to the Indians, his Peace Commission initially reported in 1868, "They have not the Bible, but their religion, which we call superstition, teaches them that the Great Spirit made us all. In the difference of language to-day lies two-thirds of our trouble."[19] Although recognition of shared beliefs appeared to move in the direction of religious toleration, the policy's goal of converting Indians to Christianity undercut any notion that the commission placed Indian religions on equal footing with Christianity. Rather, the Great Spirit served as a conceptual bridge across which missionaries could lead Indians into salvation. In 1923, the prominent Protestant missionary Gustavus Elmer Emmanuel Lindquist proudly claimed a history of conversions built on supposed proto-Christian beliefs:

> The religious instinct is of the very fiber of the race. The crude Messianic beliefs prevalent among many Indian tribes responded readily to the teachings of the early missionaries, and the Indian of to-day continues to respond by "out-ward and visible signs" to the "inward and spiritual grace" bestowed upon him through increasing knowledge of the word of the "Great Spirit."[20]

Similar religious ideas found a home in public classrooms. At a 1922 conference on children's reading, R. Ray Baker prescribed the approach that teachers should

---

18. Henry Wadsworth Longfellow, *Longfellow: Poems and Other Writings* (New York: Library of America, 2000), 144–47.

19. Peace Commission, "Report of the Indian Peace Commission," in *Documents of United States Indian Policy*, ed. Francis Paul Prucha (Lincoln: University of Nebraska Press, 2000), 106.

20. Gustavus Elmer Emmanuel Lindquist, *The Red Man in the United States: An Intimate Study of the Social, Economic, and Religious Life of the American Indians* (New York: George R. Doran, 1923), xv.

take with Native American stories. Baker proposed that certain stories provided rich opportunities for students to appreciate Indians, since at least some tribes seemed primitively touched by God's hand:

> The aboriginees [sic] in their primeval state, were considered pagans, and doubtless many of them were. However, some of the tribes, particularly those of the Iroquois confederacy, held many ideas which tho [sic] crude, are associated primarily with Christian belief. For instance, the Iroquois had one god, who was omnipotent, beneficent, and permeated the universe and most of the tribes of North America held a belief in immortality and a heaven which they designated as "The Happy Hunting Grounds." Also, the mythology of various tribes contain legends of a Messiah.[21]

Here Native American religious beliefs remained in the realm of mere superstition. However, the stereotyped concept of "Happy Hunting Grounds" becomes a Christian Heaven, and the Christian notion of a supreme God appears automatically accompanied by idea of a worldly messenger sent by that God to save Indians in general. Yet by the early twentieth century, anthropologists and ethnologists had amassed a substantial body of well-researched studies that cumulatively argued for the recognition of Indian spiritual beliefs, devoid of any supposed Christian equivalencies, as equal in value, on their intrinsic merits, to those of Christianity, or to any of the world's other religions.

Anthropologist Franz Boas (1858–1942) claimed that different social and geographical environments produced different cultures. One culture did not rate higher than another. Boas' "democratization" inspired many scholars to reevaluate existing ideas about Indians and their beliefs. His theory, known as cultural relativism, challenged the earlier anthropological theory chiefly associated with Lewis Henry Morgan (1818–81). Morgan argued for an evolutionary model of social development, according to which humankind passed through three great stages: savagery, barbarism, and civilization. Sometimes savages and barbarians froze permanently at their levels. Occasionally, others advanced to civilization, the highest stage.[22] Morgan dismissed "primitive religions"—Native American religions fell into this range—as "grotesque

---

21. R. Ray Baker, "What Is the Educational or Moral Value for Boys and Girls in Reading the Books about the American Indian?" in *Public Libraries: A Monthly Review of Library Matters and Methods*, vol. 27 (Chicago: Library Bureau, 1922), 324.

22. Morgan's attempt to apply the theory of biological evolution to society did not wear well, and most serious scholarship eventually rejected it. In 1918, anthropologist Berthold Laufer attacked cultural evolution as "the most inane, sterile, and pernicious theory ever conceived in the history of science." Berthold Laufer, "Culture and Ethnology by Robert H. Lowie" (review), *American Anthropologist* 20 (1918): 90. However, Morgan conducted pioneering ethnological research in Iroquoian kinship structures. His *The League of the Ho-de-no-sau-nee or Iroquois* (1851) remained a classic for generations of scholars. His *Ancient Society* (1877) built on his kinship research to fully construct his evolutionary theory.

and to some extent unintelligible."[23] Whereas Boasian relativists compared Native American and Christian beliefs, they did not rank them.[24] Without placing undue emphasis on the mainstream impact of an academic theory, it suffices to say that cultural relativism at least shared the stage with growing White curiosity about Native American religious practices.

This curiosity—especially about Southwestern Indians—drove increasing numbers of White Americans to travel to and to personally experience some of the "exotic" tribes that they previously viewed only in magazines and books. By 1884, the Southern Pacific and the Atlantic and Pacific railroads completed their Southwestern lines. Moreover, after the U.S. military captured the Apache leader Geronimo in 1886, and with the collapse of the Ghost Dance movement following the Wounded Knee Massacre in 1890, the Indian Wars of the previous decades effectively ended. These final military defeats signaled new tourist opportunities for White Americans, as Western boosters widely advertised that any fear of Indian attacks belonged to a bygone era. Railroads financed Southwestern hotels and resorts. As noted in Chapter 3, they launched massive advertising campaigns throughout the United States. Brochures featured exotic descriptions of ancient Native American ruins. The Denver & Rio Grande Railroad romanticized Mesa Verde as the heart of "the mystical Southwest" and urged tourists to experience "America's sublime antiquity [which] has the lure of a mystery greater than the ruined cities of the old world."[25]

By 1907, both Mesa Verde and Chaco Canyon became national parks. Along with venturing through their Ancestral Puebloan ruins, the avid tourist likely took in a Hopi Snake Dance, often advertised as the essential Native American religious experience. Travel writer Charles Francis Saunders commented in 1912:

> Were it not for the annual Snake Dance of the Hopis, it is probable that few travellers except those of the fireside would have any knowledge of these people. As it is, the Snake Dance has been so industriously written up and talked over that it has become a magnet which, every August, draws more or less of a crowd of tourists and holiday-makers across the

---

23. Lewis Henry Morgan, *Ancient Society, or Researches in the Lines of Human Progress from Savagery to Barbarism to Civilization* (New York: Henry Holt, 1907), 5–6.

24. As anthropologists Margaret Mead—Boas' most famous student—and John Whiting summarized, "We have stood out against any grading of cultures of the world in a descending scale according to the extent to which they differ from ours." Margaret Mead and John Whiting, "The Role of South Sea Cultures in the Post War World," *American Anthropologist* 45 (1943): 193. For another instructive example, see James Mooney, *The Ghost-Dance Religion and the Sioux Outbreak of 1890* (Lincoln: University of Nebraska Press, 1991). First published in 1897, the book remains an essential ethnographic study. He writes, "The doctrines of the Hindu avatar, the Hebrew Messiah, the Christian millennium, and the Hesunanin [Wovoka] of the Indian Ghost dance are essentially the same, and have their origin in a hope and longing common to all humanity." Ibid., 657.

25. Quoted in Jenkins, *Dream Catchers*, 66.

desert sands to witness this most entrancing and most dramatic half-hour entertainment that America has to offer.[26]

Saunders then added his voice to the growing number of those who defended Native American religions when he chastised "the average white onlooker" for seeing only entertainment in: "a solemn and religious rite—the public *dénouement* of a nine-days' secretly-conducted intercession for the divine favour."[27]

Many onlookers believed that the rituals they witnessed belonged to nearly extinct peoples. Operating here to enhance the tourist experience, the Myth of the Vanishing Indian complemented the Mystical Indian. According to this view, Native American dances and ceremonies, however profound and religiously valid, belonged to the past. Destined to fade with the onslaught of modernity, the last of these living religious relics must be seen *now*. The urgency resulted in part from the mistaken belief that the religious practices of Indians persisted unchanged throughout time. Native Americans somehow remained immune to the historical fluidity of religious doctrines and practices common to the rest of the world. Local variations of the same general beliefs, and influence from other beliefs—transmitted through communication and trade routes—have produced often incremental but at times dramatic changes in the world's rich and dynamic array of religious expressions. However, in the popular imagination, Indian religions by some unexplained means remained "pure," and because of their fragile state they must be recorded for posterity before being lost forever.

At the same time, considering the often-brutal suppression of Native American religions across the centuries, the tenuousness of their survival remained real. Yet grim assessments sometimes relied on preconceptions of Indians as passive receptors of the many egregious federal policies that outlawed their religions. Discounting the historical agency of Indians, White commentators often prophesized their inability to retain traditional religious beliefs.

Fearing the disappearance of these beliefs, a sense of urgency drove not only tourists to the Southwest. By the early twentieth century, an enclave of artists, writers, and intellectuals developed in Taos, New Mexico, drawn there by the climate and landscape and by their interest in the region's Indian cultures. With the founding of the Taos Society of Artists in 1914, and through the attention brought to it by a wealthy and erudite benefactor, Mabel Dodge Luhan, the media often highlighted the society's interest in Indians. This press coverage proved beneficial to the tourist trade. In turn, Indian religions proved lucrative to commercial interests.

But the establishment of the Taos art colony—and of another one in Santa Fe—belongs primarily to the Atchison, Topeka, and Santa Fe Railway (ATSF), which retained a vested interest in promoting the image of the Mystical Indian.

---

26. Charles Francis Saunders, *The Indians of the Terraced Houses* (New York: G. P. Putnam's Sons, 1912), 203.

27. Ibid.

In this poster, the horse-mounted Indian warriors remain sidelined in the past. The Warbonnet locomotive debuted in 1937. It came in two major models, the *Super Chief* and the *Chief*. The caption reads: "Headed by the *Super Chief* and *The Chief*, the Santa Fe great fleet of trains between Chicago and California offers a choice of fine accommodations to satisfy every taste and fit every pocketbook. And between Chicago and Texas, it's the *Texas Chief*. For smooth riding comfort . . . friendly hospitality . . . delicious Fred Harvey meals . . . fascinating scenery . . . travel Santa Fe—*the Chief Way!*" "Chiefs Poster," Santa Fe System Lines. http://www.american-rails.com/images/ATSFINDADCHIEF.jpg.

Beginning in 1898, the railway brought painters to northern New Mexico and commissioned them to produce travel posters. Many featured idealized images of Indians. Even the Santa Fe's "Warbonnet" locomotive design drew directly on Indian stereotypes.

Dozens of artists transformed the inequitable social conditions of the region's Indians into paintings that often conveyed an enticing sense of mystery about the Southwest. Reproduced as color lithographs in ATSF calendars, brochures, menus, and train folders, these images tempted tourists to travel, to see the land with their own eyes, and to watch the Indians perform their exotic ancient rituals.[28] The process of mystification came easily to artists who preferred to idealize their subjects, to blur the uncomfortable realities of an arid, isolated, underdeveloped frontier region. Indeed, early Anglo artists in Taos fought against efforts to bring electrification and modern plumbing to the town, placing them at odds with the local progressive Hispanic population. The artists, as arch-conservationists, wanted to preserve the region's rustic charm. They fled the expensive urban East to live in the Wild West and to paint Indians according to their own Romantic visions. They happily sold their paintings to wealthy Eastern patrons but preferred the inexpensive living conditions in Taos. Impoverished Hispanic and Native American workers built houses, hired out as servants, and acted as models for the painters.[29] Rusticity must be preserved. It provided cheap labor. The artists invested as heavily in the Myth of the Authentic Indian as in the Myth of the Mystical Indian.

The artists transformed the region's economic liabilities into assets by flooding the marketplace with their imaginative works. Their paintings meant passenger revenue for the ATSF. Affiliated with the ATSF, the Fred Harvey Company—the world's first chain restaurant—also profited mightily from the tourist trade. Moreover, tourists booked rooms in ATSF-affiliated hotels throughout the Southwest. The Myth of the Mystical Indian meant big money in many pockets.

Indians served as the mystical Other, not as regular human beings. Most paintings and photographs did not convey realistic portraits of them as they actually appeared in everyday life. Romantic compositions presented them in prototypical dress and tended to portray them as ideal types in harmony with nature, caught in pristine, eternal moments. Mass marketing and the tourist industry helped to transform Native Americans from devilish savages to sublime priests. The transformation set the stage for the Mystical Indian as the featured image in lucrative publishing, consulting, and advertising enterprises. Indeed, the state of New Mexico apparently channeled the Mystical Indian into its motor vehicle department in 1941, when it initiated the license plate logo, "Land of Enchantment."[30]

Rainbow Warriors

William Willoya and Vinson Brown's *Warriors of the Rainbow: Strange and Prophetic Dreams of the Indian Peoples* (1962) claims to present an authentic Native American prophecy. As the authors explain, "The story told below, we believe actually happened,

---

28. Keith L. Bryant, Jr., "The Atchison, Topeka, and Santa Fe Railway and the Development of the Taos and Santa Fe Art Colonies," *Western Historical Quarterly* 9 (1978): 437.

29. Sylvia Rodríguez, "Art Tourism, and Race Relations in Taos: Toward a Sociology of the Art Colony," *Journal of Anthropological Research* 45 (1989): 78–89.

30. Ibid., passim.

although not in these exact details. We have deliberately named no tribe in this story because we want it to mean the same to all tribes, to all the Indians."[31] Willoya and Brown's story involves a wise old woman and a boy who share a vision as they peer skyward to the east and behold "a great flaming rainbow." The description reveals the book as a thinly veiled Christian treatise:

> "The rainbow is a sign from Him who is in all things," said the old wise one. "It is a sign of the union of all peoples like one big family. Go to the mountain top, child of my flesh, and learn to be a Warrior of the Rainbow, for it is only by spreading love and joy to others that hate in this world can be changed to understanding and kindness, and war and destruction shall end!"[32]

Willoya and Brown purportedly compared American Indians with Indigenous Peoples elsewhere in the world, claiming that they all shared a vision of "brotherhood and love between all races." Only God's mystical influence in the lives of these ancient peoples could explain their inherently peaceful and spiritual natures.[33]

Regardless of Willoya's Eskimo heritage, *Warriors of the Rainbow* belongs to the genre of fakelore, manufactured folklore that masquerades as authentic traditional beliefs. His coauthor, a White biologist, shared Willoya's evangelicalism. Together they produced one of the most influential books in the burgeoning Mystical Indian marketplace. Moreover, the book's romanticized fabrications inspired one of the world's most visible environmentalist organizations, Greenpeace. As Robert Hunter explains in *Warriors of the Rainbow: A Chronicle of the Greenpeace Movement* (1979), Greenpeace "attempted to fulfill an ancient North American Indian prophecy of an age when different races and nationalities would band together to defend the earth from her enemies."[34] Willoya and Brown's fiction lives on as the name of Greenpeace's famous ship, *Rainbow Warrior*. And the book serves as a fundamental text for the Rainbow Family, a countercultural movement that originated in the early 1970s.

Rainbow Family members also call themselves "the Rainbow Nation" or the "Rainbow Tribe." Their gatherings, held throughout the United States, attract thousands of mostly young White adherents. Although influenced by mixtures of religious and philosophical notions drawn from sources throughout the world, many of the Rainbow people especially idealize Native Americans and identify closely with them. But not only do Rainbows play Indian, they have sometimes regarded themselves as saviors guided by prophecies to bring Indians into their own tribe.

---

31. William Willoya and Vinson Brown, *Warriors of the Rainbow: Strange and Prophetic Drams of the Indian Peoples* (Happy Camp, CA: Naturegraph, 1962), 2.

32. Ibid., 15.

33. Ibid., 1.

34. Robert Hunter, *Warriors of the Rainbow: A Chronicle of the Greenpeace Movement* (New York: Holt, Rinehart, and Winston, 1979), ix.

For its 1972 gathering at North Table Mountain near Golden, Colorado, Rainbow Family members received a booklet, *The Rainbow Oracle of Mandala City*. Probably with its evangelical subtitle, *New Jerusalem*, in mind, the booklet includes a section called "The Tablet." It proclaims that the Rainbow Tribe might be destined to aid the beleaguered Hopi, in accord with Hopi prophecy:

> We hear of the Hopi prophecy that the Warriors of the Rainbow are to come bearing a sacred stone tablet, a red blanket and a hat. Well, my brother Barry [Adams] has this hat and blanket that match the prophecy too. So we travel to the Hopi lands and meet with the elders who tell us that it is not their stone tablet but one that belongs to someone who will come to us. Perhaps it is our tablet, perhaps the world's.[35]

A Moses fantasy, "The Tablet" appears hewn from the same missionary material found in *Warriors of the Rainbow*. Indeed, *The Rainbow Oracle* quotes Willoya and Brown's work at length.

Thomas Banyaca (1909–99), one of four Hopi men selected by the Kikmong-wis (Hopi spiritual leaders) in 1946 to interpret traditional prophecies for nontribal people,[36] did not recall any visit by Barry Adams. Moreover, he pointed out, Hopi beliefs include nothing about so-called Warriors of the Rainbow. Banyaca did remember speaking with Willoya and Brown. He speculated that their book, which he held in low regard, fueled the notion that somehow the Hopi originated the rainbow story. *Warriors of the Rainbow* also lists Banyaca in its acknowledgments, something that he found offensive: "It's not right. . . . We hope they will stop it."[37]

"The Resurrection of the American Indian," an illustration from *The Rainbow Oracle of Mandala City*, features a floating Indian head topped by a haloed figure. With arms uplifted, the figure faces backward, apparently focused on the distant circle of dancers and a cross on a hill in the upper left. In the middle plain stand tipis. A war-bonnetted Indian sits cross-legged beside a fire. In the foreground rests a shield and tomahawk in a cross formation, a further mixture of Christian symbols with iconic Native American images. The encircling inscription reads:

> The Family is the union of all races and all peoples—unto the Family is reborn the true spirit of the Indians. Thus it is foretold—the true light family will come bringing the long-lost STONE TABLET—symbol of the land, and return it to the Indians. The GREAT SPIRIT watches

---

35. "The Tablet," *The Rainbow Oracle of Mandala City: Table Mountain, Rocky Mountain Nat'l. Park: New Jerusalem* (Eugene, OR: Rainbow Family of Living Light, 1972), no pagination, http://imgur.com/a/ITJnD (accessed November 9, 2016).

36. "Thomas Banyaca biography page," http://banyacya.indigenousnative.org/bio.html (accessed November 9, 2016).

37. Michael L. Niman, *People of the Rainbow: A Nomadic Utopia* (Knoxville: University of Tennessee Press, 2011), 135–35.

"The Resurrection of the American Indian," from *The Rainbow Oracle of Mandala City*. *The Rainbow Oracle of Mandala City*, no pagination, http://imgur.com/a/ITJnD

over all of his children all of the time. From the heart center comes the RAIN-BOW joining all hands and hearts and minds.

Messianic ambitions found additional expression through the proliferating numbers of "New Age" Euro-American shamans. Although individuals who identify with the New Age might also take interest in paranormal experiences, extraterrestrials, crystals, and goddess worship, an attraction to Native American spirituality remains their common denominator. A movement only in its loosest sense, the New Age gained popularity in the early 1980s among its mostly middle-class, moderately affluent White adherents. Since most New Age related material—books, CDs, DVDs, tarot cards, crystals, aura photos, gemstones, psychic readings, workshops, concerts, seminars, and sweat lodges—require purchase, New Ageism remains rooted in consumerism, a fundamental irony since New Agers tend to censure materialism, the foundation of consumer society.[38]

Some Native American activists refer to the self-styled shamans, like the aforementioned Brooke Medicine Eagle, as "Shake and Bake Shamans," or as "Plastic Medicine People."[39] In 1980, an intertribal group of Native American elders issued the "Resolution of the Fifth Annual Meeting of the Traditional Elder Circle." The resolution strongly condemned the White usurpation of Native American religious practices:

> Various individuals are . . . purporting to be spiritual leaders. They . . . are gathering non-Indian people as followers who believe they are receiving instructions of the original people. We the Elders and our representatives sitting in Council give warning to these non-Indian followers that it is our understanding this is not a proper process and the authority to carry these sacred objects is given by the people and the purpose and procedure is specific to time and the needs of the people. The medicine people are chosen by the medicine and long instruction and discipline is necessary before ceremonies and healing can be done. These procedures

38. Lisa Aldred, "Plastic Shamans and Astroturf Sun Dances: New Age Commercialization of Native American Spirituality," *American Indian Quarterly* 24 (2000): 330.

39. Ibid., 331.

are always in the Native tongue; there are no exceptions and profit is not the motivation.[40]

Lynn V. Andrews, known by her critics, as well as by some of her followers, as the "Beverly Hills shaman," has published books listed as bestsellers by *The New York Times*. With her mentors Agnes Whistling Elk and Ruby Plenty Chiefs—supposedly Cree medicine women—she battles an evil sorcerer, learns more secrets from a flying horse that shape-shifts into a rainbow, and transmits the dreams of Australian Aborigines to her readers through a eucalyptus tree antenna. She learns how to make another antenna out of a Mayan pyramid/mesa. Zoila, her pyramid instructor, explains the procedure in both Mayan and English:

> "On this top mesa, or top triangle if you prefer, is the gatherer pyramid. It essentially brings in power and holds it. Because of this you place antennalike objects there—candles, canes, sticks, feathers, prayer sticks—whatever pulls energy down from the universe and into your prayers." Zoila pointed again. "The bottom triangle is your personal giving of power toward the center, where the pyramids converge and meet. Your shooting crystals go here, as well as your personal arrows. . . . In the center of any mesa goes your translator. This is your hermaphrodite or androgynous power representative."[41]

Andrews claims that her books only carry out Agnes Whistling Elk's demand to "Give the spirit world to your people. Let your message fly."[42] The Lynn Andrews website offers a full line of her products and services.[43]

Her work appears heavily influenced by Carlos Castaneda (1925–98), whose first book, *The Teachings of Don Juan: A Yaqui Way of Knowledge* (1968), describes the author's apprenticeship to Don Juan, a Yaqui shaman. With Don Juan's guidance, Castaneda ingests peyote, and this opens the door to his encounters with often-horrifying mystical creatures that guide him into increasingly deeper realms of spiritual knowledge. Castaneda continued his supernatural experiences with Don Juan in two other books: *A Separate Reality: Further Conversations with Don Juan* (1971) and *Journey to Ixtlan: The Lessons of Don Juan* (1972). He wrote the trilogy as a graduate student in anthropology at UCLA and presented it as authentic ethnological research;

---

40. "Resolution of the Fifth Annual Meeting of the Traditional Elder Circle," https://www.cultural-survival.org/publications/cultural-survival-quarterly/united-states/resolution-fifth-annual-meeting-elders-circle (accessed November 10, 2016).

41. Lynn V. Andrews, *Jaguar Woman and the Wisdom of the Butterfly Tree* (New York: Harper and Row, 1985), 113.

42. Lynn V. Andrews, *Medicine Woman* (New York: Harper and Row, 1981), 204.

43. *Lynn Andrews: Ancient Teachings for a Modern World*, http://lynnandrews.com/ (accessed November 10, 2016).

with it he earned a Ph.D. in 1972. Moreover, the University of California Press published all three volumes.[44]

But after he published several more books purporting to explore other visionary experiences with Native American spirit guides, questions arose regarding the authenticity of his work. He never met Don Juan because Don Juan never existed. He produced works of fiction, not anthropological research. Regardless, he remained a wildly popular author, especially on college campuses. His many defenders shrugged off any criticism of his work as mere signs of jealousy. As charges of fraud accumulated, Carlos Castaneda amassed a fortune from book sales. Indeed, all of his books remain in print, thanks primarily to an enthusiastic New Age audience.[45]

Castaneda's work stands at the forefront of fictional shaman narratives. The genre's crowded marketplace easily includes hundreds of authors. Mary Summer Rain claimed shamanic credentials through her apprenticeship to No-Eyes, a blind Indian woman who teaches her to help lost spirits in the afterworld. After their adventures together in *Spirit Song: The Introduction of No-Eyes* (1985), No-Eyes, who attended the Tonto school of Indian dialect, says: "Summer, No-Eyes be done with stuff. No-Eyes finish here. No-Eyes *all* done."[46] However, Summer Rain recalls more about her time with No-Eyes in *Phoenix Rising: No-Eyes' Vision of the Changes to Come* (1987). Here No-Eyes warns her student about the dangers of the modern world: "Summer, people gone too far too fast. They gone too fast in wrong direction. They miss right road way back in time."[47] Humanity must turn back, start over, and follow the ancient Native American paths of peaceful coexistence and harmonious relationships with Mother Earth. However, as Summer Rain explains in *Daybreak: The Dawning Ember* (1991), the Phoenix Days, destined to trigger humanity's reroute, involve a polar shift which:

> will occur moments before Armageddon in [a time frame that] may be altered by God Himself. . . . Considering that God will be walking among us during this portion of the Phoenix Days, it would naturally stand to reason that all negativity and evil will be banished from His Realms of Creation. . . . Entities such as the Inner Earth dwellers

44. Dean Chavers, "The Fake Carlos Castaneda," *Indian Country Today Media Network*, March 24, 2011, http://indiancountrytodaymedianetwork.com/2011/03/24/fake-carlos-castaneda-24168 (accessed November 10, 2016).

45. Nimen, *People of the Rainbow*, 140; *Carlos Castaneda Bibliography*, http://www.biblio.com/carlos-castaneda/author/243 (accessed November 10, 2016).

46. Mary Summer Rain, *Spirit Song: The Introduction of No-Eyes* (Norfolk, VA: Hampton Roads, 1985), 152.

47. Mary Summer Rain, *Phoenix Rising: No-Eyes' Vision of the Changes to Come* (Norfolk, VA: Hampton Roads, 1987), 43.

(Sasquatch, Little People, Fairies, etc.) . . . will join us only if they perceive it as God's will.[48]

Self-help guides claiming insight derived from traditional Native American religious ideas also flood the marketplace. The book titles themselves often make unequivocal promises for DIY shamanism. A few canonical texts include Wolf Moondance's *Rainbow Medicine: A Visionary Guide to Native American Shamanism* (1994); Thomas E. Mails' *Secret Native American Pathways: A Guide to Inner Peace* (1988); Sun Bear's *The Path to Power* (1997) and his *Dancing with the Wheel: The Medicine Wheel Workbook* (1992).[49] *Rainbow Medicine* drew exclusively from the imagination of Euro-American writer Charlene Vara, aka Wolf Moondance. Euro-American Thomas E. Mails served as a Lutheran minister in Minnesota and California. He wrote several highly romanticized accounts of Native American history. His *Secret Native American Pathways* merely perpetuates stereotypical notions about Indian spiritual beliefs.

Vincent LaDuke (1929–92), of Ojibwe descent, went by the name Sun Bear. After a brief career as a movie actor, he founded the Bear Tribe Medicine Society near Sacramento, California in 1970. Through it he attracted a White clientele—mostly college students—eager to learn about Native American religion. As the tribe's self-appointed shaman, he drew on a number of Native American religions to create a hybrid based on the central symbol of the medicine wheel. During the 1980s, and until his death in 1992, he led medicine wheel rituals throughout the West Coast, attracting thousands of mostly young White attendees. But while becoming a New Age celebrity shaman, and marketing his books, seminars, and rituals, he drew the ire of Native American activists.[50] They disrupted his seminars and ceremonies, accusing him of inventing and selling a sham religion. As one activist declared, "Use of the term 'Shaman' alone is a good indicator of fraud. Native leaders don't use the term."[51] Admission to a Sun Bear medicine wheel ceremony cost $100, the fee for a Sun Bear vision quest ran for $150, and $50 covered a sweat lodge ceremony.

New Age shamans commonly market sweat lodge ceremonies and claim an authentic Native American cleansing experience for participants. Entrance fees vary. In October 2009, about fifty people participated in a sweat lodge ceremony during a "Spiritual Warrior" seminar near Sedona, Arizona. Participants paid up to $10,000

---

48. Mary Summer Rain, *Daybreak: The Dawning Ember* (Norfolk, VA: Hampton Roads, 1991), 138–39.

49. Wolf Moondance, *Rainbow Medicine: A Visionary Guide to Native American Shamanism* (New York: Sterling, 1994); Thomas E. Mails, *Secret Native American Pathways: A Guide to Inner Peace* (Tulsa, OK: Council Oak Books, 1998); Sun Bear, Wabun Wind, and Barry Weinstock, *The Path to Power* (New York: Prentice Hall, 1997); Sun Bear, Wabun Wind, and Crysalis Mulligan, *Dancing with the Wheel: The Medicine Wheel Workbook* (New York: Simon and Schuster, 1992).

50. Jenkins, *Dream Catchers*, 172–74.

51. Quoted in Jenkins, *Dream Catchers*, 237.

apiece for five days of shamanic guidance by self-help celebrity James Arthur Ray. Ray instructed:

> The true spiritual warrior has conquered death and therefore has no fear or enemies in this lifetime or the next, because the greatest fear you'll ever experience is the fear of what? Death. You will have to get a point to where you surrender and it's OK to die.[52]

The temperature inside the lodge reached 200 degrees. Ray refused to let participants leave. Eighteen required hospitalization and three people died, including one hospitalized person who died a week later. Found guilty on three counts of negligent homicide, he served a two-year sentence. Upon release in 2013, he returned to the self-help seminar circuit.[53] After the sweat lodge deaths, Navajo journalist and president of *Three Sisters Media* Valerie Taliman wrote:

> It was a bastardized version of a sacred ceremony sold by a multimillionaire . . . for his "Spiritual Warrior" retreat. Alvin Manitopyes, a healer from the Cree, Anishnawbe and Assiniboine nations, explained that "in a sweat lodge ceremony [the intent] is to purify ourselves inside and out and restore balance within ourselves. . . . Our elders conduct sweat lodge ceremonies out of love for their people to help them in their healing and spiritual growth. When someone attaches a price tag to the ceremony, then the sacredness is gone and it comes down to them playing around with our sacred ceremonies."[54]

The Myth of the Mystical Indian distorts and commoditizes traditional Native American religious beliefs and practices. It blurs distinct geographical and cultural lines between multiple Indian religions. This leads to simplified and formulaic concepts that non-Native American audiences often find attractive. Generally, the attraction stems from dissatisfaction with mainstream White Judeo-Christian culture.

By making a colonialist assumption, the myth takes control of the Indian's spiritual realm in a manner similar to the historical expropriation of Indigenous land. The myth often imports Christian values and symbols into Indian belief systems. Sometimes this provides a missionary tool for converting Indians to Christianity. Perhaps more frequently, however, individuals and groups combine their notions of

---

52. Quoted in Felicia Fonseca, "Self-Help Guru Convicted in Sweat Lodge Deaths," *Associated Press*, 2011, http://www.nbcnews.com/id/43501833/ns/us_news-crime_and_courts/t/self-help-guru-convicted-sweat-lodge-deaths/#.WCSwteErJBw (accessed November 10, 2016).

53. Matt Stround, "Self-Help Author Imprisoned for Sweat Lodge Deaths Is Making a Comeback," *Bloomberg*, March 3, 2015, http://www.bloomberg.com/news/articles/2015-03-03/self-help-author-imprisoned-for-sweat-lodge-deaths-is-making-a-comeback (accessed November 10, 2016).

54. Valerie Taliman, "Selling the Sacred," *Indian Country Today Media Network*, October 14, 2009, http://indiancountrytodaymedianetwork.com/opinion/selling-the-sacred-15597 (accessed November 10, 2016).

the Mystical Indian with any number of religious and cultural ideas from regions and historical periods throughout the world. Often these practitioners mistakenly believe that their work honors Native Americans. In sum, the myth paternalistically assumes control of Indian religions. It manipulates them in accord with Euro-American value systems, and many who promote the myth often do so in the pursuit of economic gain.

Epilogue

James Earle Fraser, *End of the Trail*, Waupun, Wisconsin.
Photograph by Shawn Conrad, Wikipedia. CC BY-SA 3.0.

The persistence of misconceptions about Native American peoples, cultures, and histories depends primarily on mainstream preferences for simplistic notions of the past. So long as individuals "learn" their history through the media of popular culture, their dependency on broad categorizations of historical—and currently living—Indian peoples remains unchecked. Thus categorizing Indians within one or several stereotypes comes easily and naturally. Indeed, as deeply ingrained cultural defaults, these stereotypes continue to find expression in print, in broadcast programming, and online, and they are sometimes produced by otherwise well-educated individuals.

As demonstrated in *Seven Myths of Native American History*, the origins of many Indian stereotypes often reach far back to the earliest days of European contact with North America's Indigenous Peoples. Habits of thinking initiated in European sources were transmitted across centuries to remain current today as inherited—and wrongheaded—views about Indians in Canada and the United States. Moreover, no utopian age awaits that will somehow illuminate the murk of mainstream misconceptions about Indians. To the contrary, enhancements of currently existing myths—or perhaps the development of new myths altogether—seem likely, given certain patterns of thinking exhibited so far in the historical record.

Notwithstanding this grim forecast, patches of our cultural landscape might experience periodically clearing skies. University courses and degree programs in Native American history that exist—and proliferate—today arose relatively recently, mostly since 1970, and often in response to demands by Native American students and communities. During the same period, some K–12 textbook publishers developed increased sensitivity to Native American history.[1] Therefore, compared to previous generations,

---

1. For some strategies for teaching Native American history in elementary schools, see Floy C. Pepper, "Unbiased Teaching about American Indians and Alaska Natives in Elementary School,"

a growing number of students might have the chance to gain a better understanding of the Indian past and of issues concerning Indians today. But this understanding depends on the quality of their classroom resources, and the uneven process of indigenizing educational sectors often faces institutional apathy and pushback.[2]

In the area of popular culture, as examined throughout this book, many films perpetuate Indian stereotypes. A few movies turn some myths on their heads or otherwise interrogate them. But such efforts often merely reshuffle stereotypes through misguided efforts to present a sensitized understanding of Indian history. These films generally idealize Indians, as in *Pocahontas*[3] and *Dances with Wolves*,[4] so that Whites, not Indians, emerge as the demonized savages. The films present only a muddy sense of history—churned up a bit.

However, within the past few decades, a number of films either defuse Indian stereotypes and myths by ridiculing them or tell stories drawn entirely from Native American worldviews, thereby dispensing with the business of White perceptions altogether. Produced by Native Americans, these films present indigenized narratives, and the best of them use innovative cinematographic techniques uniquely suited to these narratives.

Skins (2002) initially tricks the viewer into thinking that the film intends to frame itself as a documentary about the impoverished Pine Ridge Reservation in South Dakota. As opening credits roll, voice-overs give statistics that include the reservation's rate of alcoholism, with death from the disease at nine times the national average; a 75 percent unemployment rate; and a life expectancy fifteen years less than that of most Americans.[5] But then the film launches into its actual story, that of two brothers, Mogie, an alcoholic Vietnam War veteran, and Rudy, a tribal police officer. They live on the fictional Beaver Creek Indian Reservation, a stand-in for Pine Ridge.

---

http://www.kidsource.com/kidsource/content3/unbiased.teaching.k12.2 (accessed December 1, 2017). For ongoing distortions in textbooks about Native Americans, see Deborah A. Miranda, "Lying to Children about the California Missions and the Indian," http://indiancountrytodaymedianetwork.com/2015/04/07/lying-children-about-california-missions-and-indian-159914 (accessed December 1, 2016). For a broad discussion about Native American history taught at the college level, see Gregory D. Smithers, "Teaching Native American History in a Polarized Age," http://tah.oah.org/content/teaching-native-american-history-in-a-polarized-age/ (accessed December 1, 2016).

2. For scholarship that explores the incorporation of Indian history in the classroom, see Susan Sleeper-Smith, Juliana Barr, Jean M. O'Brien, Nancy Shoemaker, eds., *Why You Can't Teach United States History without American Indians* (Chapel Hill: University of North Carolina Press, 2015). For issues regarding racism, ethnic fraud, and activism in the Native American academic world, see Devon Abbott Mihesuah and Angela Cavender Wilson, eds., *Indigenizing the Academy: Transforming Scholarship and Empowering Communities* (Lincoln: University of Nebraska Press, 2004). See also http://www.niea.org/students/native-american-studies.aspx (accessed June 20, 2015).

3. See Chapter 1, pp. 10–11.

4. See the Introduction, pp. xxvii–xxviii.

5. *Skins*, directed by Chris Eye, 2002.

In one scene, Rudy washes his face in his bathroom sink. A spider crawls along the faucet. Introducing a flashback, Rudy narrates: "Iktomi, the trickster spider, a Lakota spirit, had reappeared in my life. I was ten years old when we first met." That meeting took place in an outhouse. A spider bit him in the testicles. In the flashback, Rudy runs out the door screaming and rolls on the ground, whereupon Mogie hauls him away on his back, "taking him to safety."[6]

Rudy is a police officer but often takes the law into his own hands, so one night he sets fire to a liquor store a few miles outside the reservation's border. Beaver Creek outlaws the sale of alcohol on its land, so the store figures as a notorious supplier to the reservation's alcoholics. To Rudy's horror, as fire devours the store, Mogie runs through the smoke on the roof. Screaming and wrapped in flames, he falls to the ground, barely alive. By coincidence, he had attempted to break into the store that night to steal liquor.

Mogie recovers from his burns but soon thereafter dies from cirrhosis of the liver. Partially carrying out his brother's wish to disfigure Washington's face on Mount Rushmore, Rudy hauls a five-gallon bucket of red paint up the slope behind the monument. Just before hurling the open can over the side, he sees a spider—Iktomi—crawl along the rim of the can and then fall into the paint. Rudy smiles and launches the paint over the edge. The next day he surveys his work. A streak of red runs down the president's nose.

The film interweaves the political and cultural effrontery that Mount Rushmore represents to the Lakota with the troubled relationship between Rudy and Mogie. Both strands interweave through the wiles of Iktomi, the trickster spider. Iktomi even tricks the viewer into expecting an "educational" documentary and then spins out an entirely Lakota world. In other words, the film does not peer *into* the Lakota world through an outside lens—a documentary lens. Rather, the story emerges from *within* the Lakota world itself. The Eurocentric stereotypes discussed in *Seven Myths of Native American History* do not function in *Skins*. The film's focus on alcoholism might be construed as a fulfillment of the drunken Indian stereotype, but *Skins* does not shy away from dealing with the disease head-on. Moreover, Mogie might be a hopeless drunk, but he remains a fully three-dimensional human being, as does his equally, if differently, flawed brother.

Atanarjuat: The Fast Runner (2001) immerses the audience in the Inuit world of the Arctic. The film's Inuit actors speak their own language, Inuktikut,[7] and the Inuit-controlled film company, Igloolik Isuma Productions, demanded the most accurate possible portrayals of Inuit culture as it appeared five hundred years ago, the film's time period. These efforts earned the film worldwide acclaim and prestigious awards.

---

6. Chris Eyre, director, *Skins* (First Look Pictures, 2002).

7. An official language of Nunavut, Canada's northernmost territory (a mainland region combined with a network of islands that covers approximately 800,000 square miles of land and water), Inuktitut nonetheless faces challenges as a living language. See Michael Robert Evans, *The Fast Runner: Filming the Legend of Atanarjuat* (Lincoln: University of Nebraska Press, 2010), 56–57.

Moreover, *The Fast Runner* continues to challenge many long-cherished conventions regarding moviemaking itself.[8]

The Fast Runner combines several variations of an Inuit legend that originated centuries ago on Igloolik Island, a small, craggy landmass in the Fury and Hecla Strait between Baffin Island and mainland Canada. Asleep in their tent, the story goes, Atanarjuat and his brother, Aamarjuaq, undergo an attack by their rivals, Uki and his brothers. The rivals kill Aamarjuaq, but Atanarjuat escapes. Naked, he flees across the ice. Famous for his speed as a runner, he outdistances his attackers, who pursue him relentlessly. Finally, he manages to elude them. Weak to the point of death, his feet bleeding and slashed by the ice, he comes across a family that nurses him back to health. He then returns to Igloolik, his village, and exacts revenge on Uki and his family.[9]

Because *The Fast Runner* tells its story on Inuit terms, not only does a non-Inuit audience confront an unfamiliar culture, but that audience must also heed the village leader's warning in the film's first scene: "I can only sing this song to someone who understands it."[10] Put another way, the intervention of spiritual powers accounts for much of the action between Atanarjuat's family and Uki's family. However, the film assumes that the audience understands the function and operation of these powers. So to the uninitiated, relationships within and between the two families appear nearly inexplicable. The rigorous conditions set by *The Fast Runner* might well leave an audience exhausted by the end of the film, as if having internalized Atanarjuat's naked and desperate run across the arctic ice.

Along the way, however, the terrain grows familiar. The Inuit shape of the story reveals itself, at least occasionally. Because the workings of an invisible, or partially visible, sprit world continually influence all Inuit affairs, the film's initial battle scene does not involve physical combat. Rather, two shamans bound in ropes draw only on their spiritual resources. They contort their faces and grunt until one of the shamans, the village leader Kumaglak, falls over dead from the metaphysical struggle. But the film provides no explanation of the scene. To all appearances, nothing much happens. Two men make animal-like noises. One falls over.

Voices and ghostly figures appear throughout the film, subtly manipulating events. Atanarjuat's dead father flickers briefly in the air during his son's naked run, urging him forward. Uki's dead father distracts the murders momentarily, allowing Atanarjuat to escape. But these and other spiritual intercessions occur with *such* subtlety that the viewer likely remains perplexed, even frustrated, while attempting to understand the course of action on the screen. Trying to comprehend the film by drawing on a background of

---

8. Ibid., passim.

9. Ibid., xv and 63–85.

10. Zacharias Kunuk, director, *Atanarjuat: The Fast Runner* (Igloolik Isuma Productions, 2001). For further discussion of this line's significance, see Michelle H. Raheja, *Reservation Reelism: Redfacing, Visual Sovereignty, and Representations of Native Americans in Films* (Lincoln: University of Nebraska Press, 2010), 212–13.

conventional cinematic narratives leads nowhere. Such narratives, which generally rely on character development and explain—in one fashion or another—the relationships between characters, do not belong to the world of *The Fast Runner*.

The learning curve remains steep throughout the film. In this manner, *The Fast Runner* expresses its sovereignty, its demand to exist on its own terms, not according to conventions imposed upon it from outside. By extension, the film makes a political statement of Inuit sovereignty, the right of the Inuit people to live according to their own laws and customs, not to those of the Canadian government or of Euro-Canadian culture. But the Inuit live fully within the modern world, as confirmed by the production and the worldwide success of *The Fast Runner*. Stereotypes and myths about Indigenous Peoples prove groundless once again.

The belief that spiritual forces influence people's lives and the world in general arises often in *Skins*, and more so in *Atanarjuat: The Fast Runner*. Yet the Myth of the Mystical Indian plays no part in either film, because the understanding of these forces resides within Native American cinematic sovereignty. Both films bypass common assumptions made by White filmmakers, who, to one degree or another, perpetuate the Myth of the Mystical Indian through romanticizing and idealizing the realms of traditional Native American religious beliefs.

Attempting to understand Native American culture and history will lead only to misperceptions as long as the cultural and historical lenses themselves remain flawed. However, a number of new historical narratives re-image, or indigenize, North American history.

I mention only two: Colin G. Calloway's Indian-centered history *One Vast Winter Count: The Native American West before Lewis and Clark*[11] ranges west from the Appalachians to the Pacific and north into Canada. It re-images Indians as pioneers who moved into a new land where they learned to use resources and build societies in nearly every environment that the continent offered. This led to the development of a complex variety of identities, economies, and technologies. Calloway delineates the trade networks that linked people who lived hundreds and even thousands of miles apart, and he traces population movements from the earliest migrations from Siberia down through the nineteenth century. The native perspective remains central when European colonials enter the picture. Calloway looks at a broad set of historical patterns among native groups, and his ethnohistorical analysis of a significant number of individual groups and their changes across time demolishes the myth that Indians somehow existed in a timeless and static state.

Daniel K. Richter's *Facing East from Indian Country: A Native History of Early America*[12] provides another example of a re-imaged and indigenized history. Richter

---

11. Colin G. Calloway, *One Vast Winter Count: The Native American West before Lewis and Clark* (Lincoln: University of Nebraska Press, 2003).

12. Daniel K. Richter, *Facing East from Indian Country: A Native History of Early America* (Cambridge, MA: Harvard University Press, 2001).

examines postcontact eastern North America from the Indian vantage point, one grounded in the reality that for nearly three hundred years after the arrival of Columbus, Native Americans continued to control most of the continent. Although European contact with Native Americans brought with it disease, dispossession, and violence, Native populations continued to recreate new communities. Differences in custom and economy between Europeans and Indians led at times to accommodation and at times to conflict. The multiple means by which Indian groups throughout the continent adapted to new historical conditions calls for a revision of the Eurocentric master narrative, one dependent on stereotypes of Indians as savages doomed to vanish as victims of westward expansion. Richter argues that the accommodation often reached between Indians and Euro-Americans has been ignored in the accepted master narrative, which emphasizes conflict between the two and de-emphasizes the historical complexity and ambiguity between the two groups.

A list of other similarly indigenized histories appears at the end of this book.

The complexity, nuance, and ambiguity that attend fact-based understandings of the past militate against easy reversions to simplistic myth-based ideas about history. Moreover, as new historical evidence comes to light, and new questions and new research methods arise, assumptions within all areas of historical study remain nearly always in a state of revision. The seven myths examined in this book represent only a handful of the misconceptions that to many appear as unquestioned facts. The work of overturning historical misconceptions might seem never ending, but now and again the possibility remains to pry a myth out of its stubborn lair and send it packing.

Suggested Reading

Guided by brevity, this list includes only books currently in print and easily accessible. It does not include journal articles, most of which would not be readily available to most readers. The intention has been to suggest only a few titles, a few likely suspects, that the curious reader might want to take a look at. Bibliographies in the listed books will provide sources for readers who wish to pursue deeper study of a given topic.

Myths about Indians

Berkhofer, Robert F., Jr. *The White Man's Indian*. New York: Vintage, 1979.

Dunbar-Ortiz, Roxanne and Dina Gilio-Whitaker. *"All the Real Indians Died Off" and 20 Other Myths about Native Americans*. Boston: Beacon Press, 2016.

Hauptman, Laurence M. *Tribes and Tribulations: Misconceptions about American Indians and Their Histories*. Albuquerque: University of New Mexico Press, 1996.

Mihesuah, Devon A. *American Indians: Stereotypes and Realities*. Atlanta: Clarity Press, 2004.

Stedman, Raymond William. *Shadows of the Indian: Stereotypes in American Culture*. Norman: University of Oklahoma Press, 1982.

Truer, Anton. *Everything You Wanted to Know about Indians but Were Afraid to Ask*. St. Paul, MN: Borealis Books, 2012.

General Native American History

Blackhawk, Ned. *Violence over the Land: Indians and Empires in the Early American West*. Cambridge, MA: Harvard University Press, 2006.

Calloway, Colin G. *One Vast Winter Count: The Native American West before Lewis and Clark*. Lincoln: University of Nebraska Press, 2003.

Richter, Daniel K. *Facing East from Indian Country: A Native History of Early America*. Cambridge, MA: Harvard University Press, 2003.

White, Richard. *The Middle Ground: Indians, Empires, and Republics in the Great Lakes Region, 1650–1815*. Cambridge, UK: Cambridge University Press, 2011.

Witgen, Michael. *An Infinity of Nations: How the Native New World Shaped Early North America*. Philadelphia: University of Pennsylvania Press, 2012.

Indian Policy

Clifton, James A., ed. *The Invented Indian: Cultural Fictions and Government Policies*. New Brunswick, Canada: Transaction Publishers, 2011.

Horsman, Reginald. *Expansion and American Indian Policy: 1783–1812*. Norman: University of Oklahoma Press, 1992.

Prucha, Francis Paul. *The Great Father: The United States Government and the American Indians*. Lincoln: University of Nebraska Press, 1986.

———. *American Indian Treaties: The History of a Political Anomaly*. Berkeley: University of California Press, 1997.

Satz, Ronald N. *American Indian Policy in the Jacksonian Era*. Norman: University of Oklahoma Press, 2002.

Indian Removal

Anderson, Gary Clayton. *Ethnic Cleansing and the Indian: The Crime That Should Haunt America*. Norman: University of Oklahoma Press, 2014.

Bowes, John P. *Land Too Good for Indians: Northern Indian Removal*. Norman: University of Oklahoma Press, 2016.

Perdue, Theda and Michael D. Green. *The Cherokee Nation and the Trail of Tears*. New York: Penguin, 2007.

Indian Boarding Schools

Adams, David Wallace. *American Indians and the Boarding School Experience, 1875–1928*. Lawrence: University Press of Kansas, 1995.

Child, Brenda J. *Boarding School Seasons: American Indian Families, 1900–1940*. Lincoln: University of Nebraska Press, 2000.

Gram, John R. *Education at the Edge of Empire: Negotiating Pueblo Identity in New Mexico's Indian Boarding School*. Seattle: University of Washington Press, 2015.

Native American Gender Identity Studies

Child, Brenda J. *Holding Our World Together: Ojibwe Women and the Survival of Community*. New York: Viking, 2012.

Denial, Catherine J. *Making Marriage: Husbands, Wives, and the American State in Dakota and Ojibwe Country*. St. Paul: Minnesota Historical Society Press, 2013.

Jacobs, Sue-Ellen, Wesley Thomas, and Sabine Lang, eds. *Two-Spirit People: Native American Gender Identity, Sexuality, and Spirituality*. Urbana: University of Illinois Press, 1997.

Kugel, Rebecca and Lucy Eldersveld Murphy, eds. *Native Women's History in Eastern North America before 1900: A Guide to Research and Writing*. Lincoln: University of Nebraska Press, 2007.

Roscoe, Will. *Changing Ones: Third and Fourth Genders in Native North America*. New York: St. Martin's Press, 2000.

Native Americans and Popular Culture

Bird, Elizabeth S., ed. *Dressing in Feathers: The Construction of the Indian in American Popular Culture*. Boulder, CO: Westview, 1996.

Kilpatrick, Jacquelyn. *Celluloid Indians: Native Americans and Film*. Lincoln: University of Nebraska Press, 1999.

McNenly, Linda Scarangella. *Native Performers in Wild West Shows: From Buffalo Bill to Euro Disney*. Norman: University of Oklahoma Press, 2012.

Raheja, Michelle H. *Reservation Reelism: Redfacing, Visual Sovereignty, and Representations of Native Americans in Film*. Lincoln: University of Nebraska Press, 2010.

Sheyahshe, Michael A. *Native Americans in Comic Books: A Critical Study*. Jefferson, NC: McFarland, 2008.

Troutman, John W. *Indian Blues: American Indians and the Politics of Music, 1879–1934*. Norman: University of Oklahoma Press, 2012.